101
QUESTIONS & ANSWERS
SERIES

ADMINISTRATIVE LAW

CHARLES P REED
LLB, Barrister

OLD BAILEY PRESS

OLD BAILEY PRESS
200 Greyhound Road, London W14 9RY

First published 1998
Reprinted 1999
Reprinted 2001

ISBN 1 85836 092 7

British Library Cataloguing-in-Publication Data

A catalogue record for this book is available from the British Library.

Printed and bound in Great Britain

Contents

Contents

101

QUESTIONS & ANSWERS
SERIES

ADMINISTRATIVE LAW

Foreword

This book is part of a series designed specifically for those students studying at undergraduate level. Coverage is not restricted to any one syllabus but embraces the main examination topics found in a typical examination paper.

This book is concerned with administrative law in the context of examinations. Each chapter contains an Introduction setting out the scope of the topic, important recent cases and articles, and other helpful advice as to likely examination questions on that topic.

Additionally, in each chapter there are Interrograms and Examination Questions. The Interrograms are designed as short questions testing knowledge of the fundamentals of the topic being covered. The Examination Questions are a selection of actual questions taken from papers set by a university, and have been selected because they represent the most typical examples of how knowledge of the syllabus is tested. It is intended that students should work through the Interrograms and Examination Questions before checking their knowledge (and presentation style) against the suggested answers contained in each chapter (skeleton answers for Interrograms, full-length essay answers for the Examination Questions). The answers state the law as at 1 January 1998.

Acknowledgement

Examination questions are the copyright of the University of London.

The questions are taken or adapted from past University of London LLB Degree for external students examination papers. Our thanks are extended to the University of London for their kind permission to use and publish the questions.

Caveat

The answers given are not approved, sanctioned or endorsed by the University of London and are entirely the Publishers' responsibility.

Table of Cases

1

Introduction to Administrative Law

Introduction

This chapter is concerned with the concepts of administrative law and in particular of judicial review. It is essential to grasp these concepts at the outset in order to understand the practical application of the subject. For example, the doctrine of ultra vires has been the basis of judicial review for many years and hence it is extremely important to understand the distinction between review (concerned with legality) and appeal (concerned with merits).

However, in recent years academics have been challenging traditional notions of administrative law. The expansion in grounds for review (for example, the rapid development of the doctrine of legitimate expectation since 1969) have led to suggestions that judges are becoming more vigorous in scrutinising administrative action and that sometimes they come very close to examining the merits of executive decisions. In 1984 the writers Harlow and Rawlings published an influential work, *Law and Administration*, in which they suggested new concepts to explain the modern operation of judicial review. These concepts were given the labels of 'red light' theory and 'green light' theory and it is one of the purposes of this chapter to explore those theories.

Unfortunately it is difficult to appreciate such conceptual ideas until after an exploration of practical case law, hence it would be a useful exercise to return to this opening chapter after working through the rest of the book. Administrative law is a very detailed subject and it may be difficult to 'see the wood because of the trees'. But if the 'red light' and 'green light' theories are appreciated at an early stage they become useful tests for assessing individual judicial approaches to particular branches of judicial review. For example, in Chapters 7 and 9 it will be seen that some judges have helped to develop a doctrine of 'substantive' legitimate expectation as a device for giving greater protection to individuals against abuse of power (a 'red light' approach). Other judges have resisted such development on the ground that it amounts to unjustified interference with legitimate executive discretion which needs to exist to ensure efficient administration (a 'green light' approach).

Since this chapter concentrates on conceptual analysis there is no set list of cases or statutes which is compulsory reading, though one recent case which offers an insight into contrasting judicial attitudes is *R v Cambridge District Health Authority, ex parte B* [1995] 2 All ER 129 – see, especially, the judgments of Laws J at first instance and Sir Thomas Bingham MR (as he then was) in the Court of Appeal. It is also important to read articles in the main law journals, particularly those that offer a critical analysis of judicial review. Among recent such articles may be mentioned ones by Harlow [1997] PL 245, Oliver [1997] PL 630, Forsyth [1996] CLJ 122, Lord Irvine [1996] PL 59, Sir John Laws [1995] PL 72 and Lord Woolf [1995] PL 57.

In regard to examinations usually essay-type questions are set requiring conceptual and critical analysis of the modern purposes and operation of public law and judicial review. At least one such question can be expected in a typical examination paper.

Questions

INTERROGRAMS

1   What are the main purposes of administrative law?
2   Distinguish between legality and merits for the purpose of judicial review.
3   What is the 'red light' theory?
4   What is the 'green light' theory?

QUESTION ONE

'Administrative law is the citizen's protection against the abuse of power.'
   Consider this view of the subject.

London University LLB Examination
(for external students) Administrative Law June 1986 Q1

QUESTION TWO

'Judicial review is concerned with the legality of a decision and not with its merits.'
   Discuss. Is it possible to distinguish legality from merits?

London University LLB Examination
(for external students) Administrative Law June 1991 Q1

QUESTION THREE

'To talk of "red light" and "green light" theories of administrative law may be helpful in identifying *theoretical* extremes, but it provides little useful guidance concerning the *practical* role that legalistic models of decision-making might play in the government of a contemporary democratic state.'
   Discuss.

London University LLB Examination
(for external students) Administrative Law June 1993 Q1

Answers

ANSWERS TO INTERROGRAMS

1   The main purposes of administrative law are to determine the framework of public authorities and to control the manner in which such bodies exercise their functions. It is a function of administrative law to define the characteristics of a public body in order to determine whether it is subject to judicial review. The doctrine of ultra vires

is the basis upon which judicial review is exercised. The purpose of the doctrine is to ensure that a public body does not exceed or abuse its delegated powers.

2   Judicial review is concerned with the legality of administrative decisions and not with their political merits. For this purpose legality is determined by the application of the established grounds for review set out in such judgments as Lord Greene MR in *Associated Provincial Picture Houses Ltd* v *Wednesbury Corporation* [1948] 1 KB 223, and Lord Diplock in *Council for Civil Service Unions* v *Minister for the Civil Service* [1985] AC 374. Examples include acting unfairly, acting in bad faith, failing to have regard to relevant considerations, fettering discretion, and acting in a totally unreasonable or irrational manner. A doctrine of proportionality may yet become a further ground for review, but so far judges have refused to develop it on the ground that it may bring them too close to examining the wisdom of political judgments: *R* v *Secretary of State for the Home Department, ex parte Brind* [1991] AC 696.

3   The 'red light' theory contends that the purpose of judicial review should be to protect individual rights against the exercise of state power, ie with the redress of grievances. This puts all the emphasis on rights and duties enforced by the ordinary courts and therefore follows Dicey's theory of the Rule of Law.

4   The 'green light' theory contends that the purpose of public law should be to facilitate efficient administration. This puts the emphasis on the need for an interventionist state operating through legislation and regulation, controlled by internal methods such as consultation with affected individuals. It is inconsistent with Diceyan concepts of the Rule of Law because it recognises the need to distinguish clearly between public law and private law and to acknowledge the roles of tribunals, inquiries and ombudsmen as devices for controlling the exercise of public powers.

SUGGESTED ANSWER TO QUESTION ONE

General Comment

A general question on the nature of administrative law. Note that the answer should really concern itself with how well administrative law performs this task, and not merely how. As always, specific examples will be needed to prevent the answer being too vague.

Key Points

- Nature and purpose of administrative law
- Scope of judicial review – *Padfield, Anisminic, CCSU* v *Minister for the Civil Service*
- Limitations of judicial review – other remedies
- Influence on daily work of civil servants

Suggested Answer

The statement under consideration expresses a widely held, but, it is submitted, possibly over-optimistic view of administrative law.

In the narrow sense when one speaks of administrative law, one means judicial review. The theory is that parliament delegates some of its powers to an inferior body, which then uses this power to make decisions affecting the rights of citizens. Should such a body exceed its delegated powers, the courts are there to quash ultra vires decisions at the behest of the aggrieved citizen.

How well this system works as a protection for the citizen against abuses of power by public bodies is largely dependent on the attitude of the judiciary. During the last 40 years, the judges have shown on a number of occasions their willingness to intervene in the decision making process on behalf of the citizen.

In *Padfield* v *Minister of Agriculture* (1968), the House of Lords showed its willingness to invalidate the decisions of a government minister even where he acted under a subjectively worded power. There are numerous cases where the courts have invalidated decisions of local authorities on the grounds of abuse of power, usually on the specific point of public spending.

The judiciary have been undeterred by efforts to exclude review, as the inventive jurisprudence of the majority of the House of Lords in *Anisminic* v *Foreign Compensation Commission* (1969) demonstrates. In *Council of Civil Service Unions* v *Minister for the Civil Service* (1985) the House of Lords extended the ambit of judicial review beyond the supervision of statutory powers, to include powers derived from the prerogative. This has led to the suggestion that the source of any given power might well be irrelevant to an application for judicial review; what is important is the effect of that power being exercised on the public.

In a broader sense, administrative law encompasses problem solving agencies such as the various ombudsmen, the Commission for Racial Equality, and the Police Complaints Authority. The very existence of such bodies highlights the shortcomings of judicial review as a safeguard for the citizen, against the abuse of power.

There are a number of dangers associated with being complacent about the ability of administrative law, and in particular judicial review, to protect the citizen. The availability of judicial review is at the discretion of the judges. Certain aspects of the administrative process are singled out as being best left in the hands of ministers or administrators, and review is refused.

In *R* v *Preston Supplementary Benefits Appeal Tribunal, ex parte Moore* (1975) the Court of Appeal declined to interfere with the tribunal's decision on the ground that the welfare benefits system should not become a 'happy hunting ground for lawyers' and should be administered with as little technicality as possible. It is submitted that this approach does not show administrative law as offering the citizen any great protection against abuse.

In *R* v *Secretary of State for the Home Department, ex parte Hosenball* (1977) the court refused an application to quash a deportation order, intimating that the Home Secretary was in the best position to judge what was in the interests of national security, and was, in any event, answerable to the House of Commons for his actions.

Other groups such as immigrants and students have also had grounds in the past to find the judges failing to live up to their reputations as the citizens' safeguard against abuse of administrative power.

Furthermore, it should be remembered that many applications for review deal only with individual cases. An administrative body may have a decision or policy declared ultra vires, but there is no guarantee that it will abide by such a ruling in future cases. Judicial review is reactionary not dynamic.

To return to the main theme, however, there is little doubt that administrative law, in its modern guise, does provide the citizen with an extensive safeguard against the abuse of power. The very existence of administrative law must have a salutary effect on decision makers within the public authorities who act in the knowledge that the means are at the citizen's disposal to challenge arbitrary, unreasonable, unfair, and biased decisions. During the 1980s civil servants in central government were provided with a booklet *The Judge over Your Shoulder* to guide them on the grounds for judicial review and how to avoid them from arising by 'structuring' the exercise of their discretionary powers in a lawful and fair manner. Hence the influence of administrative law may be more profound than the case law suggests.

SUGGESTED ANSWER TO QUESTION TWO

General Comment

A question of a general nature requiring an explanation of what judicial review is supposed to deal with and what it actually deals with. Examples are clearly needed to illustrate the points made.

Key Points

- Consider the nature of review and appeal
- Give examples of areas where review is more 'objective'
- Explain the nature of review concerned with reasonableness and the inevitable examination of merits
- Consider the use made by the courts of the distinction

Suggested Answer

The primary purpose of judicial review is to ensure that public bodies act within the law, and this can be achieved by quashing a decision so that it has to be taken again, properly; ordering the performance of a duty; or prohibiting a proposed course of conduct which would be unlawful.

It is to be contrasted with an appeal which can not only overturn an earlier decision, but result in the substitution of the appellate body's decision for the original. On review the court cannot replace the original decision with its own.

An appeal can therefore consider the merits of a decision, review is only concerned with legality. Further, review is a common law right, appeal is only available where statute so provides.

Review is not concerned with compensating the individual for any loss he may have suffered. As a general rule damages are not available for loss resulting from acts that are ultra vires per se.

The ground upon which an application for judicial review may be brought can generally be described as 'abuse of power'. An allegation that a public body has abused its powers inevitably involves an allegation that it has acted illegally, and in this sense it is true to say that judicial review is concerned with the legality of administrative action. There are situations, however, where it becomes very difficult to separate the issue of legality from the question of whether or not the decision under consideration is a 'good' one or a 'bad' one.

It is submitted that where the courts are concerned with objective criteria there is less scope for them to question the merits of the decision before them. Three examples will help illustrate this point.

First, the courts will review the legality of the actions of a public body on the grounds that it has been guilty of procedural impropriety. The public body may have failed to follow some procedural step laid down by its enabling Act. Such a failure does not automatically render a decision ultra vires. The courts distinguish between mandatory requirements, which must be observed, and directory requirements which are more flexible. The question is generally a straightforward one, however, in the sense that the court is examining whether or not a step in the procedure laid down by Parliament has been complied with or not.

Secondly, the courts can review the actions of a public body on the ground that it has committed a jurisdictional error. This arises where a body makes an error as to the extent of its powers. An enabling Act may provide that a tribunal has jurisdiction to determine the fair rent for dwellings within a certain area. The tribunal may decide to assess the rent to be paid for a dwelling that is in fact outside their area of control; in so doing they would have committed an error as to the scope of their jurisdiction – hence a jurisdictional error. Again, the court in such a case is not questioning the merits of the decision, ie 'was the rent fair?', but is looking at whether or not the body in question was empowered to deal with the matter at all.

Thirdly, the courts will review administrative action where it appears that the decision maker may have been biased. Again the court is looking at some aspect of the procedure that has been followed rather than looking at the merits of the ultimate decision.

There are other grounds of review, however, where the dividing line between legality and merits becomes very difficult or even impossible to draw.

Where administrative action is challenged on the ground that there has been some error of law on the face of the record, the supervisory jurisdiction of the High Court extends to quashing decisions even though they are intra vires, provided these errors are apparent on the 'record' of its proceedings. In all such cases it is for the court to decide whether or not an error has been made. If it decides to intervene and quash a decision it is essentially because it prefers its own interpretation of a particular provision to that provided by the decision maker. The court is dealing with the legality of the decision, but is also saying it is a bad decision on its merits because it has been arrived at by adopting an incorrect legal test.

Where the allegation is that an individual has been denied a fair hearing, perhaps because he has not been granted a hearing or has not been allowed legal representation, the function of the court might be seen as questioning legality and merits. If it quashes such a decision it might be said that it has done so simply on the grounds of a procedural error, but it can also be said that these errors have combined to produce a decision which is therefore flawed in some way, and therefore lacks merit.

The confusion of legality and merits becomes more apparent when one considers review on the ground of irrationality or unreasonableness, because here, although in theory the courts are only concerned with legality, they will be involved in making value judgments as to what is 'reasonable' and what is 'fair'.

The established test for reasonableness in administrative law is derived from the Court of Appeal's decision in *Associated Provincial Picture Houses Ltd* v *Wednesbury Corporation* (1948). The local authority had the power to grant permission for the opening of cinemas, subject to such conditions as they saw fit to impose. The plaintiff sought a declaration that a condition imposed on a grant of permission to open one of their cinemas, namely that no child under fifteen was to be allowed in without an adult, was ultra vires. In the course of holding that the conditions imposed were intra vires, Lord Greene MR stated that it was important to bear in mind that Parliament had entrusted the local authority with the discretion to impose conditions because of its knowledge of the area's needs, and (impliedly) because having been elected it reflected the views of the area's inhabitants. It was his view that the courts should therefore be slow to intervene to quash a condition imposed by such a body, but would do so where a condition was seen to be totally unreasonable. This meant that the condition would have to be one that was so unreasonable, no reasonable authority would have imposed it, and to prove a case of that kind would require evidence that was overwhelming.

Whilst this is laudable as an example of the courts recognising the boundary between the function of reviewing legality and examining merits, it will be seen at once that it is in reality almost impossible to separate the two. There are many examples of the courts intervening on the grounds that the decision maker had made a 'bad' decision. In *Secretary of State for Education and Science* v *Tameside Metropolitan Borough Council* (1977) the House of Lords upheld Lord Denning's view, expressed in the court below, that the Secretary of State must have misdirected himself on the interpretation of 'unreasonableness', and that there was no evidence on which the Secretary of State could declare himself satisfied that the council were proposing to act unreasonably. One might be tempted to ask how it was that the court knew better than the minister.

The theoretical distinction between merits and legality is one that can be relied upon by the reviewing court where it chooses not to intervene. In such cases it can decline to interfere with a decision on the basis that to do so would be to usurp the role of the decision maker appointed by Parliament. As Lord Brightman stated in *R* v *Hillingdon London Borough Council, ex parte Puhlhofer* (1986):

> 'Where the existence or non-existence of a fact is left to the judgment and discretion of a public body and that fact involves a broad spectrum ranging from the obvious to the debatable to the just conceivable, it is the duty of the court to leave the decision of that fact to the public body to whom Parliament has entrusted the decision making power save in a case where it is obvious that the public body, consciously or unconsciously, are acting perversely.'

Perhaps in the light of this, the question posed should be answered by saying that whilst judicial review is concerned with legality and not merits, the distinction cannot always be maintained.

SUGGESTED ANSWER TO QUESTION THREE

General Comment

This question is not as intimidating as it appears at first glance. It concerns the way in which authorities may make rules governing the exercise of their powers. These rules might be described as 'legalistic' in the sense that they have the same effects as, and in some cases are difficult to distinguish from, legislative codes of rules governing decision-making. The answer should display an understanding of the different kinds of rules in use, the justification for their use and the control exercised over them by the courts. Note that the 'red light' and 'green light' theories were conceived by Harlow and Rawlings, *Law and Administration* (1997, 2nd ed).

Key Points

- The different kinds of rules
- Scrutiny of the rules
- Formation of policy
- The right to be heard

Suggested Answer

That administrative bodies should develop rules governing the exercise of their decision-making powers is inevitable. In a large number of cases such rules will be legalistic in the sense that the results of the decision-making process will be dictated to a very great extent by the application of the rules to the situation under consideration. Thus to an observer the process may seem to be little more than a purely mechanical exercise similar to the observation of traffic lights, with no genuine consideration of the merits of any particular claim. It is clear from a consideration of the authorities that this view is simplistic; rules are acceptable, but they must not allow a decision-maker to evade the responsibility of exercising discretion.

There are a number of different kinds of rules governing decision-making. Parliament frequently empowers ministers to make rules and regulations governing particular areas of administrative law. Such rules will often be embodied in Statutory Instruments, and will be subject to the scrutiny of Parliamentary Select Committees and ultimately of the House of Commons itself. The Statutory Instruments Act 1946 defines specific classes of delegated legislation that are subject to parliamentary controls, and which will be published. These rules will be legalistic in the truest sense of the word, and will be applied in the most mechanical fashion; they are also subject to a greater degree of control and certainty than any other kinds of rules, and the legality of their application can be more readily scrutinised and enforced by the courts. Such rules will often confer rights upon individuals, who can enforce their application by applying for an order for mandamus.

Of greater interest to the administrative lawyer are the kinds of rules that do not fall into the categories defined by the Statutory Instruments Act. Some such regulations will be made pursuant to a statutory provision; although these are not subject to parliamentary scrutiny, the courts will scrutinise them to ensure that they are not ultra vires (see *Commissioners of Customs and Excise* v *Cure & Deeley* (1962)). Other kinds of rules may be manufactured with various degrees of formality; they may consist of fairly certain and routine rules which are published in circulars and which are to be applied in each case, or they may consist of no more than officially understood policy operating within a department. These rules may bear all the hallmarks of delegated legislation and yet fall short of it (see *R* v *Secretary of State for the Home Department, ex parte Hosenball* (1977)). Such rules are the inevitable and natural product of well-developed bureaucracy, and usually arise in cases where an authority has a power of discretion. They are helpful in two ways: they assist the decision-maker in reaching decisions consistently, and thus in promoting fairness; they also promote efficiency, since they streamline the decision-making process.

The difficulty with such rules arises in defining their role in such a way as to ensure that the use of rules does not in itself become an abuse of power. This involves balancing the interests of consistency with those of exercising discretion in a way that is sensitive to individual cases. Since the only real scrutiny that the rules come under is that of the courts, it will always be ex post facto and in that sense second best. Since these non-legislative rules will usually govern the exercise of a power or discretion, difficult questions may arise as to their enforcement.

The courts have not found the development of administrative rules objectionable, but have tended to encourage it. Thus in *British Oxygen Company* v *Minister of Technology* (1971) the House of Lords held that the minister was entitled to form a policy. Such a policy might be restrictive, in the sense that its operation was a purely mechanical assessment of whether an applicant fulfilled certain criteria for the making of a grant, but the minister's exercise of discretion could not be impugned so long as he listened to anybody with something new to say in the matter. There must be a genuine exercise of discretion, and it must not be exercised in bad faith, but the existence of rules guiding that discretion was acceptable. As a matter of practical reality, a moment's consideration will show that the formation of policy rules will often be essential since it will be impossible to approach each and every case as if it were the only case to be decided.

One of the problems faced by potential applicants is the extent to which they may have knowledge of pre-existing rules of policy. Usually these will not be published but will be circulated internally. An individual may be prejudiced not only by the application of these rules but also by the failure to apply them, and therefore it will clearly be to his advantage to know in advance what they are. There is no duty to publish such rules, and in theory there is no duty to apply them, since the public body must exercise its discretion. The courts have mitigated this second problem by developing the concept of legitimate expectations. In *R* v *Secretary of State for the Home Department, ex parte Khan* (1985) it was held that where an authority has a settled policy which it wishes to change it may be under a duty to hear what an applicant has to say on the matter. Thus, while rules may govern the exercise of discretion, an authority must listen both to those who might be prejudiced by the exercise of those rules and to those who might be prejudiced by their not being exercised. In other words, the authority must keep its mind open in all the circumstances; it may not simply apply a blanket 'red light/green light' test to applicants. This may be contrasted with the position where rules of a legislative nature are promulgated by a minister conferred with authority to do so: there is no duty at common law to accord a hearing prior to their promulgation (see *Bates* v *Lord Hailsham* (1972)).

It can be seen that there are many different ways in which rules governing decision-making may come to exist. These rules may make decision-making 'legalistic', and they may present democratic problems in the sense that they are not subject to parliamentary scrutiny. The rules themselves are usually a healthy means of adding efficiency and consistency to the decision-making process, and in that sense have an important role to play within the decision-making process. It is clear, however, that decisions must be made by the appropriate decision-maker; discretion must be exercised, and 'red light' and 'green light' theories have little to say about the majority of cases, since any novel circumstances in an individual application must be taken into account, and an individual with something new to say must be heard.

2

Public Interest Immunity

Introduction

This chapter is concerned with the historical development of Crown privilege into the modern concept of public interest immunity (PII). Although essentially a rule of evidence relating to discovery of documents, it has wider importance when considered in the context of open government, because there is an obvious risk of abuse of power if information is withheld from a court action other than on genuine grounds of public interest. The task of the judge has become extremely contentious insofar as he/she has to balance competing interests in deciding whether to order disclosure.

What are those competing interests? From the view of the individual litigant there is a demand for full and frank disclosure by the state of all relevant information. From the view of the state there is a demand to protect certain types of information from disclosure either on the ground of national security or because of the need to ensure the proper functioning of the public service. Whilst genuine claims of national security will rarely be contested by the trial judge, claims based merely on the need for confidentiality in government will be treated with more scepticism, particularly if it appears that the state is using PII as a cloak to cover politically embarrassing secrets.

Although PII cases are predominantly found in the civil law, it is possible for a PII claim to be made in a criminal case and this happened, amid great political controversy, in the Matrix-Churchill trial in 1993 concerning illegal arms sales to Iraq. The affair led to a public inquiry under Sir Richard Scott V-C, and his Report, published in February 1996, was very critical of government use of PII certificates. The government accepted Scott's finding that ministers are not under a duty to claim PII whenever national interests are involved. Rather, ministers have a policy discretion not to claim the immunity if satisfied that there is a clear balance in favour of disclosure for the administration of justice. New government guidelines were issued to make this clear and the result may be more open government and fewer claims to PII.

The Matrix-Churchill case naturally invoked renewed academic interest in the subject of PII, and among useful articles on the subject are those by Sir Jack Jacob [1993] PL 121, Simon Brown LJ [1994] PL 579 and Zuckermann (1994) 54 MLR 703. On the Scott Report's findings on PII, see Scott [1996] PL 427, Ganz (1997) 60 MLR 552 and Forsyth [1997] CLJ 51.

Important recent cases on PII are: *R v Chief Constable of West Midlands Police, ex parte Wiley* [1994] 3 All ER 420; *Kaufmann v Credit Lyonnais Bank* (1995) The Times 1 February; *O'Sullivan v Metropolitan Police Commissioner* (1995) The Times 3 July; and *Taylor v Anderton* [1995] 2 All ER 420.

In regard to examinations the tendency has been to set essay-type questions requiring a critical analysis of the way in which judges have approached the balancing exercise when deciding whether to order disclosure. During the 1990s the subject received much media and political attention, and hence it is still reasonable to expect at least one such questions on PII in a typical examination paper.

Questions

INTERROGRAMS

1 What is the nature of the burden on an applicant requiring disclosure of documents for which public interest immunity is being claimed?
2 What is a 'contents' claim and how will it be decided by a trial judge?
3 What is a 'class' claim and how will be be decided by a trial judge?
4 Can public interest immunity be claimed in a serious criminal trial?

QUESTION ONE

'Although judges have sometimes deferred to claims of public interest immunity, such claims are never really in the public interest.'
    Discuss.
London University LLB Examination
(for external students) Administrative Law June 1988 Q1

QUESTION TWO

Has the law on public interest immunity helped or hindered the development of judicial review in the last sixty years?
Adapted from London University LLB Examination
(for external students) Administrative Law June 1990 Q3

Answers

ANSWERS TO INTERROGRAMS

1 The burden is on the applicant to establish at least a prima facie case on his own evidence without the aid of discovery and then to go on to show reasonable grounds for requesting discovery of the documents in question. Reasonable grounds include:

    a   a reasonable likelihood that the documents will assist his case;
    b   that the documents will put him on enquiry as to further evidence to assist his case; or
    c   that disclosure will damagee the other side's case.

    See further *Air Canada* v *Secretary of State for Trade (No 2)* [1983] 1 All ER 910.
2 A 'contents' claim is one in which the ministerial certificate is seeking to protect from disclosure a particular document which contains material of such a sensitive nature that it ought not to become public knowledge, eg for national security reasons. Although such a claim can be challenged it would be rare for a trial judge to

dispute it, and in obvious cases the trial judge would probably refuse even to investigate the claim.

3   A 'class' claim is a claim that a particular document should not be revealed in a particular case because it belongs to a class of documents which, of its character, ought to be protected, such as Cabinet documents, Foreign Office despatches and the like. The protected classes are now well settled and it has been said that judges will not recognise new class claims unless there is 'clear and compelling evidence' that non-disclosure is necessary in the public interest: per Lord Woolf (as he then was) in *R* v *Chief Constable of West Midlands Police, ex parte Wiley* [1994] 3 All ER 420 at 446.

4   Although it would be rare for a government to claim PII during a criminal trial (because of the risk that an innocent accused may be wrongly convicted), it is possible and did happen during the Matrix-Churchill trial in 1993. In such a case the trial judge will be particularly sensitive to the risks of a miscarriage of justice and will be 'vigorous' in examining the PII claim, since the balance of competing interests will be tilted heavily in favour of disclosure to ensure the fair administration of justice. When the trial judge in the Matrix-Churchill trial adopted this approach and ordered the disclosure of some of the material in question, the prosecution decided to drop its case rather than let the information become public knowledge.

SUGGESTED ANSWER TO QUESTION ONE

General Comment

A question that requires at least an outline of how claims of public interest immunity are dealt with by the courts, before the more contentious aspects of the views it expresses can be considered. Specific examples are required in order to test the truth of the claims made in the question, and caution is needed to avoid falling into the trap of thinking that all cases in which discovery of documents is successfully resisted by the Crown have been decided on the basis that such discovery would not be in the public interest.

Key Points

- Process of discovery of documents
- 'Contents' claims and 'class' claims
- Judges' powers to overrule ministerial claims to public interest immunity
- The 'candour' in government argument
- Cabinet papers
- Heavy burden of proof on applicant for disclosure
- No new 'class' claims – *ex parte Wiley*

Suggested Answer

A claim of public interest immunity can arise in the course of litigation where the Crown, whether it is a party to the litigation or not, objects to the disclosure of certain evidence on the ground that such disclosure would not be in the public interest. The stage at which such a claim is usually made in civil proceedings is discovery of documents, a matter governed by O.24 of the Rules of the Supreme Court, under which discovery of documents will not be ordered by the courts unless it can be shown that disclosure is necessary for fairly disposing of the case or for saving costs.

Claims of public interest immunity will normally be based on one of the two criteria established in *Duncan* v *Cammell, Laird & Co Ltd* (1942). In that decision a distinction was drawn between an objection to the production of a document on the basis of its contents (a 'contents' claim), and objection to the production of a document on the basis of its classification (a 'class' claim). The former might involve material such as plans for military hardware. The latter would be documents that had to kept confidential because of the need for the efficient running of the administration, for example communications between civil servants and ministers. The argument was that if such communications were made public, it would affect the candour with which civil servants gave their advice to ministers.

In *Conway* v *Rimmer* (1968), the House of Lords made it clear that if there was a dispute between a minister and a litigant as to the desirability of a document being disclosed, it was ultimately for the courts to resolve the matter. Where a ministerial certificate is produced claiming privilege for certain documents, a trial judge is at liberty to inspect the material in question and either accept the certificate or grant discovery of the documents. *Conway* v *Rimmer* further suggests that if a claim of public interest immunity is put forward on a 'contents' basis, the judiciary might be more prepared to bow to the better judgment of the relevant minister. Where, however, the claim to immunity is put on the basis of 'class' of documents to which the material belongs, the courts would be more likely to assert their independence and if necessary override the minister's objections.

The statement under consideration suggests that even where judges do defer to ministerial claims of public interest immunity, such deference is not justified. It is submitted that such a statement goes too far. *Duncan* v *Cammell Laird & Co Ltd* (above) provides a clear example of a situation in which most would agree that the granting of public interest immunity was fully justified. The plaintiff was the widow of a sailor who had drowned when the submarine 'Thetis' sunk during trials. In the course of her action for negligence against the manufacturers of the vessel, she sought discovery of the designs of the submarine's torpedo tubes. The court refused to permit discovery of these documents however, following an affidavit submitted by the First Lord of the Admiralty to the effect that the information contained therein would be of assistance to the enemy.

More questionable, perhaps, are those cases where litigants have sought discovery of communications between civil servants and ministers, and this has been refused by the courts on the ground that publication of such material would hamper the efficient administration of government. There is a compelling argument that if documents of this nature contain evidence of unlawful action on the part of government departments their contents should be made public. In *Burmah Oil* v *Bank of England* (1980), both Lord Scarman and Lord Keith felt that too much emphasis had been placed in the past on the need to secure the confidentiality of government papers so as to ensure candour on the part of civil servants when advising ministers. Lord Scarman suggested that such an approach might only be tenable where matters of national security were involved. Balanced against this, however, are two important constitutional conventions. The first is that civil servants are traditionally anonymous, and are not identified as responsible for particular policies or decisions; production of communications between civil servants and ministers might seriously undermine this position. Secondly, the production of documents might undermine the doctrine of collective responsibility where it reveals differences of opinion between various government departments on matters of policy.

With this latter point in mind, it is submitted that claims of public interest immunity are likely to be more compelling where the material involved comprises Cabinet Papers. As Lord Reid stated in *Conway* v *Rimmer* (above) no government could contemplate with equanimity its innermost workings being exposed to the gaze of those ready to criticise without adequate knowledge of the background and perhaps with some axe to grind. Are Cabinet papers, therefore, in a special category that ensures that they will never be disclosed in litigation without the consent of the government? Lord Widgery clearly thought so in *A-G* v *Jonathan Cape Ltd* (1976), when he stated that:

'It is quite clear that no court will compel the production of cabinet papers in the course of discovery in an action.'

But this is to be set alongside by the observations of Lord Fraser in *Air Canada* v *Secretary of State for Trade (No 2)* (1983):

'I do not think that even Cabinet minutes are completely immune from disclosure in a case where, for example, the issue in a litigation involves serious misconduct by a Cabinet minister ... while Cabinet documents do not have a complete immunity, they are entitled to a high degree of protection against disclosure.'

It is important to bear in mind when considering the statement contained in the question that in a number of significant recent cases discovery of documents has been refused, not so much on the ground of public interest immunity, but on the basis that the plaintiff has failed to make out a sufficiently compelling case for discovery. In *Burmah Oil* v *Bank of England* (above), discovery of documents containing details of the formulation of government policy was refused on the ground that Burmah Oil had failed to establish how such disclosure would advance its case.

Similarly, in the *Air Canada* case (above), the House of Lords stressed that the onus was on the party seeking disclosure of documents to show that it would be likely to support its case, or at least that there was a reasonable probability that it would do so. Lord Fraser expressed the view that documents sought should be, '... very likely to contain material that would give substantial support ...' to the applicant's case. A further ground for refusing discovery of the documents sought in that case was the view of their Lordships that most of the information contained therein was already available to the plaintiffs elsewhere.

It is submitted, therefore that the statement contained in the question rather misses the point as to how the courts are currently dealing with claims of public interest immunity made by government departments. Rather than deciding what is and what is not in the public interest, the courts are shifting the argument to whether or not the applicant can show why disclosure is necessary.

Following the public controversy during 1993–1994 over the use of public interest immunity in trials involving arms sales to Iraq, the judges began to reflect public concern by insisting that no new class claims should be recognised unless there is clear and compelling evidence that non-disclosure is necessary in the public interest: see, for example, per Lord Woolf (as he then was) in *R v Chief Constable of West Midlands Police, ex parte Wiley* (1994).

SUGGESTED ANSWER TO QUESTION TWO

General Comment

An unusual question since the main authorities on public interest immunity, with the exception of the *Air Canada* case have nothing to do with judicial review. Added to this, discovery has only been available on an application for review since 1977. Nevertheless one can argue that discovery is now a valuable weapon in support of an application for review.

Key Points

- Explain problems associated with the question
- Note that authorities are not review cases
- Explain the nature of immunity
- Explain changes in the application for review
- Interrelate the two issues with the *Air Canada* case
- Recent case law: *ex parte Wiley, Taylor* v *Anderton*

Suggested Answer

To consider the relationship between judicial review and the law relating to public interest immunity during the past 60 years may, at first sight, appear to be a pointless exercise. At the outset it has to be accepted that the landmark decisions on what was Crown immunity, such as *Duncan* v *Cammell, Laird & Co Ltd* (1942) and *Conway* v *Rimmer* (1968), both involved actions in tort, not judicial review. *Burmah Oil* v *Bank of England* (1980) concerned an action for relief in respect of an unconscionable bargain. That there is a link between the two becomes more apparent perhaps when one looks not so much at the subject matter of the individual cases dealing with claims of public interest immunity, but at the way in which the law has developed to open up decision making to the public gaze.

A claim of public interest immunity can arise in the course of litigation where the Crown, whether it is a party to the litigation or not, objects to the disclosure of certain evidence on the ground that such disclosure would not be in the public interest. The stage at which such a claim is usually made in civil proceedings is discovery of documents, a matter governed by O.24 of the Rules of the Supreme Court, under which discovery of documents will not be ordered by the courts unless it can be shown that disclosure is necessary for fairly disposing of the case or for saving costs.

Claims of public interest immunity will normally be based on one of the two criteria established in *Duncan* v *Cammell, Laird & Co Ltd*. In that decision a distinction was drawn between an objection to the production of a document on the basis of its contents (a 'contents' claim), and objection to the production of a document on the basis of its classification (a 'class' claim). The former might involve material such as plans for military hardware. The latter would be documents that had to be kept confidential because of the need for the efficient running of the administration, for example communications between civil servants and ministers. The argument was that if such communications were made public it would affect the candour with which civil servants gave their advice to ministers.

In *Conway* v *Rimmer*, the House of Lords made it clear that if there was a dispute between a minister and a litigant as to the desirability of a document being disclosed, it was ultimately for the courts to resolve the matter. Where a ministerial certificate is produced claiming privilege for certain documents, a trial judge is at liberty to inspect the material in question and either accept the certificate or grant discovery of the documents. A minister is free to appeal against any such order for discovery, however. *Conway* v *Rimmer* further suggests that if a claim of public interest immunity is put forward on a 'contents' basis, the judiciary might be more prepared to bow to the better judgment of the relevant minister. Where, however, the claim to immunity is put on the basis of 'class' of documents to which the material belongs, the courts would be more likely to assert their independence and if necessary override the minister's objections.

Have such issues arisen in the context of proceedings for judicial review? The procedure of applying for judicial review is used in order to test the legality of the actions taken by a public body or officer. In the vast majority of cases there will be no dispute as to fact and hence no need for cross examination upon facts. On this basis there is likely to be little need for discovery of documents or the administering of interrogatories. Furthermore, until the reforms instituted in 1977, an application for discovery of documents could not be made in proceedings for the prerogative orders, hence, strictly speaking, it would be impossible to consider the relationship between judicial review and public interest immunity over a 50-year period. In the course of his speech in *O'Reilly* v *Mackman* (1982), Lord Diplock adverted to the matter in these terms:

> '... the procedural disadvantages under which applicants for (certiorari) laboured remained substantially unchanged until the alteration of Order 53 in 1977. Foremost among these was the absence of any provision for discovery. In the case of a decision which did not state the reasons for it, it was not possible to challenge its validity for error of law in the reasoning by which the decision had been reached. If it had been an application for certiorari those who were the plaintiffs in *Anisminic* would have failed; it was only because by pursuing an action by writ for a declaration of nullity that the plaintiffs were entitled to the discovery by which the minute of the commission's reasons which showed that they had asked themselves the wrong question was obtained.'

The position now therefore is that discovery is available in judicial review proceedings, and a number of cases have arisen where applicants have been successful in obtaining evidence relating to administrative procedures and decision making. In *R* v *Secretary of State for Social Services, ex parte Hincks* (1979), a large number of documents were produced where the applicant was attempting to establish that the minister was in breach of his duty to provide health services. Similarly in *Williams* v *Home Office (No 2)* (1981), the applicant was permitted access to Home Office records concerning his transfer to a special control unit, despite the fact that this might affect the working of the prison service.

In the light of the above it is submitted that in the period between 1942 and 1977 the law relating to public interest immunity neither helped nor hindered the development of judicial review. What hindered the usefulness of judicial review was the availability of discovery altogether. If one looks at those categories of cases where public interest immunity is likely to prevail, such as national security, or the conduct of foreign affairs, judicial review proceedings would in any event be unlikely to succeed since such issues are largely non-justiciable.

In the modern context, the law relating to public interest immunity can help or hinder the development of judicial review depending upon whether it enables or prevents a litigant from gaining access to documents indicating the thinking behind, for example, a ministerial policy. On the basis of what is now the leading authority on this point, the conclusion might well be that it is a hindrance.

In *Air Canada* v *Secretary of State for Trade (No 2)* (1983) , where a number of airlines sought to establish that the minister had acted ultra vires in ordering an increase in landing charges at Heathrow Airport, the House of Lords stressed that the onus was on the party seeking disclosure of documents to show that it would be likely to support its case, or at least that there was a reasonable probability that it would do so. Lord Fraser expressed the view that documents sought should be, '... very likely to contain material that would give substantial support ...' to the applicant's case. In a sense a litigant has to know of the evidence of illegality before he can apply for its production. A note of encouragement was sounded by Lord Fraser, however, when he stated:

'I do not think that even Cabinet minutes are completely immune from disclosure in a case where, for example, the issue in a litigation involves serious misconduct by a Cabinet minister ... while Cabinet documents do not have a complete immunity, they are entitled to a high degree of protection against disclosure.'

In *R* v *Chief Constable of West Midlands Police, ex parte Wiley* (1994) Lord Woolf (as he then was) said that the 'class' categories of public interest immunity are today well settled and new ones should not be recognised unless there is clear and compelling evidence that non-disclosure is necessary in the public interest. However, the need to safeguard the proper functioning of public administration may be recognised as a sufficient public interest justifying non-disclosure: *Taylor* v *Anderton* (1995).

Hence one could conclude that the law relating to public interest immunity may have made judicial review more effective since many of the old obstacles to obtaining evidence have been removed; but the judiciary hold the balance, and there is clearly a heavy burden resting upon any applicant for review who needs evidence in normally confidential government papers to support his case.

3

Tribunals and Inquiries

Introduction

This chapter is concerned with the functions of tribunals and inquiries as devices for resolving disputes and ensuring participation for the ordinary citizen in important decision-making processes. The system of tribunals and inquiries is regulated by statute (currently the Tribunals and Inquiries Act 1992), and rules made under that statute. However, the statute is not comprehensive and common law plays an important part in controlling the manner in which tribunals and inquiries operate.

The history of tribunals and inquiries needs to be considered in order to evaluate their contribution to modern society. A useful starting point is the Franks Report (1957) Cmnd 218, which was the basis for many statutory reforms in this area, notably the setting up of the Council on Tribunals in 1958. The Council acts as an independent supervisory 'watchdog' over tribunals and inquiries, and it is useful to compare its role with that of the courts in assessing the effectiveness of external controls. A useful article on the Council on Tribunals is by Foulkes [1994] PL 564. A useful recent article on inquiries is by Sir Richard Scott (1995) 111 LQR 596.

The subject should be studied from a general historical perspective. There are no recent statutes or cases of special noteworthiness.

In regard to examinations, essay-type questions are the usual means of testing knowledge of this subject. Sometimes the question may be on tribunals only, or on inquiries only, or both, or even on the Council of Tribunals, though the tendency seems to be to ask for a critical analysis of the operation of the tribunal and inquiry system.

Questions

INTERROGRAMS

1 What are the main functions of a tribunal? How does it differ from a court of law?
2 What are the main functions of an inquiry? How does it differ from a tribunal?
3 What were the main recommendations of the Franks Report (1957)?
4 Describe the composition and functions of the Council on Tribunals.

QUESTION ONE

The Prime Minister appoints a Committee of Inquiry under Dame Margaret Obscure to 'investigate the reasons why tribunals have been created, examine their operation and effectiveness, and consider any proposals for reform'. Dame Margaret Obscure asks you, as the senior civil service lawyer seconded to the Committee, to prepare a briefing paper for the members of the Committee, outlining the role of tribunals in the administrative process and commenting on any reforms which seem desirable to you. Draft a memorandum in response to her request.

London University LLB Examination
(for external students) Administrative Law June 1987 Q6

QUESTION TWO

'Inquiries are a waste of time and money. They merely give the illusion of participation.'
   Discuss.

London University LLB Examination
(for external students) Administrative Law June 1987 Q5

QUESTION THREE

A new Transport Accidents Prompt Inquiries Act establishes an inspectorate for 'major disasters caused by any mode of transport'. Immediately after such disasters as an airplane, train or boat accident, an inspector is appointed to hold an inquiry into the causes of the accident and report to the relevant minister. The M25 motorway which encircles London is congested, so a new motorway has been built above the existing road, supported by stilts. A small portion of that higher road, the M50, collapses in the middle of the night. Fortunately, nobody is injured. An inspector is appointed and during the inquiry he refuses to let counsel for the engineers involved in the building of the M50 cross-examine eye-witnesses. The statute states that 'The inspector shall conduct the inquiry in whatsoever way he thinks fit'. The inspector explains that the purpose of the Act is to establish quickly whether there is any further danger to the public and there is no point in prolonging proceedings when counsel for the inquiry has already cross-examined those witnesses to the satisfaction of the inspector. The engineers seek judicial review of the inquiry, claiming that it is being conducted in breach of natural justice and that, in any event, it is ultra vires since an accident in which nobody is harmed cannot be a 'major disaster' and that Parliament meant vehicles, not roads, when enacting the phrase 'mode of transport'.
   Advise the engineers as to the likelihood of success.

London University LLB Examination
(for external students) Administrative Law June 1990 Q9

QUESTION FOUR

'Tribunals and inquiries merely give the citizen the illusion of participation in the administrative process.'
   Discuss.

London University LLB Examination
(for external students) Administrative Law June 1988 Q3

QUESTION FIVE

Compare and contrast the contribution of tribunals and inquiries to administrative law in the years since the Franks Report.

London University LLB Examination
(for external students) Administrative Law June 1989 Q6

Answers

ANSWERS TO INTERROGRAMS

1   The main functions of a typical tribunal in such fields as housing and social welfare disputes are to provide a cheap and efficient system for resolving such disputes, at the same time exercising a degree of discretion to ensure a fair and flexible administration of policy and justice. The typical tribunal will follow an adversarial procedure similar to that of a court of law, but the emphasis on cheap and speedy resolution of disputes means that a tribunal may take a more relaxed attitude towards rules of evidence and may discourage legal representation. Even where legal representation is permitted legal aid may not be available (which is the case with most typical tribunals). Tribunals therefore offend Dicey's concept of the rule of law, which put the emphasis on 'regular' courts of law as the most appropriate means of protecting individual rights in disputes against the state or other powerful institutions.

2   The main functions of a typical inquiry in an area such as planning law are to enable individual citizens to have their say in the decision-making process, and to inform the minister with the necessary facts and the views of those consulted so that the minister is better placed to decide a number of policy issues arising from, for example, a decision to build a new motorway.

   An inquiry is therefore different from a tribunal because, whereas a tribunal follows an adjudicatory procedure to resolve a dispute, an inquiry follows an inquisitorial process to determine facts, sound out opinions, and make recommendations. The final decision rests with a minister and it is often impossible to deduce the degree to which he/she has taken account of objectors' views – indeed, many cynics dismiss the typical inquiry as mere 'window-dressing', a charade which has no real influence on the final decision, which is determined by governmental policy needs.

3   The Franks Report (1957) made a number of important recommendations, most of which were later implemented by legislation. On tribunals, the outstanding recommendation was that tribunal procedures should be 'open, fair and impartial' so as to avoid the risk of arbitrary decisions-making. On inquiries, the Report recommended that inspectors holding inquiries should follow clear rules of procedure ensuring objectors' rights to call witnesses, to cross-examine opposing witnesses, to be legally represented and to be provided with reasons for the inspector's recommendations. Some of the Report's findings were not acted on, eg legal aid for tribunals operating in important fields of social welfare. Other findings were very speedily accepted, eg the Council on Tribunals was set up in 1958 to

implement the Report's view on the need for an independent supervisory body over the whole system of tribunals and inquiries.

4   There is a maximum of 16 members of the Council on Tribunals, many of whom work on a part-time basis. There is a lay majority. There is also a small secretariat to support Council members. The main functions of the Council are to keep under review the constitution and operation of most tribunals and inquiries. It can make annual reports on matters of general concern, as well as individual reports on specific matters, perhaps arising from a visit to a particular tribunal or local inquiry.

SUGGESTED ANSWER TO QUESTION ONE

General Comment

A question calling for an examination of how and why tribunals are used, and also some consideration of their shortcomings.

Key Points

- Principal finding of Franks Report
- Advantages of tribunals over courts of law
- Functions of tribunals
- Control of tribunals
- Reform proposals
- Role of Council on Tribunals

Suggested Answer

In many ways the question seems to be asking what would the Franks Committee on Tribunals and Inquiries report if it were to examine the tribunal system today. The Franks Report found that:

> 'Tribunals [were] not ordinary courts [of law], but neither [were] they appendages of Government Departments ... the essential point is that ... Parliament has deliberately provided for a decision outside and independent of the department concerned' ((1957) Cmnd 218, para 40).

The form that tribunals might take varies from one area of activity to another; whilst some decision making bodies are termed 'Authorities', possibly because they have a wide range of responsibilities – the Civil Aviation Authority provides an example – some bodies are referred to as 'Commissions', the Foreign Compensation Commission being a well known example.

The decision to allocate certain functions to a tribunal is one based on government policy. Frequently the policy is based on a desire to have matters decided by an independent body without having to resort to the complex procedures of the courts.

Tribunals enjoy many advantages over the courts of law in their role of forums for dispute resolution. Whilst judges are expert in law, tribunal members are frequently chosen because of their practical expertise in a given area, for example industrial relations, or local property values. The result is that they should be able to reach more well informed decisions on the matters before them. Tribunals handle approximately six times as many cases as the courts, indicating that they offer a very cost efficient method of solving disputes. Particularly in the case of welfare benefit appeals, the court system with its inherent delays, high costs, and formality would prove quite inappropriate as a means of providing redress.

Tribunals thus perform two functions. First, somewhat contrary to the desires expressed in the Franks Report, disputes which might once have been resolved by the courts have been allocated to tribunals – the system of Industrial Tribunals being an example. Secondly, the tribunal system deals with issues which would not, in the normal course of events, give rise to litigation anyway; for example the referral of a planned merger to the Monopolies and Mergers Commission. As has been observed by many writers, tribunals occupy a 'no man's land' between law and administration. They are creatures of the administration being established as a consequence of a policy decision, yet they are required and expected to act in a judicial fashion, without however becoming embroiled in the problems that beset the judicial process.

By a combination of the Tribunals and Inquiries Act 1992 and the inherent supervisory jurisdiction of the High Court in respect of inferior bodies, the tribunal system is overseen by the courts so as to ensure that they keep within the limits of their powers. Tribunals listed in the 1992 Act can be required to give reasoned decisions (a traditional safeguard against arbitrariness) and a right of appeal on a point of law lies from their decisions to the High Court. The power of review is sometimes used sparingly by the courts for fear of over-judicialising tribunal procedures which are meant to be uncomplicated (see *R* v *Preston Supplementary Benefits Appeal Tribunal, ex parte Moore* (1975)), but the existence of such a supervisory jurisdiction is in itself important.

Turning to reforms of the tribunal system, a number of issues arise for consideration. First, it is still true to say that there has been a proliferation of tribunals with little attempt to introduce uniformity in procedure, such as has been achieved in respect of inquiries by the adoption of the Town and Country Planning (Inquiries Procedure) Rules 1992. Further there is no uniformity in the provision of appeals from tribunal decisions. Where no right of appeal is provided, the only way in which an individual can challenge a decision is by appealing on a point of law, or applying for judicial review. The result is that if he is complaining about a tribunal decision on a question of fact, he is unlikely to be able to overturn it, judicial review being in theory only concerned with the legality of a decision, and not with its merits. A possible reform would therefore be the drafting of a model tribunals procedure, and the provision for a right of appeal on the merits of all decisions.

Whilst one of the oft-quoted advantages of tribunals is that they can act more swiftly than the courts of law and are less daunting to the ordinary person appearing before them, this lack of judicialisation does not always work to the advantage of the individual. Tribunals are not, for example, bound by the strict rules of evidence, but it has been suggested that decisions should not be based on hearsay evidence. Further, there may be situations where evidence should be given on oath. Franks thought that all tribunals should have the power to administer the oath, but confusion still exists on the question of whether or not some can. The difficulty here is in striking a balance between procedural propriety and informality.

Proceedings before tribunals attract qualified privilege (see *Royal Aquarium Society v Parkinson* (1892)), but may not in every case attract absolute privilege (see *Trapp* v *Mackie* (1979)). This is clearly in contrast with proceedings in court, and again the suggestion is that tribunals might work more effectively if those taking part in hearings felt the same freedom to speak as those in formal court hearings.

Given that the English legal system is one based on common law and adherence to precedent, it is somewhat surprising that tribunals remain, for the most part, free to operate without such constraints. The key lies of course in the absence of any reporting of decisions. In some areas, for example Industrial Tribunals and Social Security, this may no longer be the case, but for other tribunals, the work of members, advocates, and the interests of the parties could be well served by greater efforts to summarise and circulate recent decisions on matters of general importance. Consistency is, after all, one of the hallmarks of justice.

The conventional view of tribunal proceedings is that the lay person should be able to present his own case. Given the complexity of the law, and the inevitable judicialisation of the processes, many now seek legal help and representation. Many now consider a reform necessary so that legal aid for representation before tribunals should be extended to all tribunals.

Finally, the role of the Council on Tribunals should be expanded, and the Council given the resources it needs to perform its supervisory functions properly. At present it represents an understaffed toothless watchdog which, beyond submitting its annual reports and liaising with the Lord Chancellor, is unable to take effective action to reform the tribunal system.

SUGGESTED ANSWER TO QUESTION TWO

General Comment

Note that the quotation makes two assertions which both have to be dealt with. Reference should be had both to the Franks Report and judicial statements in assessing the accuracy of the assertions.

Key Points

- Types of inquiry
- Findings of the Franks Report
- Small scale and large scale inquiries – different purposes
- *Bushell*'s case
- Conclusions and reform suggestions

Suggested Answer

The quotation, in declaring inquiries to be a waste of time and money, is a gross overgeneralisation, as will be explained below; it does however echo a general disillusionment with the inquiry process, and the reasons why this should have arisen have to be considered. The charge of overgeneralisation stems from the fact there are a wide variety of inquiries, serving a number of functions; these range from the local planning inquiry held on behalf of the minister into the refusal of planning permission, to an inquiry into a large scale development, the application for which has been 'called in' by the minister. The Franks Report ((1957) Cmnd 218, para 269) expressed the view that the intention of Parliament in providing for an inquiry was twofold; to ensure that the interests of the citizens closely affected should be protected by the grant to them of a statutory right to be heard in support of their objections, and to ensure that the relevant minister should be better informed of the facts of the case. Many of the recommendations of the Committee were implemented by the government, with the result that the inquiry process became more judicialised in nature, this judicialisation arising in no small part from the imposition of far more stringent procedural requirements upon statutory inquiries.

The Franks Report did alight upon what has continued to be the main tension in the continuing debate on the nature and purpose of public inquiries: why are they held? The assertion that they are a waste of time and money because they provide only the illusion of public participation presupposes that such inquiries are held for the purpose of facilitating public participation. Such a view may be a serious misconception.

In the case of small-scale local planning inquiries, which do not raise issues of regional or national significance, it may be more realistic to talk in terms of those attending having some participatory role in the ultimate decision that is made. The Secretary of State will almost certainly have delegated the function of determining the outcome of the inquiry process to the inquiry inspector, who will decide the matter on the basis of the evidence before him. In such a case the procedure becomes much more adversarial than it might be at other inquiries, and those submitting evidence are entitled to feel that their contributions are likely to have some effect on the outcome.

As regards the more large-scale inquiries, such as those into proposals for new motorways, or large scale projects such as nuclear power stations, the participatory model seems inappropriate. Here the inquiry serves much more the purpose of informing the minister's mind. The key difference is the role of government policy. In, for example, the case of an inquiry into a proposed nuclear power station, the Secretary of State may have already made plain that government policy is in favour of developing nuclear power, the purpose of the inquiry being as to the suitability of a particular site. Indeed, government policy may be in favour of the site, in which case the participation in decision making by objectors is reduced to producing evidence at the inquiry which might persuade the minister to think again. In *Bushell* v *Secretary of State for the Environment* (1981), Lord Diplock made it clear that objectors at public inquiries into large-scale projects having national significance (in this case a planned motorway) should not view the proceedings at the inquiry as if they were at a court hearing.

The purpose of the inquiry, he explained, was to provide the minister with as much information about the objections as would ensure that in reaching his decision he would have weighed the harm to local interests and private persons who may be adversely affected by the scheme, against the public benefit which the scheme would be likely to achieve.

It is submitted that many view such inquiries as a waste of time and money because of the misconception that they are participating in the decision-making process, when in fact they are merely informing the minister of their views. It is this failure to grasp the fact that the minister will be deciding the matter on the basis of policy and national interest that leads many to regard the inquiry process as pointless. What can they say at an inquiry that will change the outcome?

The cynical would perhaps agree with the quotation on the basis that large-scale inquiries are an empty exercise in consultation, providing pressure groups and objectors merely with the opportunity to 'let off steam'. The feelings of frustration by those putting forward objections is evidenced by the unruly behaviour that sometimes erupts at such hearings. There can be no doubt that the supposed 'battle' between the government and objectors is an unfair one, in that the latter group will have only limited resources and information with which to fight their case. Again the expenditure of large sums of money on presenting objections at large public inquiries to no effect increases the sense of futility. On the other hand many of those promoting large-scale developments point to the delays that these consultation exercises cause, and contend that the economic progress of the country is frequently hampered as a result.

The answer may lie first in re-educating the general public in what can realistically be achieved by bringing forward objections at large scale public inquiries, and secondly by perhaps dealing with large scale public debates on developments of national significance in a different way. It may be better to adopt a procedure more similar to the examination-in-public, where there is no pretence of one side winning the argument, merely parties invited to make representations to the Secretary of State.

SUGGESTED ANSWER TO QUESTION THREE

General Comment

An unusual question that requires detailed consideration of two issues. Jurisdictional error and the application of natural justice to inquiries. There are basically two main authorities, and as such they need to be referred to in some detail.

Key Points

- Problem of who the respondent body will be
- Jurisdictional error
- Breach of natural justice
- The application of *Bushell*

Suggested Answer

The information given indicates that the engineers seek judicial review of the inquiry. The information indicates that the engineers think that they have been treated unfairly, by not being permitted to conduct cross-examination at the inquiry, and further that the inquiry had no jurisdiction to investigate the road collapse in any event.

Lack of jurisdiction
The enabling Act indicates that the inspectorate can conduct inquiries into 'major disasters caused by any mode of transport'.

The engineers' contention is that an accident such as occurred with the M50, in which nobody was harmed, cannot be a 'major disaster' and that Parliament when enacting the phrase 'mode of transport' meant this to refer to accidents caused by vehicular failure, not roads.

The terms 'major disaster' and 'mode of transport' refer to jurisdictional facts which must be established before the inquiry can have the power to investigate the matter. Clearly an inferior body, such as an inquiry, cannot be left to take the final decision on a question relating to the extent of its own jurisdiction, as this would make the supervisory role of the courts otiose. If one takes the example of a rent tribunal, a jurisdictional fact would be whether property is furnished or not; only when a conclusion that it is furnished has been reached can it proceed to determine a 'fair rent' for the premises.

The court's decision in *White & Collins* v *Minister of Health* (1939) is particulary helpful in analysing the problem raised by the engineers. A borough council exercised powers of compulsory purchase over land owned by the appellants. Under the statute these powers were not to be exercised over land forming part of (inter alia) any park, garden, or pleasure ground required for the amenity or convenience of any house. The appellants contended that some of the land over which the council had exercised its powers constituted parkland, and thus could not be acquired in this way.

A public inquiry was held into objections to the scheme, but the Minister confirmed the compulsory purchase order. The land owners applied to quash the Minister's confirmation. The Court of Appeal held that the order would have to be quashed. As Luxmoore LJ explained:

> 'The first and most important matter to bear in mind is that the jurisdiction to make the order is dependent on a finding of fact; for, unless the land can be held not to be part of a park ... there is no jurisdiction in the borough council to make, or in the Minister to confirm, the order. In such a case it seems almost self-evident that the Court which has to consider whether there is jurisdiction to make or confirm the order must be entitled to review the vital finding on which the existence of the jurisdiction relied upon depends. If this were not so, the right to apply to the Court would be illusory.'

In the present case it must be up to the courts to determine whether or not the facts which are preconditions to the exercise of discretion exist. Whether or not the engineers succeed with their challenge will depend largely upon the affidavit evidence put forward at the time of the application for review.

Breach of natural justice

If the engineers lose their argument as to lack of jurisdiction, the emphasis will shift to their contention that in any event they were not given a fair hearing at the inquiry because of the denial of their request to cross examine witnesses. The leading authority on this issue is the House of Lords' decision in *Bushell* v *Secretary of State for the Environment* (1981).

Objectors to a proposed motorway attended an inquiry, and sought to cross-examine the witnesses from the Department of the Environment on the need for the motorway. In particular they sought to question the validity of the department's traffic flow predictions. The inquiry inspector refused to allow cross-examination of the departmental witnesses on the grounds that government policy could not be questioned at the inquiry, and their cross-examination on the accuracy of the traffic flow forecasts would serve no useful purpose. The objectors claimed, inter alia, that the inquiry had not been conducted fairly.

Lord Diplock explained that with such inquiries the procedure to be adopted must necessarily be left to the discretion of the inspector appointed to hold the inquiry. In exercising that discretion, as in exercising any other administrative function, the inspector was under a constitutional duty to perform it fairly and honestly and to the best of his ability.

Lord Diplock warned against applying to procedures involved in the making of administrative decisions concepts that were appropriate to the conduct of ordinary civil litigation between private parties. His Lordship felt that the phrase 'natural justice' was inappropriate to describe the procedural niceties that had to be observed at such inquiries, preferring instead the view that the procedure adopted should simply be fair to those who have an interest in the decision that will follow it, whether they have been represented at the inquiry or not. What was a fair procedure to be adopted at a particular inquiry would depend upon the nature of its subject matter.

What is of vital significance in the present case is that the inquiry does not involve a lis inter partes but is merely an investigation. It is not clear what action might follow the inspector's report. On this basis it is submitted that the courts are unlikely to find a refusal of cross-examination to be unfair. To insist on cross-examination would be to run the risk of what Lord Diplock described as the 'overjudicialising' of the inquiry.

In conclusion, therefore, refusal by an inspector to allow a party to cross-examine orally at an inquiry a person who has made statements of facts or has expressed expert opinions is not unfair per se.

SUGGESTED ANSWER TO QUESTION FOUR

General Comment

Tribunals and inquiries are such different animals that it is wise to consider each separately. In relation to inquiries, emphasis should be placed on the significance of government policy to the final outcome. In relation to tribunals, emphasis should be placed on attendance, appearance, and membership.

Key Points

- Inquiries
  - impact of Franks Report
  - problems of facing objectors
- Tribunals
  - impact of Franks Report
  - attendance, appearance and membership

Suggested Answer

The statement in question refers to both tribunals and inquiries, however, given the difference in the nature of the proceedings of these two administrative devices, the question of public participation will be considered separately in relation to each.

Inquiries

Although inquiries can differ enormously in nature they will normally involve an investigation into a set of proposals affecting the public or a section of the public. Amongst those of chief concern to the administrative lawyer are those concerned with land use. The most significant investigation of the workings of such inquiries in recent years was that carried out by the Franks Committee in 1957. In its report ((1957) Cmnd 218) the Committee commented that it did not see public inquiries into land use as being either wholly judicial or administrative in nature. Inquiries were not judicial proceedings because any final decision would be taken after the hearing, possibly on the basis of factors not considered during the inquiry, such as ministerial policy, on the other hand they were not purely administrative, because they provided for a special hearing process prior to any decision making, a feature not normally encountered in the administrative process.

The Committee further recognised that the intention of Parliament in providing for the holding of a public inquiry was two-fold; to ensure that the interests of citizens closely affected by any proposals should be protected by giving them an opportunity to be heard in support of their objections, and to ensure that the relevant minister should be better informed as to the public's view before coming to any final decision. Too close an adherence to the 'administrative' view of inquiries would result in the role of participants being under-emphasised; too close an adherence to the 'judicial' model would result in participants wrongly viewing the inquiry inspector as a kind of judge having the power to determine the issues involved.

As a result of the Franks Committee's recommendations, certain persons can attend public inquiries as of right, but in addition, any person may attend at the discretion of the inquiry inspector: Town and Country Planning (Inquiry Procedure) Rules 1992, made under the Town and Country Planning Act 1990. In theory, therefore, there is considerable scope for public participation at inquiries. A number of factors, however, prevent this from becoming a reality in a number of cases.

A fundamental problem arises in relation to the public's conception of the inquiry process. Where, for example, an inquiry is held to consider objections into a proposed new highway development, many objectors will attend the inquiry in the mistaken belief that by expressing their anger and/or fear at the proposals, the building of the road can be prevented. There appears to be a widespread failure on the part of the public to grasp the significance of central government policy in relation to the issues considered by inquiries. The Town and Country Planning (Inquiry Procedure) Rules 1992, expressly state that if a representative of a government department attends to give evidence at a public inquiry held pursuant to the Rules, he is not to be required to answer any questions dealing with the merits of relevant government policy. Thus whilst members of the public can express their views as to proposed development, and lead evidence as to why it should not proceed, it is not the purpose of the public inquiry to provide an opportunity for members of the public to persuade government departments to change the policy upon which particular proposals are based.

The decision of the House of Lords in *Bushell* v *Secretary of State for the Environment* (1981) underlines the gap between the purpose of the public inquiry as seen by the courts and as seen by objectors appearing at the inquiry. It was held that objectors who had not been permitted to cross-examine a government official as to the need for a proposed motorway had not been treated unfairly because, in the view of Lord Diplock, it was wrong to equate a public inquiry with a court of law where a matter could be proved to be right or wrong. In his Lordship's opinion all that was required of the inquiry process at common law was that objectors should be able to state their case before the inspector. Lord Diplock emphasised that when a minister finally came to take his decision, following an inquiry inspector's report, he had to have regard not only to the interests of those members of the public who had attended the inquiry and stated their views, but also the wider public who had not attended, and who might yet have a significant interest in the outcome of the proceedings.

These limitations upon what can be achieved by the inquiry process are more likely to cause disillusionment amongst individual members of the public than organised pressure groups, who will have had more experience of such processes, yet even for organised objectors, effective participation in the inquiry process may be difficult to achieve. One obvious problem is that of resources. To mount an effective campaign of opposition to a proposal at a public inquiry may require a great deal of expensive research and preparation, and in addition expensive legal representation if it is to be put forward convincingly. Such limited resources are likely to be stretched even further where the inquiry into objections to proposals for a development such as a new motorway, is held at various points along the proposed route. Organised opposition may require attendance at each hearing.

Whilst the emphasis of the foregoing has been upon the inability of members of the public to participate in decisions based upon policy, it should be noted that any submissions made to an inquiry on a matter of fact can have a significant affect on the outcome. A minister is at liberty to reject an inquiry inspector's recommendations on a matter of policy, but under the 1992 Rules mentioned above, can only reject the inspector's findings on a matter of fact if he first allows interested parties to make fresh representations to him and provides his reasons for rejecting the recommendations.

Similarly, where a public inquiry concerns developments of a purely local nature, involving little or nothing in the way of central government policy considerations, the direct contribution of members of the public attending the inquiry is likely to have a far greater affect on the eventual outcome, as the inspector will be basing his recommendation on the evidence adduced before him. Indeed, there is an increasing tendency for ministers to exercise their discretion to delegate the actual decision-making function to inquiry inspectors in some cases, thus making the links between those attending public inquiries and those determining the issues even closer.

In conclusion, the prospect of public participation in the inquiry process is real as regards questions of fact, but illusory as regards issues of policy.

Tribunals

As regards access to tribunals, the Franks Committee recommended that as a general rule, their proceedings should be open to the public, so as to ensure public confidence in the fairness of the proceedings. The Committee recognised that there were three situations where the right of the public to attend should be curtailed. Proceedings in camera might be justified where issues relating to national security arose; where intimate personal or financial details were to be disclosed; and in cases involving questions of professional capacity and reputation. Subject to these three categories the Committee felt that the exclusion of the public should be a matter within the discretion of the chairman of the relevant tribunal.

The Council on Tribunals tries to ensure that procedural rules for new tribunals allow the public a right to attend, but if the public are allowed to attend at a tribunal hearing, the room for them to do so is likely to be extremely limited. It is certainly not a requirement of natural justice that tribunal hearings should be open to the public.

As regards participation in the actual decision-making by tribunals, members of the public appearing before them clearly enjoy a greater degree of participation than is the case with inquiries. Most tribunal proceedings are adversarial in nature, and if a citizen, who is appearing against a government department before a tribunal, can adduce sufficient evidence and establish the legal position in his favour, he will clearly achieve the result he seeks. As is the case with inquiries, however, if there is a high degree of policy underlying the tribunal's decision-making, the role of the citizen will clearly be diminished; see for example the role of the Civil Aviation Authority in licensing airline operators.

A third aspect of public participation in the decision-making processes of tribunals is as members. Some tribunals do provide for lay membership, but such members will normally have some expertise in the relevant subject area. In the case of Industrial Tribunals for example there will be, in addition to a legally qualified chairman, a representative from an employers' organisation and a representative from the trade unions. In this respect it is submitted that participation by the citizen in the processes of tribunals is very real and effective.

SUGGESTED ANSWER TO QUESTION FIVE

General Comment

This straightforward question requires a comparison of the effectiveness of tribunals and inquiries as administrative devices and the extent to which this has been affected by the implementation of recommendations in the Franks Report.

Key Points

- Rule of tribunals and inquiries in public administration
- The Franks Report
- Summary of key reforms to tribunals
- Remaining problem areas
- Advantages over courts

- Problems of large-scale planning inquiries
- Conflicting expectations
- Small-scale inquiries

Suggested Answer

Administrative law is essentially concerned with public administration. Two administrative devices which have assumed increasing importance in recent years are tribunals and inquiries; the former were conceived as an alternative form of dispute resolution while the latter are generally used to conduct some sort of public investigation as a prelude to decision making, particularly in the planning context.

Concerns about defects in the operation of inquiries and in particular of tribunals led to the setting up of the Committee on Administrative Tribunals and Inquiries (the Franks Committee) which produced a report containing a large number of recommendations for reform: (1957) Cmnd 218. These subsequently led to the creation of the Council on Tribunals to review the constitution and working of certain tribunals and inquiries and to the enactment of the Tribunals and Inquiries Act 1958 (the Act) (now consolidated by the Tribunals and Inquiries Act 1992).

In the case of tribunals, the main achievement of the Council of Tribunals has been the promotion of the presidential system of organising tribunals (thereby providing for better communications between tribunals of the same class), the publication of guidelines for members and the provision of assistance in organising, training sessions and meetings of chairman. However, despite the Council's efforts, there is still no standardised procedure before tribunals and no consistency in the quality or training of tribunal members. Similarly, although the Act has improved the accountability of tribunals in terms of requiring them to give reasons and subjecting their decisions to appeal to the High Court on points of law, these provisions only apply to certain tribunals listed in the Act.

Furthermore, there continue to be a number of other problem areas where the impact of reforms has been minimal. For example, there are still serious concerns about independence arising from the method of appointment of tribunal members (presidential members are selected from a list drawn up by the Lord Chancellor, but other members are appointed at the discretion of the minister), their lack of security of tenure and their close associations with government departments. In addition, the lack of availability of legal aid to cover representation at many tribunals, when combined with the increased judicialisation which has taken place in their procedures, has tended to undermine their objective of providing a cheap and accessible alternative to the courts. It should also be noted that problems as to how to strike an appropriate balance between procedural propriety and formality and between consistency and flexibility still remain largely unresolved.

Nevertheless, tribunals have made an invaluable contribution to public administration in terms of providing an avenue of dispute resolution which is more informal, cheaper, speedier and more accessible to applicants than the courts. It is also a mechanism which is capable of being more efficient in terms of allowing for adjudication by persons who have a special expertise in the subject matter of the dispute. Furthermore, to the extent that their procedures and staffing have been improved by the reforms which followed the Franks Report, their contribution has become more effective.

In the case of inquiries, their major contribution has been as a device which allows for the injection of public input into governmental decision-making, particularly in the context of land use planning. However, their effectiveness in the context of large-scale inquiries has been hampered by an apparent divergence between the objectives which would appear to underlie the more judicialised procedures introduced in the post Franks era, and the views of the government and the courts as to the purposes they are intended to achieve.

The problem in brief is that the adversarial type procedures which are used give rise to an expectation on the part of members of the public that the inquiry will take the form of an adversarial contest and that the final decision will be based on the evidence and facts raised. This view is at odds with that taken by the government and the courts, which is that they are essentially an information-gathering process which is designed to ensure that the decision-maker arrives at a more informed decision, and that it is not their purpose to ensure that members of the public have any say in the final decision (see *Bushell* v *Secretary of State for the Environment* (1981)).

In view of the above, it would seem that there are serious deficiencies in the inquiry mechanism. If it is the purpose of inquiries to allow for public participation in the policy-making process then this needs to be more clearly expressed in the relevant legislation. If, on the other hand, inquiries are simply designed as information-gathering exercises then their procedures should be altered to reflect this fact, and the public should be re-educated accordingly. In the meantime, it is arguable that inquiries are unduly expensive and time consuming as an information-gathering mechanism, and that they create unrealistic expectations which are evidenced in the unruly and disruptive behaviour which sometimes erupts at such hearings.

It should, however, be noted that these criticisms do not apply with the same force to small-scale local planning inquiries. As these do not involve broad policy issues, it is more likely that the courts will accept that those attending should have some participating role in the ultimate decision. As a result these have not attracted the same degree of criticism and have, arguably, made a more effective contribution to administrative law than the large-scale inquiry.

4

Statutory Corporations

Introduction

This chapter is concerned with the implementation of local authority powers and duties. The framework of local government and its relationship with central government are essentially matters of constitutional law and are therefore not dealt with here. Instead the emphasis is on the concept of public authority liability and, in particular, the way the courts have limited the legal responsibility of public bodies for the negligent exercise of power.

It should be noted that public authority liability is a concept stretching beyond local government, and that some of the leading cases concern other types of statutory corporation (eg those responsible for the few remaining nationalised industries) or even the Crown itself through the central government departments: see, eg, *Home Office v Dorset Yacht Co Ltd* [1970] AC 1004. Hence, a background knowledge of the Crown Proceedings Act 1947 is useful when examining these analogous cases.

However, the bulk of authority consists of local authority cases and the main theme of academic interest in this context is the way in which judges first developed and then refined what has become known as the 'policy/operation' dichotomy in public law. Briefly, the rule is that tortious liability will attach only to a negligent implementation of policy. Negligence in the policy-making process itself is a matter of public law and judicial review rather than private law and writ procedures: *Anns v Merton London Borough Council* [1978] AC 728. Although this case was later overruled insofar as it held local authorities liable for pure economic loss (*Murphy v Brentwood District Council* [1991] 1 AC 398), it was not overruled so far as it concerned the policy/operation test. However, the test has remained controversial, and in later cases judges began to express their dissatisfaction with it and to substitute new tests.

There are several recent cases which illustrate this trend away from *Anns v Merton London Borough Council*, most notably: *X v Bedfordshire County Council* [1995] 3 All ER 353; *Stovin v Wise* [1996] 3 All ER 801; *Welton v North Cornwall District Council* [1997] 1 WLR 570; *Barrett v Enfield London Borough Council* [1997] 3 WLR 628; and *Capital and Counties plc v Hampshire County Council* [1997] 2 All ER 865.

Recent articles exploring the policy/operation dichotomy include ones by Convery (1997) 60 MLR 559, Harris (1997) 113 LQR 398, Cane (1996) 112 LQR 13 and Hopkins [1996] CLJ 425.

It should also be noted in the context of public authority liability that one of the few cases in which damages may be awarded under the public law process of judicial review is where the ultra vires decision consists of deliberate or grossly negligent misuse of power amounting to the tort of 'misfeasance in a public office'. The elements of this special tort were recently examined in *Three Rivers District Council v Bank of England (No 3)* [1996] 3 All ER 558: see further Hadjiemmenuil [1997] PL 32.

In regard to examinations, essay-type questions on public authority liability generally may be expected, although it is an area which lends itself well to problem-type questions involving local authorities. At least one question on public authority liability can be anticipated in a typical examination paper.

Questions

INTERROGRAMS

1   What do you understand by the policy/operation dichotomy in public law?
2   What is the effect of *X* v *Bedfordshire County Council* on the policy/operation test?
3   What is the effect of *Stovin* v *Wise* on the policy/operation test?
4   Can damages be recovered if a public body commits a breach of a statutory duty?
5   What are the ingredients of the tort of misfeasance in a public office?

QUESTION ONE

a   Under the Road Traffic Regulation Act a highway authority is empowered to place double white lines on roads. Some twenty years ago the Department of Transport issued guidelines in the matter, recommending that roads less than twenty feet wide should not have double white lines. Gravel DC then resolved to adhere to those guidelines and accordingly did not provide such lines on a particular stretch of road. Over the years, minor road repairs there had caused the width of the road to exceed twenty feet but double white lines were not provided.

   Evan was injured in a road accident at that spot, and alleges that if double white lines had been provided, the accident would not have taken place. He wishes to sue Gravel DC. Advise him.

b   Write an account of the tort of misfeasance in a public office.

London University LLB Examination
(for external students) Administrative Law June 1985 Q6

QUESTION TWO

A local authority has statutory power, if it is satisfied that the electrical installations in any dwelling house are below acceptable safety standards, to require the householder to carry out repairs and, if he fails to do so within seven days, to enter the premises, if need be by force, and arrange for the work to be carried out at the householder's expense.

On receipt of information from a council employee who had been working in Joseph's house, the Public Safety Committee of the Bullying District Council sent a notice to Joseph requiring him to make arrangements for the rewiring of his house. Joseph was not allowed to make representations to the Council. Two weeks later, council officials arrived. Joseph refused to allow them to enter; the officials forced their way in and permitted Kevin, an electrician, to carry out the necessary work, for which Joseph has been sent a bill. In the incident Joseph received a dislocated shoulder and his door and hallway were damaged. Kevin has done much work of this kind for the council and is the brother-in-law of Lee, a member of the Public Safety Committee.

Advise Joseph what remedies he may have and what would be the most appropriate course of action for him to take.

London University LLB Examination
(for external students) Administrative Law June 1992 Q9

QUESTION THREE

The (fictitious) Building Inspection Act 1995 empowers councils to inspect new buildings to ensure they meet statutory standards. Two years ago Northam Council decided to exercise this power and council surveyors inspected a new Basset plc housing development in the village of Sunnyside. Acting on Planning Committee instructions, the surveyors inspected only one in three of its houses. In January last year the council stopped all inspections, claiming it could no longer afford the service.

The council learned in March last year that one surveyor had falsely reported inspecting some houses. The council took no action. This information was subsequently leaked to the Local Government Ombudsman, who concluded that the council's failure to act was maladministration. The council still took no action.

In May this year, Sunnyside was battered by a hurricane. Fred's Basset house collapsed entirely. Jill, who was staying with Fred at the time, was hit by falling masonry. In addition to suffering a broken leg, she was hospitalised for three weeks and was unable to go on the foreign holiday she had booked in April. Ben's house remains intact, but repair costs are estimated at £10,000.

Fred and Ben subsequently discovered that the houses' foundations did not meet national standards, being two rather than three feet deep. They also established that Fred's house would have been inspected in February last year had the service not been discontinued, and that Ben's house was one of the properties falsely reported as inspected.

Advise Fred, Ben and Jill if they could successfully establish a claim for liability in negligence against the council.

Adapted from London University LLB Examination
(for external students) Administrative Law June 1993 Q9

Answers

ANSWERS TO INTERROGRAMS

1 The policy/operation dichotomy was first explored by the House of Lords in *Home Office* v *Dorset Yacht Co Ltd* [1970] AC 1004 and later developed, notably by Lord Wilberforce, in *Anns* v *Merton London Borough Council* [1978] AC 728. Essentially the rule is that no private law liability can arise from negligent policy-making unless so extreme as to constitute the tort of misfeasance in a public office, for which damages are available under a judicial review: *Dunlop* v *Woollahra Municipal Council* [1981] 1 All ER 1202. Private law liability will attach to negligent operation of policy decisions. However, the distinction between policy and operation is a very fine one and may be said to be a question of fact and degree.

2   In *X* v *Bedfordshire County Council* [1995] 3 All ER 353 the House of Lords appeared to move away from the policy/operation test by asking instead whether it was 'fair, just and reasonable' for the common law duty of care to be imposed in the situation in question, even if that situation concerned a clearly operational decision. Under the 'fair, just and reasonable' test it is open to the court to have regard to the special responsibilities that may burden the public authority in question. This consideration may persuade the court to exempt the public body from private law liability.

3   In *Stovin* v *Wise* [1996] 3 All ER 801 a majority of the House of Lords disapproved of the policy/operation test as formulated in *Anns* v *Merton London Borough Council*, and instead put the emphasis on the rationality of the decision not to exercise the power in question and on whether there were exceptional grounds justifying the award of compensation to persons who suffered loss because of the failure to exercise the power in question, eg had it been appreciated by the public body that there had been general reliance on it to exercise the power in issue? It was also open to the court to take account of any budgetary constraints facing a public body, which might have justified the failure to exercise the power in question.

4   Both *X* v *Bedfordshire County Council* and *Stovin* v *Wise* indicate that the courts will be reluctant to impose liability for breach of statutory duties where the duties in question involved onerous responsibilities designed to protect society generally or promote public welfare (*X* v *Bedfordshire County Council* concerned child care responsibilities of local authorities and *Stovin* v *Wise* concerned the duties of a local highway authority). In other words, the statutory duty is not by itself a sufficient basis for establishing liability; a plaintiff must be able to satisfy common law requirements of foreseeability and proximity, as well as the common law test of whether it is fair, just and reasonable to impose liability for the breach. If (as is probable) the breach of statutory duty is discernible only after an examination of the relevant framework of public law discretions, then the matter can only be determined by public law and it may turn out that there is no private law action for breach of duty at all: see *O'Rourke* v *Camden London Borough Council* [1997] 3 All ER 23, overruling *Thornton* v *Kirklees Metropolitan Borough Council* [1979] QB 626 and disapproving *Cocks* v *Thanet District Council* [1983] AC 286 (see further Chapter 5).

5   The tort of misfeasance in a public office is committed if *either* the defendant intended to injure the plaintiff (or a person in a class of which the plaintiff was a member) *or* the defendant knew that he had no power to do the act complained of and that the act would probably injure the plaintiff.

For the purpose of proving intention it is sufficient that the defendant had actual knowledge that the act was unlawful or that the defendant did not take such steps as a reasonable and honest man would have taken to ascertain whether, in case of doubt, the act was beyond his power. Malice, in the sense of an intent to injure, and knowledge (actual or imputed) that a certain activity is ultra vires, are alternative, not cumulative, bases for an allegation of misfeasance.

Finally, the plaintiff must prove not only that he suffered loss or damage as a result of the misfeasance but also that he has a sufficient right or interest to maintain an action for misfeasance.

The authority for the above propositions is *Three Rivers District Council* v *Bank of England (No 3)* [1996] 3 All ER 558.

SUGGESTED ANSWER TO QUESTION ONE

General Comment

Part (a) requires a clear explanation of the policy/operation dichotomy that arises in any discussion of the negligent exercise of statutory powers by local authorities.

Part (b) requires specific knowledge of the more obscure aspects of liability; care must be taken to distinguish between misuse and usurpation of power.

Key Points

a • Policy/operation
   • Dichotomy
   • *Dorset Yacht* case
   • *Anns* v *Merton London Borough Council*
   • Public law challenge
   • Problems with imposing duty of care
   • Policy decision by highway authority
   • *West* v *Buckinghamshire County Council*
b • Assumption and misuse cases
   • Availability of damages
   • Problems of proving malice
   • Current position
   • *Three Rivers District Council* case

Suggested Answer

a   Generally, local authorities can incur tortious liability in the same way as any other body possessing legal personality. Where the exercise of statutory powers is being considered, however, some special considerations may come into play.

Following Lord Diplock's speech in *Home Office* v *Dorset Yacht Co Ltd* (1970) a distinction may be drawn between the actions of a public body and those of a private body. The rules of liability in negligence, which was essentially a private law concept, could not be applied to the exercise of statutory powers by public bodies without some degree of modification.

When public bodies exercise their statutory powers, they may be taking two different types of decision. First, they may be taking policy decisions, such as what sort of regime ought to be operated in a juveniles prison. Secondly, there were decisions that were 'operational'. Thus where discretion was delegated to a prison officer as to how he supervised individual inmates, his decisions would fall within the operational sphere. The consequence of this distinction is of significance. Where an exercise of discretion falls within the 'policy' sphere, it can only be attacked, if at all, on a public law basis. This means that an individual wishing to establish that the policy was illegal would have to apply for judicial review to have it declared ultra vires. He may have suffered loss as a result of an ultra vires policy being adopted but that of itself does not entitle him to an award of damages. In *Dunlop* v *Woolhara Municipal Council* (1981) the Privy Council held that damages were not payable to Dr Dunlop who had suffered financial loss as a result of the imposition of ultra vires building regulations by the local authority, and Lord Diplock went on to state that even if the local authority had failed to take reasonable care in imposing the regulations (which he found they had not) he doubted whether any duty of care was owed to Dr Dunlop anyway. Policy decisions therefore cannot be challenged by way of a private law action in negligence.

In *Anns* v *Merton London Borough Council* (1978) Lord Wilberforce explained that it was easier to impose the private law concept of duty of care onto operational activities, such as the inspection of building foundations by a local authority inspector, but even then, no action in negligence would lie until it could be shown that the inspector was acting beyond the scope of the discretion delegated to him.

Although the policy/operation test has come in for much criticism (eg see *Rowling* v *Takaro Properties Ltd* (1988), *X* v *Bedfordshire County Council* (1995) and *Stovin* v *Wise* (1996)), it is suggested that it remains a useful guide in cases such as the present, where the facts are mundane and straightforward.

Applying these considerations to the problem in question, the decision of Gravel DC not to place double white lines on the road would seem to fall within the 'policy' area. Evan could challenge the decision by way of judicial review, but is unlikely to succeed because the authority have had regard to the central government guidelines, and there is no evidence of a history of accidents on the stretch of road in question, and in any case the remedies available would not include damages unless he was able to show that they would have been available by way of an action started by writ.

In *Anns* v *Merton London Borough Council* both Lord Wilberforce and Lord Salmon tend towards the view that a policy decision by a local authority not to exercise its powers would not give rise to any action in negligence by an individual who had suffered loss as a result.

Almost identical facts fell to be considered by the court in *West* v *Buckinghamshire County Council* (1984) wherein Caulfield J held that the decision by a highway authority not to place double white lines on a road was a policy decision which it was entitled to take in pursuance of its statutory powers, and therefore no duty of care arose.

b The tort of misfeasance in public office is a matter which comes before the courts only rarely, thus the available law on the nature and extent of the remedy is perhaps inconclusive. The paucity of case law is testament either to the quality of administration, or ignorance as to its existence as a remedy.

The cases seem to fall into two categories. First there are the situations where an official purports to exercise power that he does not in fact possess. The tort can be committed even where the defendant believes himself to be acting for the good of the community. This is illustrated by *Roncarelli* v *Duplessis* (1959) where the Premier of Quebec personally intervened to order the revocation of a liquor licence because he had been helping a religious sect offensive to the Quebec government.

It would appear that where the defendant purports to use powers that he does not possess, but is ignorant of the fact that he is not so empowered to act, no action for damages will lie simply because his actions are ultra vires, see *Dunlop* v *Woolhara Municipal Council* above.

The second type of case is where the defendant misuses power he does in fact possess. The English courts have been slow to recognise such action as giving rise to a claim in damages: see *Davis* v *Bromley Corporation* (1908). In *Smith* v *East Elloe Rural District Council* (1956), the House of Lords declined to strike out a claim against the Council's clerk that he had been involved in the making and confirming of a compulsory purchase order in bad faith, although ultimately the action was unsuccessful: see *Smith* v *Pywell* (1959).

In *Asoka Kumar David* v *Mamm Abdul Cader* (1963), a Privy Council decision concerning allegations that the plaintiff had been refused a cinema licence out of malice, their Lordships chose not to follow the approach in *Davis* v *Bromley Corporation*, and instead looked at the rights created between the two parties by the relationship under which one wished to operate a licence to do so, and the other had the statutory responsibility for deciding how to deal with the application. The precise scope of the tort of misfeasance in public office was examined in *Three Rivers District Council* v *Bank of England (No 3)* (1996), where it was held that although it has similarities with private law torts which require proof of an intention to injure, the tort of misfeasance in public office is primarily concerned with deliberate and dishonest abuse of power. Malice, in the sense of an intent to injure, and knowledge that a certain activity is ultra vires, are alternative, not cumulative, bases for an allegation of misfeasance.

SUGGESTED ANSWER TO QUESTION TWO

General Comment

This problem centres on the liability of a council to pay damages in particular circumstances. It also raises the issue of the interaction between private and public law remedies. To what extent is a council liable for actions of its employees? Misfeasance in public office must also be briefly considered.

Key Points

- Public law and private law remedies
- Ultra vires decision
- Council employees
- Misfeasance

Suggested Answer

Two general observations may be made be begin with. The first is that Joseph may have a claim for damages. Clearly, if possible, it will be to his advantage to bring such claims against the Bullying District Council, since they should be able to satisfy judgment whereas the other parties involved might not be able to do so. Secondly, Joseph's remedies will lie both in judicial review proceedings and in the civil courts for damages. In *O'Reilly* v *Mackman* (1983) it was held that, as a general rule, judicial review must be used as the only remedy if the public law issues in the case are the only issues or the predominant ones, but, since Joseph's injuries and loss appear to give rise to private law rights which are more than merely subsidiary to the public law issue of ultra vires, he is entitled to issue a writ for damages in the ordinary civil court as an alternative to seeking judicial review.

Turning now to the remedies Joseph may have. There are clear indications that the Council has proceeded in an unlawful manner. Where an authority proposes to interfere with a person's property rights, it must give that person an opportunity to be heard in the matter in accordance with the principle expressed in *Cooper* v *Wandsworth Board of Works* (1863). Failure to do so is a breach of natural justice which renders the decision ultra vires. As a result of this entry upon the premises and carrying out works thereon pursuant to the council's decision is itself unlawful, and therefore amounts to trespass. As a council is vicariously liable for the torts of its employees committed in the course of their employment, Joseph has an effective remedy against the council.

The question of the injuries Joseph has suffered, and the damage to his house, is more serious. We are not told how these injuries arose, or who caused them. If they arose as a result of an assault committed upon Joseph then in theory he may sue his assailant. Again, if the assault was committed by the council officials, and was committed in the course of their duties, then the council will be vicariously liable. The argument might be raised that the council is empowered by the statute to use force in order to carry out its duties. Two points may be stated in response to this. The first is that, as stated above, the council's actions were ultra vires in this instance and therefore entry into Joseph's premises by force is itself unlawful as carried out pursuant to an unlawful decision. Secondly, even if the decision were lawful, by analogy with a number of nuisance cases, the council may only escape liability for the injuries suffered if they were an inevitable result of the exercise of its powers under the statute: *Manchester Corporation* v *Farnworth* (1930). Judging from the severity of the injuries sustained, it is doubtful whether they can be said to be inevitable even if the statute provides that force may be used.

If the injuries result from the negligent actions of the council officials, then the council will be liable. The inevitability argument does not fall to be considered because negligence is held never to be inevitable: *Geddis* v *Proprietors of Bann Reservoir* (1873). If the injuries and damages were suffered solely as a result of Kevin's actions, then Joseph will have to sue him.

Finally, there may be the tort of misfeasance in public office, given the relationship between Kevin and Lee. There is only a bare suspicion of this, but the test will be that in *Three Rivers District Council* v *Bank of England (No 3)* (1996), which requires proof of deliberate abuse of power by public officials. Malice, in the sense of an intent to injure, and knowledge that a certain activity is ultra vires, are alternative, not cumulative, bases for an allegation of misfeasance. The question will be whether Lee has acted maliciously, or with knowledge that what he was doing was unlawful and knowing that his actions would harm Joseph. Given the breach of natural justice that has occurred, and the possibility of bias arising out of the relationship between Kevin and Lee, there is a hint of misfeasance. But it is only a hint, and on the facts given Joseph's claim on this point would not appear to be strong.

I would therefore advise Joseph that he has a strong claim in damages and that he should bring proceedings against the council, its officials and Kevin for trespass and for assault or negligence.

SUGGESTED ANSWER TO QUESTION THREE

General Comment

This question requires a consideration of the relationship between negligence and the exercise of statutory powers (as opposed to duties). Consider the various ways in which the council may have been negligent, and the strength of the claim arising out of that negligence. There is a difference in preliminary decisions (such as resource allocation) and in the execution of the power, but to what extent does the rule in *Anns* v *Merton* continue after *Murphy* v *Brentwood District Council*?

Key Points

- Liability dependent upon causation
- Resource allocation
- Ben
  - vicarious liability of council
  - misrepresentation
  - negligent failure to inspect
  - negligent advice
  - economic loss or physical damage?
- Jill and Fred – council policy

Suggested Answer

Each of these parties must be able to satisfy the general criteria of negligence in addition to the specific rules relating to administrative authorities. In particular, it will be necessary to show that had the foundations met national standards, then the hurricane would not have caused the damage.

The council's decision to inspect only one in three of the houses appears to have no bearing on any of these potential claims. If it does have, such a decision could not of itself make the council liable. Given that the statute gives the council a power, as opposed to imposing a duty, its discretion on how to allocate its resources so as to exercise that power generally cannot be impugned; but the power must not be exercised in an ultra vires manner (see *Rowling* v *Takaro Properties Ltd* (1988)).

Ben may have a number of grounds for claiming against the council. The first is that, if the surveyor in question was a council employee, as seems to be the case, then the council will be vicariously liable for torts committed by him in the course of his employment. The surveyor's misrepresentation that he had inspected Ben's house may amount to tortious fraud in respect of which the court will award damages.

Secondly, once the council discovered that the surveyor had falsely reported Ben's house as inspected, it may have been under a duty to order a proper inspection of the building. *Anns* v *Merton London Borough Council* (1978) held that an authority with a discretionary power to inspect buildings had a duty to consider properly whether or not to use that power. Although *Anns* has been formally overruled by *Murphy* v *Brentwood District Council* (1990), the point at issue appears to have survived the latter case. If that is so, then it may be argued that once it became known that the surveyor's report was false the council should have ordered inspection of the premises, and was negligent in not doing so. This argument derives force from the findings of the Ombudsman. However, claims for pure economic loss, as distinguished from direct consequential loss, are not recoverable as against the council: *Murphy* v *Brentwood District Council*, above, overruling *Anns* on this point.

Thirdly, when statutory powers are conferred and exercised, they must be exercised with reasonable care. Although this appears to be a case of nonfeasance it is plainly a misrepresentation to report that a house meets national standards without actually checking whether that is the case. Since the power to inspect was conferred for the purpose of ensuring compliance with national standards, such a misrepresentation could be argued to be a negligent exercise of the statutory power. As stated above, the council will be vicariously liable for the surveyor's negligence if he is an employee. Even if this is not the case, by not taking action once it was found that the surveyor had made a false report, the council may be said to have acted negligently.

The only difficulty that Ben might face is in categorising the damage that he has suffered. It is not clear whether the loss is purely economic, or whether physical damage has occurred. If the house needs to be repaired because physical damage has occurred, then there should be no bar to Ben's recovery of damages under any of the heads of negligence set out above. If the loss is purely economic Ben's claim will fail because it is now clear that a council cannot be made liable for pure economic loss caused by negligent exercise of statutory powers (*Murphy* v *Brentwood District Council*).

Fred and Jill will be unlikely to be able to claim against the council. The only thing that can be impugned is the council's decision to discontinue the service. This would appear to be a policy decision on the allocation of financial resources. Such decisions are beyond the scope of negligence unless they are ultra vires (*Rowling* v *Takaro Properties Ltd*), and there is no apparent ultra vires in this case. Fred and Jill should consider their remedies against Basset plc.

5

Introduction to Judicial Review

Introduction

This chapter is concerned with the procedural rules for making an application for judicial review under RSC O.53 (s31 Supreme Court Act 1981). This is a very important area because over the years, particularly recent years, it has thrown up a number of complex issues concerning the scope of judicial review, the degree to which O.53 is an exclusive procedure for public law cases, the distinction between public and private law, and the definition of legal standing (locus standi) for the purpose of making an O.53 application.

It is probably the most difficult part of the syllabus if only because of the volume of recent case law concerning the interpretation of complex procedural rules. It is, therefore, a challenging area, not only because of the amount of detail that needs to be grasped, but also because of the controversial character of many of the decisions which demand critical analysis.

On the scope of judicial review it is essential to understand the *Datafin* principle (*R v Panel on Take-overs and Mergers, ex parte Datafin plc* [1987] 2 WLR 699), which contains the modern test for recognising when a particular institution has a sufficient 'public' character as to be amenable to judicial review. This test examines the *functions* being performed and is different from the traditional test which examined the *source* of the institution's powers. However, it must not be assumed that the source of power is an irrelevant factor in determining the public or private character of an institution – note especially *R v Disciplinary Committee of the Jockey Club, ex parte The Aga Khan* [1993] 2 All ER 853. A useful recent article examining *Datafin* is by Forsyth [1996] CLJ 122.

On the exclusivity principle the case of *O'Reilly v Mackman* [1983] 2 AC 237 needs to be carefully analysed, not only to understand the scope of that principle and the exceptions to it but also the reasons why the principle was propounded. Are those reasons cogent? They have come in for much academic criticism and there appears to be a judicial trend away from a rigid interpretation of the *O'Reilly v Mackman* rule to a more flexible approach which concentrates on the question of whether it would be an 'abuse of process' to permit a challenge to proceed by way of private law methods rather than by judicial review. Recent cases on this point include: *Mercury Communications Ltd v Director-General of Telecommunications* [1996] 1 All ER 575; *British Steel plc v Customs and Excise Commissioners* [1996] 1 All ER 1002 (QBD); [1997] 2 All ER 366 (CA) (see further Bamforth [1997] PL 603); *O'Rourke v Camden London Borough Council* [1997] 3 All ER 23; *Trustees of the Dennis Rye Pension Fund v Sheffield City Council* [1997] 4 All ER 747; *R v Wicks* [1997] 2 All ER 801 (see further Bradley [1997] PL 365 and Craig (1997) 113 LQR 521). The issue of whether the defence can challenge the validity of a bye-law in criminal proceedings will be settled when the case of

Boddington v *British Transport Police* (1996) The Times 23 July is heard by the House of Lords (judgment expected in April 1998). It is possible that the House will overrule *Bugg* v *DPP* [1993] QB 473, which received strong criticism in *R* v *Wicks* (1997).

On locus standi recent case law reveals a judicial trend in favour of a more liberal interpretation of rules of standing so as to enable 'sincere citizens' or 'reputable pressure groups' to make judicial review applications on behalf of the public interest in matters of serious concern. This has given rise to the concept of 'public interest standing': see, for example, *R* v *Secretary of State for Foreign and Commonwealth Affairs, ex parte Rees-Mogg* [1994] 2 WLR 115. Recent cases involving pressure groups include: *R* v *Inspectorate of Pollution, ex parte Greenpeace Ltd (No 2)* [1994] 4 All ER 329; *R* v *Secretary of State for Foreign and Commonwealth Affairs, ex parte World Development Movement Ltd* [1995] 1 All ER 611.

However, it is important to distinguish between public interest standing (recognised in the above cases) and 'associational standing' which does not amount to a sufficient interest for the purpose of legal standing: *IRC* v *National Federation of Self Employed and Small Businesses* [1981] 2 WLR 722: see further articles by Cane [1995] PL 276 and Schiemann [1996] PL 240.

Finally, it is important to note that recommendations on procedural reform made by the Law Commission: (1994) Report No 226; and see further articles by Hare (1995) 54 CLJ 268, Emery [1995] PL 450, Bamforth (1995) 58 MLR 722 and Fredman (1995) 111 LQR 591. Note also views of Woolf Report, *Access to Justice* (1996): see Blake [1997] PL 215.

In regard to examinations it is reasonable to expect at least two questions on purely procedural issues, although other questions involving grounds of review may also require knowledge of procedure. The tendency is for essay-type questions requiring critical and conceptual analysis of the *Datafin* or *O'Reilly* v *Mackman* principle, or the modern case law on locus standi, especially public interest standing. Sometimes the issues may be explored in a problem-type context.

Questions

INTEROGRAMS

1   Explain the significance of the *Datafin case* (1987) in English administrative law.
2   What is the rule in *O'Reilly* v *Mackman*?
3   How was that rule interpreted in *Roy* v *Kensington and Chelsea and Westminister Family Practitioner Committee* [1992] 1 All ER 705?
4   In view of recent case law would it be true to say that *O'Reilly* v *Mackman* is no longer of importance when making a judicial review application?
5   What is the definition of locus standi under RSC O.53 and how it the issue of legal standing determined?
6   Is 'public interest standing' sufficient for the purpose of an O.53 challenge?

QUESTION ONE

Explain whether O.53 proceedings are appropriate in respect of the following claims:

a   X, a senior employee of a District Health Authority, claims that his dismissal was ultra vires.

b   A local authority, acting under statutory powers, set up a citizens' advice centre. Y sought advice as to whether planning permission was necessary for a proposed development. He now claims damages, alleging that the advice was negligent, and caused him loss.

c   Z, a tenant of a local authority, has been served with notice to quit. By way of defence to the proceedings he claims that the notice is ultra vires.

London University LLB Examination
(for external students) Administrative Law June 1986 Q8

QUESTION TWO

'The story of administrative law in the 1980s was the story of the rise of regulatory agencies.'
    Discuss.

London University LLB Examination
(for external students) Administrative Law June 1989 Q1

QUESTION THREE

'*O'Reilly* v *Mackman* (1983) is the worst decision in administrative law since the Second World War. It should be overruled.'
    Discuss.

London University LLB Examination
(for external students) Administrative Law June 1990 Q5

QUESTION FOUR

Why should it be thought important to distinguish between public law cases and other cases? Is it possible to draw such a distinction in a coherent way?

London University LLB Examination
(for external students) Administrative Law June 1991 Q6

QUESTION FIVE

To what extent have the courts' decisions post-*O'Reilly* v *Mackman* fashioned a coherent distinction between matters of public law and of private law?

London University LLB Examination
(for external students) Administrative Law June 1993 Q3

QUESTION SIX

Explain how the courts determine who has standing to apply for judicial review. Is there any need to restrict standing?

London University LLB Examination
(for external students) Administrative Law June 1990 Q6

QUESTION SEVEN

Legislation provides that, before a new road is built through an area of historical importance or outstanding natural beauty, a public enquiry must be held at which objections can be heard from 'local residents, landowners or other persons with sufficient interest'. The minister can dispense with an enquiry 'if he is satisfied that no useful purpose would be served'. It is proposed to build a new road across Ugly Moor in the north of England, which is believed by a minority of historians to have been the scene of a mediaeval battle and which is noted for the rare species of heather which grow there. No local people object but there is an objection from the Wild Flowers Studies Association. The minister decides that no public enquiry need be held.

Advise (i) the Wild Flowers Studies Association; and (ii) Muddle, the Professor of History at London University, whether they can take any legal action and what remedies, if any, may be available to them.

London University LLB Examination
(for external students) Administrative Law June 1991 Q9

QUESTION EIGHT

Why are applicants for judicial review required to have standing? Are the present English rules of standing satisfactory?

London University LLB Examination
(for external students) Administrative Law June 1992 Q1

QUESTION NINE

'The effective preservation of the rule of law demands that any citizen should be seen as having "sufficient interest" in seeking judicial review of government decisions which he or she considers unlawful. Standing rules should therefore be abolished.'

To what extent would you agree with this contention?

London University LLB Examination
(for external students) Administrative Law June 1993 Q6

Answers

ANSWERS TO INTERROGRAMS

1   Until the Court of Appeal's decision in *R* v *Panel on Take-overs and Mergers, ex parte*

Datafin plc [1987] 2 WLR 699 the issue of whether an organisation was a 'public authority' amenable to judicial review was determined by reference to the source of its power, on the ground that the ultra vires doctrine could only be applied to bodies created by statute or royal prerogative. However, *Datafin* suggested a new test based on the functions performed by the body in question and the significance of its decisions as regard the public. Hence, in *Datafin* itself, the Panel on Take-overs and Mergers was an unincorporated association with no statutory or prerogative powers, but was held to be subject to judicial review because it was performing a public duty when administering the voluntary code on Take-overs and Mergers, and no appeal was available against its decisions. Whilst the decision may be seen as a triumph for the rule of law over the risk of arbitrary decision-making, it calls into question the entire basis of the ultra vires doctrine and some judges have continued to use the traditional 'source of power test' to determine justiciability: see *R* v *Disciplinary Committee of the Jockey Club, ex parte The Aga Khan* [1993] 2 All ER 853.

2   Prior to *O'Reilly* v *Mackman* [1983] 2 AC 237 a litigant wishing to challenge a decision of a public body had a choice of procedures with which to do so. It was possible to seek judicial review under O.53 or initiate an action by way of writ or originating summons claiming the private law remedies to damages, or injunctions, or declarations. *O'Reilly* v *Mackman* decided that O.53 was intended to be exclusive procedure for public law challenges against public authorities and that it would be an abuse of process to use private law methods to pursue such challenges. The only exceptions were where both parties consented to the use of private law procedures instead of judicial review, or when the public law issue of ultra vires is collateral to predominant private law issues, although the House of Lords left open the possibility that other exceptions might be developed on a case-by-case basis. The immediate effect of the decision was to introduce a rigid distinction between public law and private law, which caused much controversy and generated considerable litigation on purely procedural matters simply because the definitions of 'public' and 'private' had never been clearly developed or settled in English administrative law.

3   In *O'Reilly* v *Mackman* Lord Diplock had implied that the exclusivity principle would apply even if private law rights were involved in the challenge, if they were subsidiary to dominant issues of public law. This 'narrow approach' was followed in cases such as *Cocks* v *Thanet District Council* [1983] 2 AC 286. However, in *Roy* v *Kensington and Chelsea and Westminster Family Practitioner Committee* [1992] 1 AC 624, the House of Lords offered relief from the rigidity of his rule by suggesting a 'broad approach' to this aspect of the exclusivity principle. In effect it was decided that it would not be an abuse of process to use private law procedures if genuine private law rights were being relied on in a challenge against a public body, even though issues of ultra vires were also being raised as part of the challenge. This suggests a much more pragmatic approach based on the suitability of the procedure chosen for making the challenge in question.

4   Although it is true to say that judgments in recent case law have expressed dissatisfaction with the rigid nature of the exclusivity principle propounded in *O'Reilly* v *Mackman*, it would be wrong to conclude that *O'Reilly* v *Mackman* is no

longer of importance. It has not be overruled, even though the House of Lords had opportunities to do so. What seems to have happened is a series of 'refinements' to the exclusivity principle which, whilst upholding the need for a public law process for purely public law cases, has recognised the costly futility of litigation over the meaning of public/private. Consequently the emphasis is on the realistic nature of the choice of procedure in question, so that, for example, if the dispute is essentially concerned with the true construction of a contract made by a public authority, the procedure by way of originating summons in the Commercial Court will be at least as well suited as, and might even be better than, the procedure by way of judicial review: see *Mercury Communications* v *Director-General of Telecommunications* [1996] 1 All ER 575. See also the call for more flexibility in respect of choice of procedures made by Lord Woolf MR in *Trustees of the Dennis Rye Pension Fund* v *Sheffield City Council* [1997] 4 All ER 747. One may conclude that, although *O'Reilly* v *Mackman* remains good law judges will no longer apply it so rigidly as to deprive a plaintiff of his remedy on purely technical grounds. The theoretical case for insisting on judicial review may have to give way to the practicalities of permitting a challenge by way of writ or other private law method.

5   Locus standi is defined as 'sufficient interest in the matter to which the application relates': O.53 r3(7) and s31(3) Supreme Court Act 1981. The judge at the leave stage will take a 'bird's eye view' of the merits of the application as part of the assessment of the issue of standing, since the question is one of fact and degree and depends on the relationship between the applicant and the matters in issue. If the application is arguable and it is clear that the applicant is a serious and concerned individual (ie not a 'mere busybody' meddling in affairs), then leave will be granted so that the issue of standing can, if necessary, be reconsidered at the full hearing when a more detailed examination of the merits becomes possible: *IRC* v *National Federation of Self Employed and Small Businesses* [1982] AC 617.

6   In a number of recent cases the courts have relaxed the test of locus standi to such a degree that it can be argued that any concerned individual will be granted leave to seek judicial review of a matter which has generated great public interest, eg any matter of great constitutional significance: *R* v *HM Treasury, ex parte Smedley* [1985] 2 WLR 576 and *R* v *Secretary of State for Foreign and Commonwealth Affairs, ex parte Rees-Mogg* [1994] 2 WLR 115.

Pressure groups may also benefit from the concept of 'public interest standing', though it may be necessary for the organisation to satisfy the court that it is a respectable and responsible one, with much experience and expertise in the issues subject to the challenge, so that it can mount a relevant and well argued application for review in a manner that will facilitate a speedy hearing and an early result: see *R* v *Inspectorate of Pollution, ex parte Greenpeace Ltd (No 2)* [1994] 4 All ER 329, and contrast *R* v *Secretary of State for the Environment, ex parte Rose Theatre Trust Co* [1990] 1 All ER 754. (There must also be some substantial default or abuse of public power.)

SUGGESTED ANSWER TO QUESTION ONE

General Comment

A fairly straightforward question requiring an application of some of the more well known decisions made in the wake of the House of Lords' decision of *O'Reilly* v *Mackman*.

Key Points

- The rule in *O'Reilly* v *Mackman*
- Dismissal of a public employee – public law or private law?
- Claims of negligence against public authorities – public law or private law?
- Raising ultra vires in collateral proceedings – an abuse of process?

Suggested Answer

In deciding whether or not proceedings under RSC O.53 are appropriate in any given case, one should always start by considering the speech of Lord Diplock in *O'Reilly* v *Mackman* (1982). His Lordship noted that O.53 was not drafted in terms of an exclusive procedure in public law cases, but added that when a case involved a public law issue and the respondent was a public law body, O.53 should be used, unless the case fell into one of the exceptions. The exceptions envisaged were, for example, where both parties agreed that the action should proceed by writ, or where the challenge to a public law decision arose as a collateral issue. Unfortunately, this decision led to much confusion as to when O.53 could, and could not, be used.

a   In this case there is little argument that the respondent body is a public authority, deriving its power from a public Act of Parliament, and is thus amenable to the prerogative orders. The real difficulty here is whether the dismissal of one of its employees is really a public law issue, or a matter of private law, specifically employment law, that can be dealt with by way of action.

In *R* v *East Berkshire Health Authority, ex parte Walsh* (1985), a senior nursing officer sought to challenge the legality of his dismissal by applying for an order of certiorari. The Court of Appeal held that O.53 was not the appropriate procedure to use in such cases. The dismissal did not become a public law issue simply because Walsh had been employed by a large public authority. The relationship between Walsh and the Health Authority was a private contract of employment, and thus any dispute should have been settled by way of action.

It should be noted, however, that there are a number of factors that might make the use of O.53 appropriate in such a case. Firstly, if an employee is very senior and actually holds an office, then there may be wide-spread public interest in his dismissal, see *Ridge* v *Baldwin* (1964) (dismissal of a chief constable). Secondly, if the employee of a public body can show that he has no remedy in private law against the public authority, he may be allowed to challenge his dismissal under O.53, as was the case in *R* v *Secretary of State for the Home Department, ex parte Benwell* (1985). Thirdly, if an employee can show that the power to dismiss him was not lawfully delegated to whoever took the decision, judicial review might be available. Finally, where conditions of service with a public authority are subject to ministerial approval, an employee might use O.53 to challenge the fact that his conditions of service differ from those agreed by the minister.

Unless X can bring his case into one of these four categories, therefore, he will have to challenge his dismissal by way of writ.

b   In advising Y as to the procedure he should use in order to recover damages for negligent advice, one has to determine to what extent he is challenging a public law decision by a public body.

Assuming the local authority is vicariously liable for the advice given by workers in its advice centre, there is no doubt that it constitutes a public body, and would thus be the subject of O.53 proceedings. The authority would doubtless argue that the issues raised here are matters of public law and hence O.53 should be used. Y might wish to argue that a private action by way of writ is permissible, as the public law issues (if any arise) are merely collateral to the main claim for damages.

Some guidance as to the possible outcome is provided by the House of Lords' decision in *Davy* v *Spelthorne Borough Council* (1984). Davy issued a writ against the local authority claiming, inter alia, damages for loss resulting from negligent advice on his position under the Town and Country Planning Act 1971. The local authority argued that such an action would be an abuse of the court process, and that it should proceed by way of O.53.

Lord Fraser was of the view that the proceedings, so far as they consisted of a claim for damages for negligence, represented a simple action in tort. Lord Wilberforce cited *O'Reilly* v *Mackman* and explained that Lord Diplock's dictum applied where it could be shown that a claim could and should be brought by way of application for judicial review. In the case of Davy's claim for damages, it could not have been brought by way of O.53 as any such claim would have to be linked with judicial review; and even if it could have been so brought, there were no reasons why it should have been.

Thus Y should be advised that an action by way of writ would be permissible in this case.

c   Once again, the local authority is a public body, and it can be argued that the provision of housing is a public law issue, thus making the notice to quit challengeable by way of O.53. In this case, however, Z seeks to challenge such a notice by way of a defence to an action. Unless it can be shown that the raising of such a defence is an abuse of the court process, Z should be allowed to proceed.

In *Wandsworth London Borough Council* v *Winder* (1985), Winder was the tenant of a council flat who was served with a notice to quit for non payment of rent. He argued that the increase in rent that he had refused to pay was ultra vires, and resisted the notice to quit on this basis. The local authority claimed that this was an abuse of the court process; a challenge to the validity of its rent increase could only be launched by way of O.53.

The House of Lords held that Winder was entitled to raise such a defence. There were a number of features that distinguished the case from those contemplated by

Lord Diplock in *O'Reilly* v *Mackman*. Firstly, there were some private rights of Winder as a tenant involved. Secondly, he had not initiated the procedure, he had merely exercised his right to raise a defence. Thirdly, the arguments in favour of producing speedy decisions on issues affecting third parties, by way of judicial review, had to be set against the right of the citizen to defend himself against unmeritorious claims. Finally, O.53 did not expressly exclude Winder's right to proceed as he had done.

Z should therefore be advised that whilst he could bring judicial review proceedings to challenge the validity of the notice to quit, he can just as easily raise its invalidity as a defence to county court proceedings for possession of the property.

SUGGESTED ANSWER TO QUESTION TWO

General Comment

A question requiring a broad perspective of the development of judicial review since 1945. It is important to establish the way in which the statement is being interpreted at an early stage in the answer. It has been assumed that the question is referring to self-regulation by private organisations, rather than by statutory bodies.

Key Points

- Impact of new conservatism
- Rise of self-regulation in place of governmental control
- Response of the judiciary
- Significance of *O'Reilly* v *Mackman*
- *Datafin* case
- Subsequent decisions

Suggested Answer

Any claim that the story of administrative law in 1980s was the story of the rise of the regulatory agencies requires careful examination of the sense in which those expressions are used. It could be argued, with some force, that the story of administrative law since the beginning of the twentieth century has been the story of state intervention in, and regulation of, the life of the citizen. In that sense the 1980s have had nothing new to offer. It is submitted, however, that if the term 'regulatory agencies' is taken to mean non-governmental agencies, a more interesting picture emerges. No observer of administrative law during the 1980s could have failed to notice the impact of the policies adopted by successive Conservative governments since May 1979.

The particular blend of conservatism popularly described as 'Thatcherism' promoted moves towards deregulation, self-regulation, and privatisation. The view was that certain aspects of economic activity were best left to control by market forces, control by those providing the services in question, or control by shareholders, subject to certain minimum statutory requirements. In short, it is submitted that the 1980s saw the rise of regulation by private bodies, as opposed to public bodies.

How has administrative law responded to these developments? Before any solution to that question can be offered, it has to be borne in mind that the 1980s has also witnessed a 'seismic disturbance' in the House of Lords' decision in *O'Reilly* v *Mackman* (1983), bringing with it the public law/private law dichotomy. As a consequence of this decision, a litigant is now required to address first the question of whether or not his case involves a public law body, and second whether or not it involves a public law issue. Should the answers to both questions be in the affirmative, the litigant would be required to challenge the decisions of the public body concerned by way of an application for judicial review. If the judges had held to the traditional view that a public law body was one created by statute or under the prerogative, many of the decisions of powerful private regulatory bodies would have fallen outside the scope of judicial review.

Predictably, the response of the courts has been to redraft the concept of the public law body. The most significant development in this direction was provided by the Court of Appeal's decision in *R* v *Panel on Take-overs and Mergers, ex parte Datafin plc* (1987). The applicants had complained to the panel about the conduct of certain other companies during the course of a contested takeover bid. The panel had rejected the complaint. The applicants then applied for judicial review of the panel's decision, but this was rejected at first instance on the basis that, as the panel was exercising neither statutory nor prerogative powers, its decisions were not amenable to judicial review. The Court of Appeal held that, despite the fact that the panel was an unincorporated association and was not exercising statutory or prerogative powers, its decisions were amenable to judicial review. The court took the view that the panel was performing a public duty when administering the Code on Take-overs and Mergers, and as there was no other means readily available by which the legality of its actions might be tested, judicial review would lie in respect of its decisions.

With this one decision, therefore, the idea that judicial review was limited to governmental bodies was swept aside. It opened up the prospect of judicial review of any organisation which had the power to take decisions affecting the public. It is submitted that the real stimulus behind the development was the reluctance of the courts to permit the exercise of such significant power go unchecked by any legal challenge. It is a prime example of judicial review operating as a residual means of control.

The decision has been followed by a number of others where this newly developed jurisdiction has been exercised. In *R* v *Ethical Committee of St Mary's Hospital, ex parte Harriot* (1987), it was accepted without lengthy argument that the decisions of the ethical committee, a non-statutory informal body, were amenable to judicial review, so that the committee's refusal to permit the applicant in vitro fertilisation treatment could be challenged.

A further example of the extension of judicial review to non-statutory self-regulatory organisations is provided by *R* v *Advertising Standards Authority Ltd, ex parte The Insurance Service plc* (1989). The Divisional Court held that the Advertising Standards Authority (ASA) was a body amenable to judicial review, since it exhibited many similarities with the Panel on Take-overs and Mergers. Like the Panel, it had no statutory or common law powers, although unlike the Panel it did have legal identity derived from its status as a company under the Companies Acts. Looking at the functions of the ASA, the court had no doubt that they fell within the sphere of 'public law'.

In conclusion, it is submitted that, whilst the post-war period can be regarded as the era in which the courts fashioned the modern concepts of irrationality and fairness to deal with the rapid growth in governmental activity, the 1980s can be seen as the era in which the courts, of necessity, extended the scope of judicial review to match the growth of significant regulatory powers in private hands.

SUGGESTED ANSWER TO QUESTION THREE

General Comment

A question that requires some explanation of the background to the decision in question, and obviously of the nature of the decision itself. The major issue is the problem of determining the public law/private law choice. Attention also needs to be paid to why Lord Diplock wanted to impose this dichotomy, and to the question of who benefits from its application.

Key Points

- Background to reforms of O.53
- Views of Law Commission
- Decision in *O'Reilly* v *Mackman* itself
- Public/private dichotomy
- What is a public law body?
- What is a public law issue?
- Movement away from *O'Reilly* v *Mackman*

Suggested Answer

In *O'Reilly* v *Mackman* (1983), Lord Diplock, speaking on behalf of their Lordships, attempted to introduce far reaching procedural changes in relation to the application for judicial review. That such a move was necessary may have seemed odd given that in 1977 the new O.53 was introduced bringing with it significant procedural changes of its own. Prior to 1977 a litigant wishing to challenge the decision of a public body, as that term was loosely understood, could either proceed by way of an application for one of the prerogative orders of certiorari, mandamus, or prohibition, or proceed by way of writ, seeking a declaration as to his rights as regards the body concerned. The reforms of 1977 were designed to encourage greater use of what became known as the application for judicial review. A wider range of remedies became available, such as declaration, injunction, and damages. Further, provision was made for an applicant for review to seek discovery of documents, or administer interrogatories, something that had previously not been possible. What is significant is that the Law Commission, which was largely responsible for these reforms, never intended that O.53 should become the only way of challenging the decisions of public bodies where no private law claim was involved.

The effect of Lord Diplock's speech in *O'Reilly* v *Mackman* was to require any litigant wishing to challenge the decision of a public body, involving substantially a question of public law, to proceed by way of an application for judicial review. It is submitted that the decision is unhelpful, to say the least, in that it assumes that there is a clear distinction in English law between public and private law, and secondly because it removes rights previously possessed by litigants, arguably for no good reason.

The public/private dichotomy

This has been an issue ever since the decision in *O'Reilly* v *Mackman*. As has been stated, subject to a number of minor exceptions, the effect of the decision was to require all cases involving challenges to decisions of public bodies based upon issues of public law to proceed by way of an application for judicial review. The need to be able to distinguish between a private as opposed to a public body, and a private law matter as opposed to one involving public law, became clear in the light of the fact that if a litigant wrongly chose to proceed with a public law matter by way of writ, his action might be struck out as an abuse of the process of the court. The difficulty for all parties lay in the fact that, historically, English law had never recognised any distinction between public law and private law. As Lord Wilberforce stated in *Davy* v *Spelthorne Borough Council* (1983):

> 'The expressions "private law" and "public law" have recently been imported into the law of England from countries which, unlike our own, have separate systems concerning public law and private law. No doubt they are convenient expressions for descriptive purposes. In this country they must be used with caution, for, typically, English law fastens not on principles but on remedies.'

The distinction between public and private law that has emerged since *O'Reilly* v *Mackman* is one based more upon pragmatism that any coherent jurisprudence.

a   *What is a public law body?*

The traditional method by which one would determine whether a body was public or private would be to consider the source of its power. Generally, bodies exercising statutory or prerogative powers would be regarded as being public bodies and thus amenable to judicial review: see *R* v *Electricity Commissioners, ex parte London Electricity Joint Committee Co (1920) Ltd* (1924), and *Council of Civil Service Unions* v *Minister for the Civil Service* (1985).

Increasingly, however, the courts have decided the question of whether a body is amenable to review by reference to its functions rather than its powers. The origins of such an approach can be found in *R* v *Criminal Injuries Compensation Board, ex parte Lain* (1967), which was cited with approval in *Council of Civil Service Unions* v *Minister for the Civil Service*, above. The fact that the Board made decisions affecting the interests of members of the public and dispensed taxpayers' money were regarded as factors that brought it within the scope of judicial review, despite the fact that it was empowered to act under the prerogative as opposed to statutory powers.

A leading authority is the Court of Appeal decision in *R* v *Panel on Take-overs and Mergers, ex parte Datafin plc* (1987). The court held that the decisions of the panel were amenable to judicial review, notwithstanding that it was not a statutory body, was not empowered to act under the prerogative, and neither did it derive its power from any contract or constitution. In fact, in the view of Lord Donaldson MR, the panel had 'no visible means of legal support'. His Lordship felt, however, that the court was justified in intervening to examine the legality of the Panel's action, on the basis of the enormous de facto power that it exercised to make decisions affecting the interests of the public, or at least sections of the public.

b   *What is a public law issue?*
Of the two problems perhaps the more difficult is that of determining whether a dispute involves primarily a question of private or public law. In *O'Reilly* v *Mackman* (above), Lord Diplock expressed the view that complaints by prisoners that they had not received a fair hearing when appearing before a prison board of visitors could only be pursued by way of judicial review, as they had no private law rights as regards the board. The prisoners' rights to a fair hearing arose under the relevant legislation, as opposed to any private agreement. With respect, however, it is submitted that such a classification is far from water-tight. If a prisoner was defamed by a member of a prison board of visitors, he would presumably be entitled to pursue a private law action for defamation. On a broader basis, what is at stake for prisoners appearing before boards of visitors is personal liberty, which could be viewed as being very much a private, as opposed to public, interest. Even more questionable is the distinction sought to be made between private and public law issues in the House of Lords' decision immediately following *O'Reilly* v *Mackman*, that of *Cocks* v *Thanet District Council* (1983). The plaintiff had sought a declaration by way of a county court action that the defendant local authority was in breach of its duty to provide him with accommodation as a homeless person. The House of Lords held that the issue of whether or not the local authority owed him any such duty was one falling within the sphere of public law, and thus his action was an abuse of process; had the local authority accepted that there was a duty to house the plaintiff but had failed to discharge that responsibility, the House felt that the matter would then have been one of private law. Presumably the matter moves from being one of public law to one of private law on the basis of the scope of the issues involved, the question of whether a person is homeless being more generalised than that of how the duty to house one individual should be discharged. It is submitted, however, that such distinctions are unclear to the point of being unworkable. Even once the duty to house an individual has been accepted, it could still be argued that the issue is one of public law as it involves the distribution of a community resource, namely public housing. This reasoning seems to have found favour with the House of Lords in *O'Rourke* v *Camden London Borough Council* (1997), in which it was held that no private law action for breach of the housing duty could arise at all. Lord Hoffmann criticised the reasoning in *Cocks* v *Thanet District Council* on this point.

The difficulty of distinguishing between private and public law has led to a relaxation of the strict rules laid down in *O'Reilly* v *Mackman*, so that, as Lord Slynn said in a recent case, the overriding question should be whether the proceedings that had been instituted constituted an abuse of the process of the court: *Mercury Communications Ltd* v *Director-General of Telecommunications* (1996). This stops short of overruling *O'Reilly* v *Mackman* with the result, for example, that the difficulties of distinguishing between public and private law rights will continue in many cases: see *British Steel plc* v *Customs and Excise Commissioners* (1997). In its 1994 Report on Judicial Review the Law Commission also stopped short of recommending abolition of the rule in *O'Reilly* v *Mackman*, instead recommending judges to continue with a flexible application of it, eg Lord Lowry's 'broad' approach adopted in *Roy* v *Kensington and Chelsea and Westminster Family Practitioner Committee* (1992). Even Lord Woolf, a supporter of the public/private divide, has accepted the need for *O'Reilly* v *Mackman* to be applied more pragmatically and not so as to deprive a litigant of a remedy on purely technical grounds: *Trustees of the Dennis Rye Pension Fund* v *Sheffield City Council* (1997).

SUGGESTED ANSWER TO QUESTION FOUR

General Comment

A question that requires a good knowledge of the issues raised by *O'Reilly* v *Mackman* and subsequent decisions, but one which is not exclusively concerned with such issues. Other areas of law where the distinction between public and private law is made need to be considered.

Key Points

* Assess the way in which the distinction has arisen
* The development of administrative law
* The areas where the distinction is made
* Assess how the distinction is maintained
* Comment on the pragmatic approach of the courts

Suggested Answer

The issues raised by the question need to be addressed in two stages.

Why is it important to distinguish public law cases?
Traditionally English administrative law has not recognised a substantive distinction between private law and public law. This may be in part due to Dicey's well known abhorrence of the idea that there might be one system of law for private individuals and another for state agencies, but it is just as likely that he was reflecting conventional wisdom at the time of writing. In the twentieth century we have become accustomed to talking of 'the State' and of 'public bodies' as useful shorthand expressions for the manifestations of government and the law that applies to them. The fundamental problem, however, is that the growth of the use of these terms has been organic. They have passed into common usage without any attempt at legal definition. We all think we know what the State is, but would find it hard to define. For example, is the British Broadcasting Corporation part of the apparatus of the State? The term public law is equally difficult to pin down. It is suggestive of a separate system of rules and courts relevant only to the activities of State bodies, but it is obvious that there is no clear

boundary between public law and private law. One should ask why it is that lawyers are at all concerned with any supposed distinction between the two. The answer lies in the fact that the courts have in certain areas used the distinction as either the determinant of which procedure should be used to launch a legal challenge, or have used it as the determinant of liability.

The effect of the House of Lords' decision in *O'Reilly* v *Mackman* (1983), was to require all cases involving challenges to decisions of public bodies based upon issues of public law to proceed by way of an application for judicial review. The need to be able to distinguish between a private as opposed to a public body, and a private law matter as opposed to one involving public law, became clear in the light of the fact that if a litigant wrongly chose to proceed with a public law matter by way of writ, his action might be struck out as an abuse of the process of the court. The difficulty is that, as pointed out above, English law has been slow to recognise any distinction between public law and private law.

The distinction has been relied upon by the courts as a factor determining the scope of liability in negligence. In *Home Office* v *Dorset Yacht Co Ltd* (1970), Lord Diplock expressed the view that if a body was exercising 'governmental functions' it would not necessarily incur liability in negligence if damage resulted. The courts would examine the case to see if the complaint related to an operational activity or was the result of a policy decision. In the latter case a private law duty of care was unlikely to be found. In *Rowling* v *Takaro Properties Ltd* (1988), the Privy Council adopted a slightly broader approach and expressed the view that in cases involving the actions of government departments the imposition of liability in negligence may not be in the public interest.

Two areas have been identified, therefore, where the public/private distinction is of relevance. But they in turn raise the questions, how does one identify a public body, and how does one know if the case involves public law issues?

Is a distinction between public law and other cases sustainable?
It is submitted that the distinction between public and private law that has emerged since *O'Reilly* v *Mackman* is one based more upon pragmatism that any coherent jurisprudence.

a *What is a public law body?*
The traditional method by which one would determine whether a body was public or private would be to consider the source of its power. Generally, bodies exercising statutory or prerogative powers would be regarded as being public bodies and thus amenable to judicial review: see *R* v *Electricity Commissioners, ex parte London Electricity Joint Committee Co (1920) Ltd* (1924).

Increasingly, however, the courts have decided the question of whether a body is amenable to review by reference to its functions rather than its powers. In *R* v *Panel on Take-overs and Mergers, ex parte Datafin plc* (1987) it was held that the decisions of the panel were amenable to judicial review, notwithstanding that it was not a statutory body, was not empowered to act under the prerogative, and did not derive its power from any contract or constitution. The court was justified in intervening to examine the legality of the panel's action, on the basis of the enormous de facto power that it exercised to make decisions affecting the interests of the public, or at least sections of the public.

b   *What is a public law issue?*

The problem of attempting to identify a distinction between public law cases and others is perhaps nowhere greater than in those instances where the dispute is as to whether the issue at stake is one of public or private law. In *O'Reilly* v *Mackman* (above), Lord Diplock expressed the view that complaints by prisoners that they had not received a fair hearing when appearing before a prison board of visitors could only be pursued by way of judicial review, as they had no private law rights as regards the board. The prisoners' rights to a fair hearing arose under the relevant legislation, as opposed to any private agreement. With respect, however, it is submitted that such a classification is far from water-tight. If a prisoner was defamed by a member of a prison board of visitors, he would presumably be entitled to pursue a private law action for defamation. On a broader basis, what is at stake for prisoners appearing before boards of visitors is personal liberty, which could be viewed as being very much a private, as opposed to public interest.

It is submitted that the search for any clear distinction between public law and private law within the English legal system is likely to prove to be something of a sleeveless errand. Where there is real doubt as to the reviewability of a particular matter, it is far better to approach the problem by asking the more generalised question, 'Is this a matter over which the courts would wish to exercise jurisdiction?' If the answer is 'Yes', then the justification for treating it as a matter falling within the sphere of public law will follow.

This 'broad' approach to the rule in *O'Reilly* v *Mackman* has found favour with the House of Lords, which, in recent decisions, has put the emphasis on 'abuse of process' as the test for striking out a private law action: *Roy* v *Kensington and Chelsea and Westminster Family Practitoner Committee* (1992) and *Mercury Communications Ltd* v *Director-General of Telecommunications* (1996). See also the Court of Appeal's pragmatic approach in *British Steel plc* v *Customs and Excise Commissioners* (1997) and *Trustees of the Dennis Rye Pension Fund* v *Sheffield City Council* (1997). In the latter case Lord Woolf MR, a supporter of *O'Reilly* v *Mackman*, acknowledged the difficulties that had been caused by the public/private dichotomy and stressed the need for flexibility in respect of choice of procedures so as to ensure that a litigant would not be deprived of his remedy on purely technical grounds.

SUGGESTED ANSWER TO QUESTION FIVE

General Comment

This question requires a clear analysis of the cases that have attempted to define the distinction between public and private law. *O'Reilly* v *Mackman* should be referred to briefly, as it provides the reason why the distinction needs to be coherent. How have the courts attempted to draw the distinction? What is the result for litigants? Is the distinction coherent?

Key Points

- Why is it essential to have a coherent distinction?
- The functional distinction: *Cocks* v *Thanet District Council* and *O'Rourke* v *Camden London Borough Council*
- Rights in issue – *Davy* v *Spelthorne Borough Council*
- Movement away from *O'Reilly* v *Mackman*
- Defences
- Is the distinction coherent?
- Recent case law

Suggested Answer

As a result of *O'Reilly* v *Mackman* (1983) it became necessary to determine from the outset of a case whether the issue is one of public law or private law. In public law cases O.53 proceedings for judicial review must be brought; litigants cannot pursue civil proceedings begun by writ as they were formerly able to do. In private law cases, subject to a few exceptions, O.53 proceedings must not be brought even where the remedies of declaration and injunction are sought. The distinction between public and private law is not part of the English legal tradition, and therefore it is not surprising that *O'Reilly* v *Mackman* has been a source of extreme difficulty and controversy in cases decided after it.

Having decided that the distinction between public and private law should be strictly observed, Lord Diplock, who gave the leading speech in *O'Reilly* v *Mackman*, refused to lay down any guidelines, saying that the distinction should be worked out on a case by case basis. The lack of guidelines has given each novel case the status of a test case. This is extremely unhealthy since it undermines the certainty that should underlie rules of legal procedure, and it has led to the drawing of difficult and illogical distinctions. This can be seen in *Cocks* v *Thanet District Council* (1983), which was decided immediately after, and on the same day as, *O'Reilly* v *Mackman*. What was under consideration in this case was a local authority's duty to provide accommodation for the applicant under the Housing (Homeless Persons) Act 1977. The House of Lords sought to distinguish between the authority's public and private law *functions*. The decision whether or not the applicant fulfilled the statutory conditions was a matter of public law; the obligation to provide housing was a matter of private law enforceable by way of injunction and damages. Since the applicant sought to challenge the authority's preliminary decision, he could only bring proceedings by way of judicial review. As he had proceeded by way of writ, his case was struck out, since O.53 does not allow cases begun by writ to proceed as if begun by O.53 application, although it does allow the reverse process to occur. This case illustrates the difficulty that can occur if the wrong procedure is chosen, but it is difficult to see how the distinction between public and private law can coherently be drawn on functional lines. An authority's public duties, including the duty to provide housing, have always been enforceable by way of the prerogative remedy of mandamus. It is entirely artificial to distinguish between the preliminary decision, as to whether a person falls into a statutory definition, and the obligation resulting out of that decision; in reality they are part of the same process and should be subject to the same legal procedure, otherwise the litigant is forced to bear the burden of distinguishing between various functions of an authority, a distinction which may be quite simply impossible.

The criticisms of *Cocks* v *Thanet District Council*, above, were accepted by the House of Lords in *O'Rourke* v *Camden London Borough Council* (1997) where it was held that no private law action was available for breach of the statutory housing duty at all. It was entirely a matter of public law, challengeable only by way of judicial review.

It might be thought that one of the simplest ways of drawing the distinction is to focus on the rights sought to be enforced. In *Davy* v *Spelthorne Borough Council* (1984) the plaintiff sued by writ for damages for negligent advice which had prevented him from appealing against an enforcement notice. He also claimed an injunction to restrain enforcement proceedings, and an order to set the enforcement notice aside on the ground that it was invalid. The last two claims were struck out as it was held that they should have been brought by way of O.53 proceedings. Lord Wilberforce stated that the distinction between public law and private law should not be drawn in terms of whether private law rights were in issue, but whether they were in issue in a way which made the public law rules of judicial review applicable. This is a particularly mystifying and circular piece of reasoning, which in effect means no more than that the public law rules of procedure should apply if they should apply, regardless of whether private law rights are sought to be enforced, and which does not improve the clarity of the distinction between public and private law. It cannot be right that a litigant should be forced to bear the expense of bringing separate actions on each occasion that he seeks a variety of relief to enforce his private law rights.

Belatedly the House of Lords has recognised some of the force of these arguments by adopting a 'broad' approach to the application of *O'Reilly* v *Mackman* so that, effectively, a writ will be struck out only where all the issues raised are clearly ones of public law only and where therefore it would be more convenient to try the case by means of judicial review, ie it would be an 'abuse of process' to try the case by writ or other private law method: see *Roy* v *Kensington and Chelsea and Westminster Family Practitioner Committee* (1992) and *Mercury Communications Ltd* v *Director-General of Telecommunications* (1996). However, the refusal to overrule *O'Reilly* v *Mackman* means that the complex task of distinguishing between public and private law issues will continue and much will depend on the pragmatic good sense of the judges in having regard to the practicalities of the procedure chosen, thereby hopefully ensuring that a litigant is not deprived of his remedy on purely technical grounds: *British Steel plc* v *Customs and Excise Commissioners* (1997) and *Trustees of the Dennis Rye Pension Fund* v *Sheffield City Council* (1997).

The position where a defendant wishes to raise a public law defence when being sued by an authority should be mentioned briefly. Here, the courts have not attempted to draw distinctions between public and private law; they have generally permitted the defence to be raised without recourse to judicial review proceedings, while admitting that the issues raised are those of public law. The defence must be a genuine defence; that is, it must be capable if proved of meeting the case put forward by the authority as a matter of law. There are some claims which fall in public law which are nonetheless capable of providing defences to private law claims. Thus, if an authority did not have power to raise its rents that would be a defence to a claim for non-payment of rent (see *Wandsworth London Borough Council* v *Winder* (1985)). If an authority failed to provide sufficient caravan sites for gypsies that would not provide at law a defence to a claim for possession, and the issue should be raised by way of judicial review (cf *Avon County Council* v *Buscott* (1988)).

In *R* v *Wicks* (1997) the House of Lords held that the invalidity of an enforcement notice could not be raised as a defence in criminal proceeding for unauthorised development of land because of the statutory framework for challenging enforcement notices (appeals or judicial review). However, on the issue of whether a defendant is ntitled to challenge the validity of a bye-law under which he is prosecuted, the Law Lords expressed views in favour of permitting such a challenge and expressed strong reservations about *Bugg* v *DPP* (1993), which had discouraged such a challenge.

It has been seen then that, with one or two exceptions, there has been a general failure on the part of the courts to provide coherent guidance as to the manner in which the distinction between public and private law is to be drawn. It is vital that consistent guidelines be devised if further injustice to litigants is to be avoided. Public bodies wield vast powers, and it is inappropriate that individuals should be saddled with the burden of defining the procedures that should be used to challenge the exercise of those powers; the litigant should know at the outset of the case which procedure to follow, and not find himself hamstrung halfway through it on purely procedural grounds.

SUGGESTED ANSWER TO QUESTION SIX

General Comment

A question requiring an account of the changes to locus standi introduced on 1 January 1978, and an explanation of subsequent developments.

Key Points

* Outline old law and 1978 changes
* *Federation* case
* Explanation by Lord Wilberforce
* Subsequent cases
* Analysis of whether any rules needed

Suggested Answer

Under RSC O.53 r3(7), the court will not grant leave to apply for judicial review unless an applicant can establish that he has, 'sufficient interest in the matter to which the application relates'. The term 'sufficient interest' replaced that of 'person aggrieved' which had been used until 1 January 1978. The implication in the change was that the new test for standing might in some respects be more liberally interpreted than that which had gone before.

The leading authority on the correct interpretation of the new formulation is the House of Lords' decision in *IRC* v *National Federation of Self Employed and Small*

Businesses (1982). The Federation sought to challenge the Inland Revenue's decision to grant a tax amnesty to casual workers in Fleet Street. In particular the Federation sought a declaration that such an agreement was ultra vires the Revenue, and an order of mandamus compelling the Revenue to collect the amount due.

In the course of his speech, Lord Wilberforce pointed out that the change in the locus standi requirement from 'person aggrieved' to 'sufficient interest' had not removed the question entirely to the sphere of judicial discretion, neither should it be assumed, he added, that because the same wording was used to describe the locus standi requirement for each remedy, that it would be applied in the same way for each remedy. His Lordship voiced his concern that litigants might view locus standi as a threshold requirement to be determined at the outset of litigation, and once satisfied, not considered again.

His Lordship stated:

> 'There may be cases in which it can be seen at the earliest stage that the person applying for judicial review has no interest at all, or no sufficient interest to support the application; then it would be quite correct at the threshold to refuse him leave to apply. The right to do so is an important safeguard against the courts being flooded and public bodies being harassed by irresponsible applications. But in other cases this will not be so. In these it will be necessary to consider the powers or the duties in law of those against whom the relief is asked, the position of the applicant in relation to those powers and duties, and the breach of those said to have been committed. In other words the question of sufficient interest cannot.be considered in the abstract; it must be taken together with the legal and factual context.'

The result of the above decision is that locus standi is a matter that falls to be considered at two stages. First there is the application for leave to apply for judicial review. The applicant should be allowed to proceed at this stage if he can show that he has an 'arguable case'. Locus standi then has to be reconsidered at a second stage, when the substantive application for judicial review is made. It is only at this second stage, in the normal course of events, that the respondent public body would be represented, and the 'other side' of the case considered. When this new evidence is before the court, it might be found that the applicant for review does not have locus standi. Furthermore,the question of locus standi is dependent to some extent on whether the applicant succeeds in establishing that the public body has acted ultra vires.

Subsequent decisions indicate that the courts have adopted a more liberal approach to locus standi. In *R* v *IBA, ex parte Whitehouse* (1985), for example, the applicant was held to have locus standi to challenge the decision of the Independent Broadcasting Authority to show the film *Scum*, on the basis that she was the holder of a television licence. In *R* v *HM Treasury, ex parte Smedley* (1985), the applicant was regarded as having locus standi to challenge the validity of payments to the European Community by the government, on the basis that he was a taxpayer. The position of pressure groups has always been more problematic. It is really a mixed question of fact and law in each case whether there is a sufficient nexus between the applicant pressure group and the public body concerned. In *R* v *Secretary of State for Social Services, ex parte Child Poverty Action Group and Greater London Council* (1985), the court held that the CPAG did have locus standi to challenge the refusal of the minister to reopen old case files to discover if applicants for welfare benefits had been underpaid in the past. The GLC was held not to have sufficient interest in relation to the same application however, because it had no express or implied status to represent welfare claimants, neither was it entitled to adopt the mantle of guardian of the public interest.

The position of pressure groups was dealt a considerable blow in *R v Secretary of State for the Environment, ex parte Rose Theatre Trust Co* (1990). During building works in the City of London developers had unearthed the remains of the Rose Theatre which dated from the seventeenth century. Despite much public campaigning for the preservation of the remains, the Secretary of State refused to exercise his discretion to schedule the site as a monument of national importance under the Ancient Monuments and Archaeological Areas Act 1979 (as amended). The applicant company had been formed by individuals opposed to any development on the site, and the company had been granted leave to apply for judicial review of the minister's decision not to schedule the site. At the substantive hearing the question of locus standi was looked at again, and Mr Justice Schiemann put forward a number of propositions. First, that locus standi did not require some financial or legal interest on the part of the applicant in relation to the matter complained of. Secondly, that merely for an applicant to assert that he or she had an interest did not of itself create such an interest. Thirdly, that a company would not necessarily have sufficient interest simply because it was formed by persons sharing a common view, even if the company's memorandum empowered it to campaign on a particular issue. The company could have no greater claim to standing than that possessed by individual members of the campaign prior to its incorporation. Fourthly, that, in the light of the above, the minister's decision was not one in respect of which the ordinary citizen had sufficient interest so as to entitle him to apply for judicial review. In his Lordship's view, the law was not there for every individual who wished to challenge the legality of an administrative decision.

However, this decision has since been confined to its special facts and the general trend has been to grant locus standi to any individual with a 'sincere concern', or any reputable pressure group with a genuine concern, with an apparent serious abuse of public power: *R v Secretary of State for Foreign and Commonwealth Affairs, ex parte Rees-Mogg* (1994); *R v Inspectorate of Pollution, ex parte Greenpeace Ltd (No 2)* (1994).

As to the question of whether or not rules of standing are necessary, the answer lies in one's perceptions of judicial review. The courts take the approach that without the rules of standing they would be besieged with busybodies, cranks, and vexatious litigants. It is submitted that this may not be the case. Litigation costs money. If a litigant is legally aided, finance will not be provided for pointless litigation. If a litigant is not legally aided, why should he be prevented from wasting his money on legal fees if that is what he wishes to do? There are very few people who genuinely want to throw their own money away on pointless litigation. Further, as some of the cases referred to above indicate, when the courts want to the rules of standing are interpreted so liberally that almost any citizen could be regarded as having locus standi, eg the *Smedley* case. On this basis they can be seen as an unnecessary procedural hurdle.

SUGGESTED ANSWER TO QUESTION SEVEN

General Comment

A question requiring a good knowledge of the law relating to locus standi, and of the principles in the *Padfield* case. Note the important factual distinction between the professor's case and that of the association; this clearly has a bearing on the merits of the challenge.

Key Points

- Procedure for challenge
- Theory of locus standi
- Leading cases and principles
- Application to the facts of the problem
- Principles in *Padfield*
- Distinguish two claims
- Relevance of remedy to standing

Suggested Answer

Both the Wild Flowers Studies Association and Muddle will be requesting the court to order the minister to hold a public inquiry into the building of the road, in the hope that the inspector appointed will recommend that it should not be built. The procedure for challenging the minister's decision not to order any such inquiry would be to apply for judicial review. Under O.53 r3(7) any person wishing to apply for judicial review must have the necessary locus standi to do so, ie:

> '... the Court shall not grant leave unless it considers that the applicant has a sufficient interest in the matter to which the application relates.'

The 'sufficient interest' criterion replaced the narrower 'person aggrieved' under the former O.53. The courts have been careful not to give restrictive interpretations to the meaning of sufficient interest; it remains in each case a question of fact and law, to be determined in the light of all the circumstances of the case.

The leading decision is that of the House of Lords in *IRC* v *National Federation of Self Employed and Small Businesses* (1982). The House of Lords held that locus standi should be considered in the first instance when leave is applied for to bring an application for judicial review. At this stage, the matter should be considered generally, and only obviously inappropriate cases dismissed. Locus standi should be considered again when the full application for judicial review was made. This was because, at this second stage, evidence from the respondent public body would be put forward which might put the applicant's claim in a different light. As Lord Wilberforce explained:

> 'There may be simple cases in which it can be seen at the earliest stage that the person applying for judicial review has no interest at all ... then it would be quite correct at the threshold to refuse him leave to apply ... But in other cases this will not be so. In these it will be necessary to consider the powers or the duties in law of those against whom the

relief is asked, the position of the applicant in relation to those powers and duties, and the breach of those said to have been committed.'

It is submitted that two factors the courts will consider, therefore, are the merits of the application and the remedy sought. Both of these issues are considered below. Before leaving this point it should be noted, however, that both applicants in the present case would be acting in the capacity of an interested pressure group and a concerned citizen rather than persons whose legal rights are directly affected by the decision. In this respect, regard should be had to the judgment of Schiemann J in *R* v *Secretary of State for the Environment, ex parte Rose Theatre Trust Co* (1990). The case concerned the extent to which the Trust Company had sufficient interest to challenge the Secretary of State's refusal to exercise his discretion to schedule the site of the Rose Theatre as a monument of national importance under the Ancient Monuments and Archaeological Areas Act 1979 (as amended). His Lordship put forward a number of propositions. First, that locus standi did not require some financial or legal interest in the matter complained of; secondly, that merely because an applicant asserted that he or she had an interest did not of itself create such an interest; thirdly, that a company would not necessarily have sufficient interest simply because it was formed by persons sharing a common view, even if the company's memorandum empowered it to campaign on a particular issue. The company could have no greater claim to standing than that possessed by individual members of the campaign prior to its incorporation. Fourthly, and in the light of the above, the minister's decision was not one in respect of which the ordinary citizen had sufficient interest so as to entitle him to apply for judicial review. In his Lordship's view, the law was not there for every individual who wished to challenge the legality of an administrative decision. As in the present case it is interesting to note that the relevant legislation gave the minister a very wide discretion to act, thus placing a heavy evidential burden upon any party seeking to establish illegality on his part.

As regards the merits of the minister's decision, the objectors would be advised to claim that the minister has thwarted the aims and objects of the legislation by not exercising his power to order an inquiry as he should have done: *Padfield* v *Minister of Agriculture* (1968). The minister may have been given widely drafted powers, but these are not to be used to thwart the policy behind the legislation. The minister in the present case could be accused of not paying sufficient regard to the purpose of the Act, viz to protect important sites.

At this point a distinction may be drawn between the claims of the Wild Flowers Studies Association and Muddle. The site of Ugly Moor is '… noted for its rare species of heather …', whilst only a '… minority of historians …' consider it to be a site of historic importance. Hence the association is likely to have a stronger case on the facts than the professor. The merit of the association's challenge is, as indicated above, a factor to be taken into account when considering the issue of locus standi; thus it may be permitted to apply for review whilst the professor might not.

The case for giving standing to the Association is also boosted by recent cases in which reputable and well-established pressure groups have been granted leave to challenge apparent abuses of public power: *R* v *Inspectorate of Pollution, ex parte Greenpeace Ltd (No 2)* (1994) and *R* v *Secretary of State for Foreign and*

Commonwealth Affairs, ex parte World Development Movement Ltd (1995). By contrast it is more difficult for a single citizen to obtain public interest standing and it appears that this will be recognised only in cases where the citizen can show a 'sincere concern for constitutional issues': *R v Secretary of State for Foreign and Commonwealth Affairs, ex parte Rees-Mogg* (1994). In the present case Professor Muddle may have a sincere concern, but it is hardly in a matter that compares in constitutional importance to Rees-Mogg's challenge to the signing of the Maastricht Treaty!

Both applicants will presumably be seeking an order of mandamus to compel the minister to exercise his discretion according to law and order the holding of an inquiry (as in the *Padfield* case).

In this respect, locus standi may be more restrictive in the case of mandamus, than certiorari or prohibition. For example in *R v Felixstowe Justices, ex parte Leigh* (1987) the court held that a journalist who was not present at a trial did not have locus standi for an order of mandamus to compel the justices hearing the case to disclose their names, but did have locus standi for a declaration that the justices' policy of maintaining their anonymity was contrary to law, thus confirming the view that the locus standi requirements are more strict in the case of mandamus than in applications for other remedies.

Even if either party succeeds in persuading the court to compel the minister to hold the inquiry, there is no guarantee that he will act in accordance with its findings. He will still have a discretion to act otherwise. In the *Padfield* case the complaint was eventually referred to a committee of inquiry which upheld the complainant's case, but the minister refused to take any further action on the matter.

SUGGESTED ANSWER TO QUESTION EIGHT

General Comment

This question requires a consideration of standing in its modern context. Is standing unique to judicial review cases? How do the modern rules operate? Do they really serve a useful function? An awareness of the rules that apply in other areas of law is helpful, as well as reference to the old rules on standing. Does standing operate in a similar way to these? Are the rules satisfactory? If not, how could they be improved?

Key Points

* Comparison with other areas
  - the old rules
  - the new rules
  - a test of merits
* Claims brought in the public interest
* Recent case law

Suggested Answer

While judicial review has its own rules of standing, the concept of standing is not unique to judicial review. Every branch of English law has similar rules which operate to narrow down the class of potential litigants by reference to their interest in or relationship to the matter. The usual technique is to require the litigant to have a cause of action. For example, where A is negligent, B will only be able to sue if certain criteria are met. A must owe B a duty of care, A's negligence must be a breach of that duty, and it must result in loss or damage to B. Thus it can be seen that in such a case, whether B has a cause of action and is entitled to sue is a function of the merits of the case. It will be argued that the same has become true of the rules of standing in judicial review cases.

The rules of standing used to be extremely technical and complex, and a different interest was required to bring the different available remedies. This is no longer the case; with the consolidation of the remedies in what is now O.53 there is no longer the clear distinction between the available remedies that justifies restrictively different rules of standing, and the modern tendency has been to adopt a liberal approach to the rules.

The statutory test of standing is now contained in O.53 r3(7). This states that the court should not *grant leave* unless it considers that the applicant has a 'sufficient interest' in the matter to which the application relates. Clearly this rule operates as a preliminary test which the court is to apply at the application for leave stage of the proceedings. 'Sufficient interest' is a test allowing a great deal of latitude to the courts; what will be a sufficient interest may differ form case to case, as will be seen.

The requirements of O.53 r3(7) were interpreted by the House of Lords in *IRC* v *National Federation of Self Employed and Small Businesses* (1982). In that case Lord Diplock spoke very clearly about the dangers of returning to the strict rules of locus standi that had applied under the old prerogative orders. This lends weight to the proposition that a uniform approach is to be applied, although it is true that some of their Lordships seemed doubtful about whether the same test would apply to all of the orders. In the end the Lords adopted a broad and uniform approach to the interpretation of the test of 'sufficient interest', and it now seems unlikely that a litigant will be hindered by the burden of having to show a different interest depending upon the remedy sought.

The test as applied by the House of Lords operates at two stages. First, at the application for leave stage. On this occasion, the test is a simple filter designed to weed out claims which are frivolous or vexatious, or those where the claimant has no genuine interest in the matter. This test will operate as a simple threshold, and given the nature of the application for leave, where evidence is given on affidavit and the application will often be decided without a hearing, it is submitted that it is right that the rules of standing should not be overly restrictive at this stage. The applicant will have little opportunity to demonstrate that she has a specific interest, but she should be able to show that the claim is not frivolous or vexatious.

It is somewhat surprising that the House of Lords held that the rules of standing should also be applied at a second stage; the substantive hearing itself. Order 53 r3(7) only speaks in terms of the application for leave. At the second stage, 'sufficient interest' must be determined by reference to the legal and factual context of the case, judged in relation to the applicant's concern with it. Thus, in the *National Federation* case, above, the applicants did not have standing because they could not show that the respondents had done anything wrong. This may be contrasted with the case of *R v HM Treasury, ex parte Smedley* (1987) where a taxpayer was granted leave to challenge an apparent illegal payment by the Treasury to the European Community. The court recognised the taxpayer's standing because he had a sincere concern with a prima facie unconstitutional use of public power.

The close association of standing with the merits of the case allows the court to take into account a range of factors that are quite subjective. This is illustrated by *R v IBA, ex parte Whitehouse* (1985). In this case it was held that any television viewer had standing to challenge a decision of the Independent Broadcasting Authority to broadcast a particular programme. But it is perhaps significant that on the merits the judge said of the film in question: 'No-one but a very odd person indeed would describe it as entertainment.' This is clearly a matter of opinion, and it is questionable how far such an approach to the question of standing can be satisfactory.

In general, however, the liberalisation of the rules of standing allows the courts a good deal of leeway in determining whether to uphold or dismiss a complaint. This is particularly important in those cases where a complainant is bringing a matter of public interest before the courts. The more liberal approach to standing means that in a suitable case the court may hear an application from a representative body. This occurred in *R v Secretary of State for Social Services, ex parte Child Poverty Action Group and Greater London Council* (1985). Here a representative action was brought by both the GLC and by the Child Poverty Action Group (CPAG). The GLC's action failed for want of standing; the GLC was held to have no special responsibility to the claimants in this case, and no right to be the guardian of the public interest. The CPAG was successful; on standing it was held to be a body which truly represented the interests of the individuals involved. Similarly, respected, well-established and reputable pressure groups have been granted standing in other cases, often because they have the resources to mount a relevant and well-argued case on behalf of concerned citizens who, as individuals, may lack such an ability: *R v Inspectorate of Pollution, ex parte Greenpeace Ltd (No 2)* (1994) and *R v Secretary of State for Foreign and Commonwealth Affairs, ex parte World Development Movement Ltd* (1995).

It can be seen that the second stage of the standing test operates in a manner similar to that in negligence or contract cases; ie it is closely tied up with the merits. It might be argued that the rules of standing have ceased to be of any effect; the leave stage will only filter out frivolous and vexatious cases, and at the second stage the merits will be considered in any event. Subject to this, in effect the rules of standing have all but disappeared. But the reality is that judicial review has itself been greatly liberalised during the last 40 years. In this context the rules are satisfactory because it is fitting that the rules of standing be not technical and complex, burdensome to both the courts and to litigants. Indeed, in the *World Development Movement* case, above, Rose LJ opined that the real question is whether the applicant can show some substantial default or abuse, and not whether his personal rights or interests are involved. This is a tremendous boost to the concept of public interest standing.

SUGGESTED ANSWER TO QUESTION NINE

General Comment

The way in which this question is framed means that issues of constitutional law must be taken into account in answering it. What aspects of the rule of law might be at play in challenging governmental decision-making? What is the function of the rules of standing? Are they useful, or merely a hindrance? When do the courts allow cases of public interest to be brought? Should democratic interest in the legality of decision-making be sufficient to justify an authority being forced to place its decisions before the courts? What about other methods of accountability – such as parliamentary control?

Key Points

- Meaning of the rule of law
- The modern rules of standing
- Public interest cases – the relator action
- Public interest cases – the rules of standing
- Type of interest required
- Should the rules be abolished?

Suggested Answer

Constitutional principles of democracy mean that every citizen has an interest in the decision-making of governmental bodies; its legality is a matter of great public interest. Furthermore, the control of such decision-making through the process of law is an aspect of the rule of law of vital importance within a healthy jurisdiction. Nonetheless, it will be argued that the rules of standing should not be abolished; they too have an important role to play within the legal system, and their existence can provide a worthwhile contribution to the preservation of the rule of law.

The rules of standing are usually thought of as being a unique and restrictive force within the sphere of administrative law. It is true that the arbitrary restriction of otherwise worthy claims with the simple aim of cutting the numbers of cases before the courts would not be a legitimate use of the rules of standing. The rule of law requires that there be effective remedies within the legal system, without arbitrary restrictions related to the capacity of the courts to deal with claims. But the rules of standing are not unique to administrative law; they are its equivalent of privity in contract and land law, or of proximity within the law of negligence. The rules of standing are as important as these equivalents in defining the class of persons entitled to bring an action in any particular case.

The former rules of standing were extremely complex and technical, and the interest required was defined differently for each of the possible judicial review remedies. The courts seized the opportunity presented by the consolidation of the remedies in O.53 (from 1 January 1978) to liberalise the rules of standing to an extent that now allows the courts a great deal of flexibility in determining whether an individual should be entitled to seek judicial review and enables them to take the initiative to a greater extent in deciding when particular claims should be heard. It is right that they should do so since the rule of law requires that the courts take responsibility for enforcing the law and thus for controlling the legality of decision-making.

Order 53 r3(7) requires that the court should not grant leave unless it considers that the applicant has a 'sufficient interest' in the matter to which the application relates. This appears to require the test to be applied at the application for leave stage of judicial review proceedings. But the House of Lords in *IRC* v *National Federation of Self Employed and Small Businesses* (1982) held that the test should be applied at two stages. At the application for leave stage, the test will operate as a simple threshold, designed to filter out claims which are frivolous or vexatious, or where there is no genuine interest in the matter. Thus at the leave stage the test is unlikely to hinder a genuine claimant, but such a test is necessary; one requirement of the rule of law is that governmental decision-making be effective, and this effectiveness would be greatly undermined if subjected to continual and frivolous challenges.

The second stage of the test will be applied at the substantive hearing, when standing will be determined by reference to the legal and factual matrix in the case, judged in relation to the applicant's concern in it. This second stage test is thus closely associated with the merits of the case. In the *National Federation* case, above, the applicants did not have standing because they were unable to show any wrongdoing on the part of the Inland Revenue.

It is submitted that this two-stage test is unlikely to have any damaging effect on the requirement of the rule of law that decision-making be subject to judicial scrutiny. The first stage should simply exclude cases where there is clearly no real merit in the application, and is appropriate as a means of preventing wasteful litigation. By the time the second stage of the test comes to be applied, the court should have looked at the factual and legal context of the case and should thus have begun its scrutiny of the decision in question.

The flexibility of this two-stage test provides the courts with a useful additional string to their bow in scrutinising cases of public interest. Judicial review proceedings in this context may be compared with the relator action in civil law proceedings. The correct approach in public interest cases is normally to use the relator action under which the Attorney-General brings the action. But there is a serious gap in this type of case in that the Attorney-General's discretion in the matter is unchallengeable (see *Gouriet* v *Union of Post Office Workers* (1978)), so there is no guarantee that the matter will reach the courts. The courts have used the more modern rules of standing to allow individuals or representative groups to bring judicial review cases of wider public importance, thus to some extent bypassing the deficiencies of the relator action. Thus in *R* v *IBA, ex parte Whitehouse* (1985) a television viewer was held to have standing to challenge a decision of the Independent Broadcasting Authority to broadcast a particular programme. However, in *R* v *Secretary of State for the Environment, ex parte Rose Theatre Trust Co* (1990) it was held that the ministerial discretion of whether or not to list a site as a protected ancient monument was one of those rare public decisions in respect of which the ordinary citizen or group of citizens did not have sufficient interest to challenge.

Clearly, therefore, there may be cases where there is a very great public interest in the legality of a decision but in which the decision will go unchallenged. Thus in *R* v *Boundary Commission for England, ex parte Foot* (1983) the applicant was held not to have sufficient interest to challenge a review of the constituency boundary lines. The applicant's interest was a purely political one, and indeed the matter was one of great political importance since the decisions of the Boundary Commission would affect the future outcome of elections. This is a case of clear public interest that has escaped judicial scrutiny, and thus arguably shows a failure of the rules of standing to uphold the rule of law. Having said that, the concern of the judiciary is with law, and not with politics. Political issues should be scrutinised and discussed by Parliament, which is the sovereign political authority in the land. It is not surprising, therefore, that a political interest is one which the courts do not recognise. Had a case been brought against the Boundary Commission by an individual who had suffered some specific tangible harm as a result of the Commission's decision, such as increased rates, then it is likely that that individual would have had a sufficient interest.

It can be seen that the rules of standing are sufficiently flexible to permit judicial review of certain kinds of decision-making that is of public interest. Where they perhaps fail is in not allowing for scrutiny of a central political issue such as the falling of boundary lines. But where an individual or representative body can show a tangible interest in the outcome of a decision, that individual or body should be permitted to bring judicial review proceedings. General democratic interest is not enough, but this is appropriate: it is for the courts to uphold legality, not individuals, and the rules of standing give the courts the necessary flexibility to do so; they should not be abolished.

6

Error of Law: Jurisdictional Error and Exclusion of Review

Introduction

This chapter is concerned with a particular ground for review, namely error of law. It has sometimes been classified as simply one among many grounds for rendering a decision ultra vires, eg it was listed as such as by Lord Greene MR in *Associated Provincial Picture Houses Ltd* v *Wednesbury Corporation* [1948] 1 KB 223 and could be regarded as an aspect of '*Wednesbury* unreasonableness'. Alternatively, any aspect of ultra vires (see Chapters 7, 8 and 9) could be regarded as a jurisdictional error of law: per Lord Reid in *Anisminic Ltd* v *Foreign Compensation Commission* [1969] 2 AC 147. The *Anisminic* case also effectively discarded the traditional distinction between jurisdictional and non-jurisdictional error so far as the decisions of inferior administrative bodies are concerned, so that any errors of law by such a body which affects its decisions will render that decision a nullity.

This branch of administrative law has usually proved troublesome for students, firstly because of the difficulty conceptual analysis contained in the leading judgments and, secondly, because it is inextricably bound up with another branch of administrative law, namely parliamentary attempts to exclude or limit judicial review. The significance of the breakthrough made by *Anisminic* cannot be appreciated except in the context of judicial resistance to ouster clauses, which were regarded as undermining the rule of law. An early example of such resistance can be found in Lord Denning's revival of the ancient doctrine of 'error of law on the face of record' as a device for ensuring the preservation of judicial review in areas where Parliament had excluded or limited challenges in the courts to decisions of tribunals: *R v Northumberland Compensation Appeal Tribunal, ex parte Shaw* [1952] 1 KB 338. After *Anisminic* all errors of law are jurisdictional, rendering decisions based on them ultra vires, so that it is no longer necessary to resort to Lord Denning's doctrine in *ex parte Shaw* as a way of reviewing what was at that time regarded as a non-jurisdictional (intra vires) error of law, and which, without Lord Denning's efforts, would have been protected from challenge by a statutory ouster clause: see further *R v Lord President of the Council, ex parte Page* [1992] 3 WLR 1112 for a useful review of the relevant authorities. A recent case on ouster clauses and jurisdictional error is *R v Secretary of State for the Home Department, ex parte Fayed* [1997] 1 All ER 228.

It should be noted that the *Anisminic* principle is applicable to inferior *administrative* bodies. Where an ouster clause purports to protect from challenge the decisions of the ordinary, regular courts it may still be necessary to prove that the error of law was a jurisdictional one in order to obtain review, so that the historic distinction between jurisdictional and non-jurisdictional error of law may remain relevant in some areas: see *South East Asia Fire Bricks Sdn Bhd* v *Non-Metallic Mineral Products Manufacturing Employees Union* [1981] AC 363 (concerning the Industrial Court of Malaysia).

Further time limits, as distinct from complete ouster clauses, will be effective to protect even ultra vires decisions after the relevant time limit has expired because of the presumed intention of Parliament to put an early end to legal disputes affecting, for example, major projects such as a new motorway. This judicial interpretation of time limits may be regarded as a pragmatic acceptance of political realities, and may be contrasted with the general judicial attitude toward ouster clauses, above: *Smith* v *East Elloe Rural District Council* [1956] AC 736; *R* v *Cornwall County Council, ex parte Huntingdon* [1994] 1 All ER 694.

In regard to examinations, essay-type questions on the *Anisminic principle* are fairly common and ouster or limitation clauses also frequently form part of problem-type questions involving various grounds for judicial review.

Questions

INTERROGRAMS

1 Explain the distinction between jurisdictional and non-jurisdictional error of law. Why was this distinction of historic importance in English administrative law?
2 What is 'error of law on the face of the record'?
3 Explain the impact of the *Anisminic* case in public law.
4 Is it possible for Parliament to oust the jurisdiction of the courts in important areas of administrative decision-making?

QUESTION ONE

The Minister for Health sends you, as her senior legal adviser, the following memorandum:

> 'I am concerned at the news that there have been one or two applications for leave to apply for judicial review of medical decisions. Admittedly, these have been unsuccessful. But who knows what the judges will do next? I do not wish the courts to challenge the priorities within hospital waiting-lists or otherwise interfere with clinical decisions. Please advise.'

Draft a memorandum in response, explaining a) whether the Minister's fears that a court might grant judicial review are justified and b) what steps, if any, the Minister could take to minimise the likelihood of judicial review.

London University LLB Examination
(for external students) Administrative Law June 1988 Q10

QUESTION TWO

'Where the existence or non-existence of a fact is left to the judgment and discretion of a public body and that fact involves a broad spectrum ranging from the obvious to the debatable to the just conceivable, it is the duty of the court to leave the decision of that fact to the public body to whom Parliament has entrusted the decision-making power save in a case where it is obvious that the public body, consciously or unconsciously, are acting perversely.' (*Puhlhofer* v *Hillingdon London Borough Council* (1986), per Lord Brightman)

Discuss.

London University LLB Examination
(for external students) Administrative Law June 1992 Q2

QUESTION THREE

'Statutory attempts to exclude the judiciary from reviewing administrative action are a threat to the rule of law. Judges rightly interpret such clauses liberally.'

Discuss.

London University LLB Examination
(for external students) Administrative Law June 1989 Q7

QUESTION FOUR

'The courts' responses to ouster clauses may appear at times to challenge the doctrine of parliamentary sovereignty, but in so doing the judges display laudable devotion to the principle of the rule of law.'

Discuss.

London University LLB Examination
(for external students) Administrative Law June 1993 Q2

Answers

ANSWERS TO INTERROGRAMS

1   If an error of law was committed by a decision-making body after having asked itself the relevant questions and applied the appropriate legal tests, for example by misinterpreting a relevant statutory provision, it was said to have committed a non-jurisdictional error and, if Parliament had protected its decisions by an ouster clause, such an error could not be corrected since Parliament had not provided a right of appeal and because judicial review was available only in respect of ultra vires (or jurisdictional) errors. An error was classified as jurisdictional if, for example, the decision-making body had asked itself irrelevant questions or applied the wrong legal tests, or acted in bad faith or in breach of natural justice, or in any of the other ways giving rise to ultra vires and void decisions described by Lord Greene MR in *Associated Provincial Picture Houses Ltd* v *Wednesbury Corporation* [1948] 1 KB 223 and by Lord Reid in *Anisminic Ltd* v *Foreign Compensation Commission* [1969] 2 AC 147. A jurisdictional error committed by an inferior administrative body was reviewable because an ouster clause was presumed to protect only intra vires determinations.

2   'Error of law on the fact of the record' is a doctrine which states that the High

Court's supervisory jurisdiction includes the power to correct the record of inferior bodies so as to remove obvious errors of law committed within the jurisdiction of the tribunal in question. Strictly speaking, the doctrine is a form of appeal rather than review since the errors of law being corrected are intra vires. It was unnecessary to use it so long as rights of appeal existed, but when Parliament tried to protect tribunal determinations during the 1940s and 1950s by taking away rights of appeal and applying 'no certiorari' clauses to them, the doctrine was reviewed so as to ensure a means of preventing injustice caused by such non-jurisdictional errors. It has become unnecessary to resort to it since the *Anisminic* case and the abolition of 'no certiorari' clauses by the Tribunals and Inquiries Act 1971.

3   *Anisminic* has had a tremendous impact on public law because it has been used as a springboard from which to launch an entirely new concept of ultra vires. After *Anisminic* any error of law which is relevant to the making of an administrative decision is a jurisdictional one, so that an ouster clause relating to the decisions of an administrative tribunal will be ineffective except possibly in respect of an error of fact (though even here it should not be too difficult to show that the error of fact was of such a kind that it prevented a fair hearing, which would then constitute an error of law and thus be reviewable).

   Anisminic is not applicable to inferior judicial bodies or, a fortiori, to superior judges of the High Court, even in their capacities as Visitors to Inns of Court when exercising disciplinary functions: *R* v *Visitors to Lincoln's Inn, ex parte Calder and Persuad* [1992] 3 WLR 994. It appears that University Visitors, whether judges or not, enjoy for historic reasons exclusivity of decision-making on questions of law and fact within their jurisdiction: *R* v *Lord President of the Council, ex parte Page* [1992] 3 WLR 1112.

4   Most types of ouster clauses will prove ineffective in the face of judicial determination to uphold the rule of law over inferior administrative bodies and to prevent injustice being caused to individuals by errors of law in the decision-making process. For example, a finality clause – 'the decision of this tribunal shall be final' – has been interpreted as being final on the merits (ie no appeal) but not on the law (so judicial review remains available): *R* v *Medical Appeal Tribunal, ex parte Gilmore* [1957] 1 QB 574.

   After *Anisminic* few ouster-type clauses could be effective to exclude judicial review since they would be presumed to apply only to intra vires decisions and any error of law by an administrative body would involve ultra vires. The House of Lords in *Anisminic* simply refused to apply a literal interpretation to the words 'this determination shall not be called into question in any court of law'. The word 'determination' was construed to mean an intra vires determination.

   However, judges have been more tolerant towards conditional ouster clauses, such as time limits, recognising a parliamentary desire for finality even at the risk of a subsequent discovery of ultra vires: *R* v *Secretary of State for the Environment, ex parte Ostler* [1977] QB 122 (where Lord Denning MR, ever mindful of the risk of injustice to the individual, advised Mr Ostler to complain of maladministration to the Parliamentary Ombudsman since judicial review was no longer available. Mr Ostler did so and was successful, receiving an ex gratia payment of compensation).

SUGGESTED ANSWER TO QUESTION ONE

General Comment

A question that calls for a general consideration of the factors which might persuade a court not to exercise its discretion to grant judicial review coupled with a consideration of the various devices at Parliament's disposal for minimising the likelihood of judicial review.

Key Points

- Scope of judicial review – sensitivity of judges to allocation of scarce resources decisions
- Various types of ouster clauses
- Judicial attitudes to ouster clauses
- The concepts of jurisdiction and error of law

Suggested Answer

The likelihood of decisions relating to the allocation of resources within hospitals being subject to judicial review.

The minister's fears as to the courts granting judicial review of decisions relating to the allocation of resources by administrators within the health service are, it is submitted, largely unfounded. The courts recognise that such bodies are having to take difficult decisions concerning the priorities to be given to different types of care, and appreciate that judges are no better qualified to take such decisions than are hospital administrators.

In *Re Walker's Application* (1987) the applicant for review was the mother of a child that needed a heart operation. The health authorities in Birmingham had already postponed the operation five times due to a shortage of trained nursing staff. The basis of the application was the alleged failure of the authority to provide an adequate service. The Court of Appeal held, in rejecting the application, that whilst the health authorities were clearly public bodies amenable to review, the rationing of resources was a matter for them and not the courts. Only if it could be shown that the allocation of funds by the authority was unreasonable in the *Wednesbury* sense (*Associated Provincial Picture Houses Ltd* v *Wednesbury Corporation* (1948)), or if there were breaches of public law duties, would the courts be prepared to intervene.

In *R* v *Cambridge District Health Authority, ex parte B* (1995) a ten-year-old girl suffering from leukaemia was refused further medical treatment on the ground, inter alia, that the cost of such treatment was too much in the light of other demands on medical services. The Court of Appeal held that this decision was lawful and Sir Thomas Bingham MR (as he then was) emphasised that it was not for judges to express opinions as to the merits of medical judgment.

Even where a health authority is under a duty to provide a certain level of health care, it is unlikely that the statutory duty will be drawn in sufficiently precise terms for it to be enforceable by the courts, and even if it is, the courts will not intervene if there is evidence that the health authority is genuinely doing its best to discharge its duties with available resources; see *R* v *Secretary of State for Social Services, ex parte Hincks* (1979).

Minimising the likelihood of such review

On the basis of the above it is submitted that little needs to be done in order to minimise the likelihood of judicial review in this context, but the following matters could be considered.

Legislation could be introduced which indicates that Parliament does not intend decisions relating to the allocation of resources within the hospital service to be questioned in the courts. Given that health authorities are administrative agencies, or 'inferior bodies' it is most unlikely that the courts would be willing to give full effect to a clause which purported completely to exclude the possibility of challenge before them. The denial of what might be considered as a 'constitutional right' to challenge decisions of the administration that affect individual interests is a very grave matter, and as will be made clear below, statutory provisions which aim to produce such a situation are likely to be successful only to the extent that the courts are willing to let them be successful.

A number of techniques are available to the parliamentary draftsman and they will be considered in turn.

a   *'Subjectively worded powers'*

Parliament may provide that the decisions of a health authority are to be made 'as it thinks fit', ie a subjectively worded power. On its face, decisions made in the exercise of such a power would seem to be immune from challenge before the courts because Parliament appears to be entrusting the decision entirely to the authority's judgment. In reality, however, such a clause would not prevent review by the courts. The decision of the House of Lords in *Padfield* v *Minister of Agriculture* (1968), illustrates the point that there is now no scope for the argument that a subjectively worded power gives rise to untrammelled jurisdiction. The courts will still 'read in' the implied limits of reasonableness and fairness.

b   *'Finality clauses'*

The relevant legislation could include a clause to the effect that the decision of a health authority on the allocation of resources is to be 'final and conclusive' on the matter. Again, it is doubtful whether such a provision would achieve the desired result. In *R* v *Medical Appeal Tribunal, ex parte Gilmore* (1957) Lord Denning MR stated that:

> 'The word "final" is not enough. That only means "without appeal". It does not mean "without recourse to certiorari". It makes the decision final on the facts, but not final on the law.'

Thus the decision of a health authority would still be subject to review on the basis that it had misdirected itself as to law in some respect.

c   *'Shall not be questioned clauses'*

A third device that might be used, and which is likely to meet with perhaps a little more success, is for an enabling Act to provide that the decision of a health authority is not to be questioned in any court of law. Such a clause was considered by the House of Lords in *Anisminic Ltd* v *Foreign Compensation Commission* (1969). Lord Reid, expressing the majority view, felt that s4(4) of the Foreign Compensation Act 1950, which provided that no determination of the Commission was to be called into question in any court of law, did not succeed in 'ousting' the jurisdiction of the courts to invalidate the Commission's actions. It was held that the term 'determination' as used in the Act referred only to a valid determination. Thus an ultra vires or invalid determination was not one protected by the 'ouster clause'. In this case it was felt that the determination of the Commission was ultra vires because it had made an error of law upon which its jurisdiction depended. The determination was therefore 'invalid' and challengeable before the courts.

In *Re Racal Communications* (1981) the House of Lords (in particular Lord Diplock) reaffirmed the correctness of the earlier decision in *Anisminic*, but added that the decision of the courts to intervene on the basis that there had been an ultra vires error of law, should be made with reference to the nature of the decision-making body. Where the decision-making body was 'judicial' in nature, such as a county court judge, the courts should be slow to by-pass 'ouster clauses' because the decision would have been taken by a body with some expertise in law. Where, on the other hand, the decision subject to challenge was taken by an administrative body, perhaps the courts should be more ready to intervene on the basis that an error of law was more likely to have been made. A health authority is almost certainly going to be regarded as an administrative body, and thus it is submitted that even if such a clause were included in the relevant legislation, it would not prevent review by the courts.

SUGGESTED ANSWER TO QUESTION TWO

General Comment

This question raises the problem of the courts interfering with findings of fact in the course of judicial review. In theory they should not do so. Why not? But there are cases in which the courts may justifiably look at the facts. When will they do so? Will they admit to doing so? An ability to grasp the issue of error of law and error of fact is needed, as is a clear analysis of the cases on this area.

Key Points

- Why the courts should not interfere with findings of fact
- The facts/law distinction
- The cases
- Unreasonableness
- No evidence

Suggested Answer

Judicial review does not operate as an appeal on the merits of a decision, it is a review of the manner of decision-making. This means that, in theory, the court may not challenge an authority's findings of fact at all. In spite of this the court does sometimes investigate findings of fact, but it will be argued that it tends to reclassify the issue as one of law thus putting it on home territory; for, while the inferior authority maybe the factfinder, the court is always the expert on law.

One justification for the court's refusal to overturn a finding of fact relates to the expertise of the inferior organisation. The High Court is the appropriate forum for questions of law, but questions of fact are often left to skilled decision-makers who are the best people to deal with them. Related to this is the peculiarly local knowledge that may be required in making certain decisions. *Puhlhofer* v *Hillingdon London Borough Council* (1986) is a particularly good example of this. The case concerned the statutory duty of local authorities to provide accommodation. The applicant argued that 'accommodation' meant 'reasonable accommodation'. The House of Lords held that the statute had not defined 'accommodation', and that whether the applicant had 'accommodation' was a question of fact for the local authority concerned. The meaning of words in a statute is normally a question of law; but the subtext of *Puhlhofer* is that each authority was responsible for allocating accommodation within its area, a matter particularly sensitive to local factors. The local authority was in the best position to assess those local factors in determining what accommodation would be available to meet the needs of particular applicants. The court's refusal to treat the meaning of accommodation as a question of law is arguably justified in this particular instance, and Lord Brightman's dictum clearly recognises the possibility of challenge should the authority behave perversely. Such perverseness might include for example unfairly favouring the needs of a council employee to those of other applicants or the provision of accommodation that is clearly unfit for human habitation.

The *Puhlhofer* case may be contrasted with *R* v *Secretary of State for the Home Department, ex parte Khawaja* (1984). In this case the court had no difficulty in reviewing a decision that the applicant was an illegal entrant. It was held that this was a question of law for the court to decide. In *Bugdaycay* v *Secretary of State for the Home Department* (1987) on the other hand, it was held that the question of whether a person who was otherwise an illegal entrant was a refugee was a matter for the immigration authorities and ultimately for the Home Secretary. In the latter case the decision of the Home Secretary was overturned on the basis that he had not taken into account evidence relating to the danger faced by the applicant if he was returned to his country of origin. The contrast between these cases may be explained on the basis that some facts are so crucial to the existence of the decision-maker's power to act that a failure to correctly establish those facts renders the decision ultra vires. In other words, questions of fact that go to the jurisdiction of the decision-maker are capable of review, since if they are not established the decision will be a nullity; this effectively reclassifies those questions of fact as questions of law, because whether an authority has acted within its powers will always be a question of law. Where, however, the analysis of specialised facts, complex issues of fact or facts within local knowledge are involved the court will be unwilling to intervene.

This analysis still leaves the matter one step removed. It does not fully explain when the courts will decide that a question of fact is so crucial that it goes to jurisdiction. This is partly a question whether the fact is preliminary to the exercise of a power; if A is an illegal immigrant then B may detain and deport A. But it is submitted that the courts also adopt a functional approach; what is the nature of the claim, and who may best determine it? Thus where important rights are at stake, eg the right to freedom

(*Khawaja*), then the courts will be more willing to investigate the facts by construing them as going to jurisdiction (sometimes known as the 'anxious scrutiny' approach). But where the power granted is a power to confer some benefit from the resources of the authority, the authority will be left to decide how to allocate its resources, as in *Puhlhofer*.

To relate this analysis to the familiar grounds for judicial review, where facts go to the jurisdiction of an authority, those facts may be challenged on the basis of illegality. Where facts do not go to the jurisdiction of the authority, the court may nonetheless find itself scrutinising findings of fact to determine whether *Wednesbury* unreasonableness (*Associated Provincial Picture Houses Ltd* v *Wednesbury Corporation* (1948)) is made out or whether there has been some form of impropriety in the procedure leading to the decision. Unreasonableness or 'perversity' will be the more likely of these grounds of challenge. It will be rare that a decision of fact will be so unreasonable that no reasonable authority could have made it. But where an authority has not considered all of the evidence available to it (as in *Bugdaycay* above) or where it has made a finding of fact in the absence of any evidence at all, then the court will no doubt be able to intervene on the basis of a failure to take into account relevant criteria, or that the fact is simply not established by sufficient evidence. The latter, known as the 'no evidence' rule, is perhaps the clearest ground upon which intervention by the court might be justified yet it has often been treated as an error of law and this further illustrates the unwillingness of the courts to be seen to handle factual issues in the process of judicial review: see *Coleen Properties* v *Minister of Housing and Local Government* (1971).

The court does not have a general power to interfere with the findings of fact of an inferior body. Thus it is rightly diffident about doing so. But the court does possess sufficient power to intervene in clear cases of perversity, unreasonableness, or no evidence. Further, there is sufficient flexibility within the notion of 'error of law' to enable the courts to review the facts of cases when they find it necessary, in order to see whether an error of law has occurred. Thus although in theory the court should not look at the facts, it is not altogether powerless to do so.

SUGGESTED ANSWER TO QUESTION THREE

General Comment

This question calls for a detailed evaluation of the approach taken by the courts to ouster and time limit clauses in the context of Dicey's formulation of the rule of law.

Key Points

- Outline of Dicey's rule of law
- Distinction between exclusion and time limit clauses
- Rationale for ouster clauses
- Criticisms of exclusion clauses
- Evaluation of contrasting approaches in *Anisminic* and *Ostler*

Suggested Answer

The law of law as formulated by Dicey is based on the notion that everyone, including government officials, should be required to act within the confines of ascertainable laws. More specifically it requires that there should be government according to ascertainable rules as opposed to arbitrary decision making and that the same law should apply to all legal entitles equally in the sense that no-one should be above the law. Any statutory attempt to exclude the judiciary from reviewing administrative action has the effect of placing the relevant decision maker in a position where he or it is above the law, in the sense of being able to act without any legal constraint, and must therefore clearly constitute a threat to the rule of law.

It is, however, necessary to distinguish between a statutory attempt to exclude judicial review and an attempt merely to limit the court's capacity to review, for example, by imposing time limits on applicants. In the latter case the decision maker is not placed above the law although he nevertheless is given special treatment. It should be noted in this regard that, although any such preferential treatment is strictly contrary to Dicey's formulation, it is now accepted that Dicey's test is based on Victorian libertarian views which have become increasingly irrelevant in the context of a modern bureaucratic society. In particular it is now recognised that government officials and agencies possess special rights and powers which are necessary to enable them to perform their functions and that the rule of law simply requires that public authorities should be subject to all normal legal duties and liabilities which are not inconsistent with their functions.

In assessing the attitude of courts to statutory attempts to exclude judicial review it is necessary to consider whether there are any valid arguments in favour of excluding judicial review on the basis that it is inconsistent with the governmental functions of the body in question. The main purpose of the exclusion clauses is to make a particular class decision final. This may be desirable if there is a need to be able to act quickly and with certainty on the basis of the decision made.

In the case of total exclusion clauses, however, there is an attempt to achieve this finally at the price of placing the authority totally beyond the reach of the law, thereby rendering meaningless any statutory constraints on the jurisdiction and powers of that body. This is contrary to any notion of rule whether based on twentieth or nineteenth century views, and would involve a fundamental change in the constitutional role of the courts as watch dogs over the executive at a time when there are serious doubts about the efficiency of parliamentary controls.

It would therefore seem that the courts have been correct in their liberal interpretation of clauses of the 'as if enacted' type which was considered in *Anisminic Ltd* v *Foreign Compensation Commission* (1969). This approach in effect sidesteps any clause which purports to exclude review for jurisdictional error. What is less clear is whether the House of Lords was correct in adopting a broad view of jurisdictional error. It is arguable that while authorities should not be free blatantly to exceed or abuse their powers, they should otherwise be free to make decisions without being subject to the constant threat of judicial review, particularly where it can be shown that this will assist them in the performance of their functions.

On the other hand, it would also seem that the courts have been correct in taking a more conservative approach to time limit clauses as illustrated in cases such as *Secretary of State for the Environment, ex parte Ostler* (1977). It is arguable that there are certain public authorities which would be severely inhibited in their ability to operate effectively if they are subject to the possibility of litigation which might delay their work for many years. In the case of these, the time limit clause represents a useful compromise in the sense of it ensuring that the authority is in fact answerable to the courts for its actions, while at the same time conferring some measure of finality. Such a clause may well offend Dicey's formulation of the rule of the law but is arguable consistent with the more modern formulation set out above.

SUGGESTED ANSWER TO QUESTION FOUR

General Comment

Here the student is required to weigh up the importance of two constitutional maxims – parliamentary sovereignty and the rule of law – as they apply to the courts' scrutiny of cases where ouster clauses apply. Distinguish ouster clauses from other clauses limiting the jurisdiction of the courts by defining them. Do you agree with the value judgment implicit in the question – that the courts *should* uphold the rule of law rather than parliamentary sovereignty?

Key Points

- What is an ouster clause?
- Errors of law within and outside the jurisdiction
- Does the distinction between errors of law survive?
- Parliamentary sovereignty challenged
- The rule of law
- Conditional ouster clauses

Suggested Answer

There are several models of legislative clause that purport to limit or to exclude the courts' jurisdiction to scrutinise the actions of administrative bodies. True ouster clauses are those that purport to exclude the courts' powers of intervention altogether. Such clauses in fact present a constitutional paradox: although parliament is sovereign, its sovereign will is enforced through the courts; yet how can the courts enforce that will if parliament deprives them of their jurisdiction? It is this paradox that has provided the courts with overt justification for evading the strongest ouster clauses, and enabled them to avoid challenging parliamentary sovereignty directly. The effect of the courts' decisions, however, has effectively been to ignore Parliament's directions, and thus in real terms to challenge parliamentary sovereignty. Given that it is one tenet of the rule of law that all inferior organisations should be subject to law, the courts are right to adopt this robust approach and to insist on preserving their powers of judicial review.

The leading case in this area is *Anisminic Ltd* v *Foreign Compensation Commission*

(1969). In this case the clause in question stated that a determination of the Commission should 'not be called into question in any court of law'. Despite the clear wording of this clause the House of Lords held unanimously that the clause would not prevent judicial scrutiny of a determination that was outside the Commission's jurisdiction. In so holding the Lords were following a long line of judicial policy which traditionally distinguished between decisions made within an authority's jurisdiction and those made outside that jurisdiction. The justification for making this distinction is to be found in the doctrine of parliamentary sovereignty itself. As Lord Pearce stated, the House of Lords was simply enforcing Parliament's mandate to the Commission. By 'determination' Parliament meant a real determination, not a purported one. The courts would ensure that the Commission did not make determinations on matters not prescribed for its attention.

This part of the *Anisminic* decision is one which was acceptable, and Parliament itself appears to have given the nod to this particular line of judicial reasoning in enacting s14 of the Tribunals and Inquiries Act 1971, which abolished pre-1958 'no certiorari' clauses as applied to tribunals. However, the House of Lords in *Anisminic* also decided that a misconstruction of the Order in Council which the Commission had to apply itself involved an excess of jurisdiction. In other words, an error of law that took the Commission outside its jurisdiction enabled the court to exercise its powers of judicial review. The House of Lords seems to have meant to preserve the distinction between errors of law within the jurisdiction of a body and those outside it, as was affirmed in *South East Asia Fire Bricks Sdn Bhd* v *Non-Metallic Mineral Products Manufacturing Employees Union* (1981). In this case the ouster clause was highly specific; it provided that an award should be final and conclusive and that no award should be 'challenged, appealed against, reviewed, quashed or called into question in any court of law'. The House of Lords held that judicial review proceedings could not be brought where there was merely an error on the face of an award; they could only be brought where there was an error going to jurisdiction. But the real effect of *Anisminic* was to bring about a sweeping change in the ultra vires doctrine. This was expressed by Lord Diplock in *Re Racal Communications* (1981), when he said that *Anisminic* for practical purposes abolished the distinction between jurisdictional and non-jurisdictional errors of law. Any error of law would result in the tribunal having asked itself the wrong question, would make its decision ultra vires and thus would enable the courts to exercise their powers of judicial review.

If Lord Diplock's reasoning is followed through to its logical conclusion, then it is apparent that ouster clauses must be meaningless. All questions of law will go to the jurisdiction of the tribunal, and will thus be subject to judicial review. In general terms questions of fact are not subject to judicial review in any event, although the court may sometimes use the 'no evidence' rule to reclassify questions of fact as questions of law in order to justify judicial review of the decision: see *R* v *Secretary of State for the Home Department, ex parte Khawaja* (1984) where the court reviewed a decision that the plaintiff was an illegal entrant on the basis of the evidence pointing to that decision.

The position reached by Lord Diplock's reasoning thus presents a very real challenge to parliamentary sovereignty, since it purports to make meaningless a provision that Parliament presumably intends to be obeyed. A later authority has stated that Parliament may exclude recourse to the courts by using clear words, and that the courts should refuse to entertain matters which Parliament has by clear words excluded from the court's jurisdiction. In *R v Registrar of Companies, ex parte Central Bank of India* (1986) the Registrar was given power under statute to decide 'all ancillary questions'; the Court of Appeal held that this included questions of law, and therefore by necessary implication excluded recourse to the courts.

That the courts should jealously cling to their powers of judicial review is justified by consideration of the rule of law. Although the courts may challenge parliamentary sovereignty, they uphold stronger considerations of lawfulness and the correct exercise of power. As Griffiths LJ has stated, citizens affected by the decisions of tribunals are entitled to expect that such decisions will be in accordance with law, and the rule of law requires that the courts speak with authority to correct decisions that are founded upon errors of law. (See *R v Knightsbridge Crown Court, ex parte International Sporting Club Ltd* (1981).)

Mention may be made of 'conditional ouster clauses'. These typically provide for a limited avenue of challenge, within a six-week period, subject to which a decision may not be questioned by prohibition or certiorari or in any legal proceedings whatsoever. Such clauses are upheld by the courts, and distinguished from the absolute type of clause considered in *Anisminic* (see *R v Secretary of State for the Environment Secretary, ex parte Ostler* (1977)). There is no linguistic reason why such a distinction should be made, but the distinction has its own logic: the courts effectively treat these clauses as limitation clauses so that an action may not be brought after expiry of the time limit, even in cases of manifest abuse of power. On the one hand this appears to be justified, since all causes of action are subject to time limits of different lengths and Parliament may be assumed to have had good policy reasons for imposing such a time limit, eg so that after expiry of such a time limit developments can go ahead without risk of subsequent challenge. On the other hand, a six-week time limit is exceptionally short, particularly in cases of concealed abuse of power. If, as *Anisminic* appears to decide, a decision that is ultra vires is not a real decision at all, then it is questionable whether the courts should interpret the conditional type of ouster clause so strictly. If the decision is not a real decision, then the courts should have no hesitation in setting it aside and preventing the authority from acting upon it.

The rule of law requires that all inferior authorities and officials should be subject to law. It is appropriate, therefore, that the courts have consistently upheld the rule of law and refused to permit inferior organisations to shelter behind ouster clauses. In doing so the courts may have challenged parliamentary sovereignty, but there is an inherent paradox in that challenge since by undermining that sovereignty on one level the courts ensure that inferior bodies remain subject to the limits imposed by Parliament on their powers. It is submitted that this is a proper and robust approach to the problem of ouster clauses.

7

Procedural Ultra Vires: Natural Justice and Fair Hearings

Introduction

This chapter is concerned with procedural ultra vires, which may occur in a number of ways:

1 failure to observe mandatory statutory requirements as to the exercise of a duty or power;
2 failure to observe common law requirements as to natural justice or fairness when exercising power.

There are several important aspects of the modern duty to act fairly, but since the scope of that duty depends on the context in which the power is being exercised it is only possible to suggest those which might be imposed; not all of the following will be applicable to a particular decision-making process:

1 the decision-maker should not be biased;
2 persons adversely affected should have the opportunity to make representations (either orally or in writing);
3 such persons need to know the factors which may be weighted against their interests;
4 there should be a reasonable opportunity for an interested party to correct or contradict opposing evidence;
5 there might be a need for such a party to be represented by a lawyer or other person;
6 there may be a duty on the decision-maker to provide reasons for the decision.

In deciding the scope of the duty to act fairly the courts have developed the doctrine of legitimate expectation, which essentially requires a higher standard of fairness from a public authority which is contemplating depriving a person of an existing benefit or advantage than when the person is merely applying to that authority for a future benefit which he/she has never had. A legitimate expectation may also arise from settled practices of consultation with interested parties or from the announcement of a general policy statement or promise to a particular person. In such cases the public body in question must act fairly before making a new decision. There are suggestions in some of the cases that the public body may not be able to make a new decision if the change would be grossly unfair to an individual citizen, and if these suggestions are correct the doctrine of legitimate expectation takes on a substantive character resembling a kind of estoppel.

Even where the court finds that there has been a breach of the duty to act fairly it should not be assumed that the decision will be quashed for being a total nullity. The courts have shown a pragmatic attitude towards the granting of remedies in this area and it might be misleading to use the labels 'void' or 'voidable' to describe decisions found to be procedurally improper.

To sum up, this is a very detailed and academically fascinating branch of judicial review which is being continually examined and developed in the modern case law. It is essential to maser the relevant cases and to appreciate the critical analysis put forward in many articles in the leading law journals.

Important recent cases include: *R* v *Secretary of State for the Environment, ex parte Kirkstall Valley Campaign Ltd* [1996] 3 All ER 304 ('real danger of bias' test applied to administrative decision-making); *R* v *Secretary of State for the Home Department, ex parte Fayed* [1997] 1 All ER 228 (affected parties entitled to receive sufficient information concerning their case to enable them to make adequate representations); *R* v *Criminal Injuries Compensation Board, ex parte Cook* [1996] 4 All ER 144 (scope of duty to give reasons); *R* v *City of London Corporation, ex parte Matson* [1997] 1 WLR 765 (scope of duty to give reasons); *R* v *Secretary of State for the Home Department, ex parte Hargreaves* [1997] 1 All ER 397 (procedural and substantive fairness); *Pierson* v *Secretary of State for the Home Department* [1997] 3 All ER 577 (HL) (procedural and substantive fairness); *Percy* v *Hall* [1996] 4 All ER 523 (effect of breach of natural justice: void or voidable?)

Important recent articles on the doctrine of legitimate expectation and substantive fairness include ones by Allan [1997] CLJ 246, Bamforth [1997] CLJ 1, Forsyth [1997] PL 375 and Foster (1997) 60 MLR 727.

Procedural impropriety forms the basis for many types of examination questions, ranging from the straightforward problem-type questions requiring identification of various kinds of unfairness to difficult conceptual essay-type questions demanding a critical analysis of, for example, the issue of whether there is, or should, be a general administrative duty to provide reasons for decisions. It is reasonable, therefore, to expect more than one question on procedural impropriety in a typical examination paper. Students need to demonstrate solid research in order to do well in such questions.

Questions

INTERROGRAMS

1   What was the effect of *Ridge* v *Baldwin* [1964] AC 40 on the applicability of natural justice?
2   What is meant by the concept of legitimate expectation?
3   What is meant by substantive fairness?
4   Is there a duty to give reasons for a purely administrative decision?
5   What is the modern test for bias?
6   Is a decision taken in breach of natural justice void ab initio?

QUESTION ONE

Explain, by reference to the cases, the distinction made by the courts between mandatory and directory procedural requirements.

London University LLB Examination
(for external students) Administrative Law June 1985 Q4

QUESTION TWO

The recent (fictitious) Street Traders Act provides that it is unlawful for any person to engage in street trading without first obtaining a licence from the district council.

Consider the following actions by Sand DC:

a   Sand DC has been concerned about the proliferation of street traders in its area (whom it believes to number 150) and resolves to limit the number of licences to 100.

Advise the Street Traders Association on the legality of that decision.

b   Alf has been a street trader for many years. He applies for a licence, and asks to be allowed to make *oral* representations in support of his application. That request is refused, as is his application. His request to be given reasons for the refusal was also refused.

Advise him.

c   Bert has also been trading for many years. Letters of objection to his application were received from Charlie (another street trader), and from the police. Bert's application is rejected. He was not told by Sand DC that letters of objection had been received by it.

Advise him.

London University LLB Examination
(for external students) Administrative Law June 1985 Q2

QUESTION THREE

a   'Natural justice is not to be confused with a vague sense of unfairness' (Stephenson LJ).

How, in the light of this statement, is natural justice related to fairness?

b   Following a sharp fall in oil prices, the government has found itself in a severe financial crisis. It has therefore decided that all civil servants below a certain grade who are over 54 are to be dismissed forthwith without notice, and the salaries of the remainder are to be cut by 10 per cent.

The Minister for the Civil Service has issued the necessary instructions, taking the view that the situation is too serious to permit consultations with the appropriate trade unions.

Consider the legality of the instructions.

London University LLB Examination
(for external students) Administrative Law June 1986 Q7

QUESTION FOUR

Section 1 of the (hypothetical) Press Council Act gives the Council statutory powers to 'establish principles of decency and fairness'. Section 2 imposes a duty on the Council to 'punish any newspaper which fails to meet the established standards of decency and fairness'. Section 3 empowers the Council to 'establish a fair procedure for hearing complaints against the press'. Section 4 states that 'the decisions of the Council shall be final and conclusive and shall not be called into question in any court of law'. A daily newspaper, The Moon, publishes photographs of naked men and women. The Council investigates a complaint. The editor of the Moon asks the Council to allow her legal representative to defend the newspaper. The Council refuses, in accordance with its code of procedure which specifically states 'So as not to intimidate any complainant, no lawyers shall be allowed to appear on behalf of newspapers.' The Moon therefore refuses to co-operate with the Council. In the absence of any representations from The Moon, the Council fines the newspaper £100,000 and requires it to 'desist from publishing such photographs forthwith'.

Advise the editor of The Moon as to whether she can successfully apply for judicial review of the Council.

London University LLB Examination
(for external students) Administrative Law June 1988 Q8

QUESTION FIVE

When is an expectation 'legitimate' for the purposes of natural justice?

London University LLB Examination
(for external students) Administrative Law June 1989 Q4

QUESTION SIX

'What administrative law really needs is for public bodies to be under a legal duty to give reasons for their decisions.' Is this already the law? Should it be the law?

London University LLB Examination
(for external students) Administrative Law June 1990 Q2

QUESTION SEVEN

'The distinction drawn by the courts between void and voidable decisions has much to commend it from the perspective of avoiding gross disruption to the government process. But as yet the case law has not provided us with any clear legal basis for the distinction.'

To what extent would you agree with these propositions?

London University LLB Examination
(for external students) Administrative Law June 1995 Q6

Answers

ANSWERS TO INTERROGRAMS

1   *Ridge* v *Baldwin* [1964] AC 40 is regarded as a landmark in English administrative law because it imposed a general duty to act fairly on all administrative bodies. Previously it had been thought that the narrow legalistic requirements of natural justice (absence of bias and duty to hear both sides of the dispute) were applicable only to judicial or quasi-judicial decisions. By formulating the required duties in broader terms of fairness it became possible to set standards appropriate to the character of each decision-making body and to the kind of decision it has to make.

2   In *Council of Civil Service Unions* v *Minister for the Civil Service* [1985] AC 374 Lord Diplock defined a legitimate expectation as some kind of established right or benefit of which it would be unfair to deprive the holder without first giving the holder a fair hearing. The established right or benefit need not be a proprietary one, such as a licence, since the doctrine of legitimate expectation is sufficiently flexible to embrace anyone who ought in fairness to be consulted before a decision affecting that person's interests, reputation or way of life is taken: see *R* v *Devon County Council, ex parte Baker* [1995] 1 All ER 73.

3   Some judges have suggested that legitimate expectation may have a substantive character so that if, for example, a public authority has announced an intra vires policy statement crucially affecting the interests of individual citizens it may be unfair to revoke that policy unless it is in the clear public interest to do so: see dicta in *R* v *Secretary of State for the Home Department, ex parte Khan* [1984] 1 WLR 1337; *R* v *Secretary of State for the Home Department, ex parte Ruddock* [1987] 2 All ER 518; and, especially, per Sedley J in *R* v *Ministry of Agriculture, Fisheries and Food, ex parte Hamble* [1995] 2 All ER 714.

    However, the concept of substantive fairness is controversial because it appears to undermine, firstly, the rule that a public body cannot fetter its discretion by a policy, contract or other representation and, secondly, the principle that a public body cannot be estopped from breaching a promise, and Sedley J's observations in *ex parte Hamble* were later overruled by the Court of Appeal: *R* v *Secretary of State for the Home Department, ex parte Hargreaves* [1997] 1 All ER 397. In *Pierson* v *Secretary of State for the Home Department* [1997] 3 All ER 577 Lord Steyn preferred to use the rule of law as a basis for enforcing substantive fairness, rather than the doctrine of legitimate expectation.

4   Traditionally there has been no common law duty on administrators to provide reasons for their decisions, but the expansion of the doctrine of procedural legitimate expectation has resulted in a duty to give reasons being imposed in many more specific situations than previously. In deciding whether fairness requires the provision of reasons in a particular case, the review court will take account of the following factors:

   a   the type of functions being performed – the closer to judicial they are the more likely reasons will be required;

   b   the trend towards greater openness in the making of administrative decisions;

   c   whether a duty to give reasons would frustrate the procedures of the decision-making body in question;

   d   whether giving reasons would be helpful in concentrating attention on the right issues;

   e   whether requiring reasons would place an undue burden on decisions-makers, eg to articulate inexpressible value judgments, or to require an appearance of unanimity where this was in fact absent; and

   f   the effect of the decision on an interested party's reputation and interests.

5   In the absence of proof of actual bias, proof of a 'real danger of bias' will suffice: *R* v

Gough [1993] 2 All ER 724. It is assumed that a direct financial interest of any kind in the outcome of the decision will constitute a real danger of bias on the part of the decision-maker having such an interest. For non-financial interests a real danger of bias requires more than a minimal risk, but less than a probability. This means that it is no longer enough to show a 'reasonable suspicion of bias', the test laid down in *R v Sussex Justices, ex parte McCarthy* [1924] 1 KB 256. The modern test is probably closer to the 'real likelihood of bias' test used in *Metropolitan Properties Co v Lannon* [1968] 3 All ER 304.

In regard to administrative decision-making there are authorities which preferred to examine whether the interests fettered the exercise of discretion rather than constituted bias, see, eg *Steeples v Derbyshire County Council* [1984] 3 All ER 468. But in *R v Secretary of State for the Environment, ex parte Kirkstall Valley Campaign Ltd* [1996] 3 All ER 304 Sedley J opined that, after *R v Gough*, the 'real danger of bias' test should apply even to purely administrative decisions.

6   At one time it was thought that a decision taken in breach of natural justice was a complete nullity, eg see per Lord Reid in *Ridge v Baldwin* [1964] AC 40. However, the granting of remedies under RSC O.53 is discretionary and there are authorities which have recognised a form of 'limited interim validity' of procedurally improper decisions as a pragmatic response to the realities of modern decision-making. For example, an invalid bye-law which had been operating for several months, and upon which the public had relied, was not declared void ab initio in *R v Secretary of State for Social Services, ex parte Association of Metropolitan Authorities* [1986] 1 WLR 1. Similarly, the internal disciplinary procedures of an inferior tribunal may have corrected a breach of natural justice that took place at first instance and this would not be possible if the first instance decision was void ab initio since there would be nothing in existence upon which to appeal: *Calvin v Carr* [1979] 2 All ER 440.

SUGGESTED ANSWER TO QUESTION ONE

General Comment

A question that requires good knowledge of specific case law for the provision of examples, but beyond that, a straightforward account of how the courts react to breaches of various statutory procedural requirements is called for. Note the inclusion in the answer of some of the difficulties that arise in the case of delegated legislation.

Key Points

- Introduction
- Explain mandatory/directory dichotomy
- Explain relevance of extent of breach
- Move to specific examples
- Time limits
- Notice in writing
- Consultation
- Appeal

- Raising revenue
- Partial invalidity delegated legislation

Suggested Answer

Procedural requirements are created for administrative bodies by statute, usually their enabling Acts, and common law in the form of the rules of natural justice. The answer to this question is only concerned with procedural requirements arising from statute, for only then is the mandatory/directory dichotomy employed by the courts.

Statutory procedural requirements may create obligations for both administrative bodies, and those individuals dealing with them; typical in the way of such requirements are that action be taken within certain time limits, with prior consultation, or only after notice of appeal or notice of a decision being taken has been provided.

The significance of the mandatory/directory dichotomy is that if a procedural requirement is classified as being mandatory, failure to observe it will render any subsequent action a nullity. Where a procedural requirement is classified as directory the failure to observe it will not invalidate any subsequent action. An initial problem, therefore, is determining whether the courts are going to regard a procedural requirement as mandatory or directory. There is no simple rule that can be applied to give an answer; much depends upon the context in which the decision is being made, and the intention of Parliament in requiring the procedural step to be complied with. In *Howard* v *Boddintgon* (1877) Lord Penzance expressed the problem thus:

> 'You cannot safely go further than that in each case you must look at the subject matter; consider the importance of the provision that has been disregarded and the relation of that provision to the general object intended to be secured by the Act.'

The problem is further complicated by the fact that a statutorily prescribed procedural requirement may be both mandatory or directory; which it will be depends largely on the extent to which it has been breached. For example, in *Cullimore* v *Lyme Regis Corporation* (1962) a local authority was empowered to carry out coastal protection work, and could levy charges on landowners within six months of the work being completed. In fact, charges were not levied until nearly two years after work had been done. The court held that the notice to pay was a nullity. Normally time limits are regarded as directory, and in this case the Court would have been willing to allow a demand for payment if it had only been a few days late, but the breach of the time limit here was so gross that the authority's demand would be held invalid.

With these considerations in mind one should now turn to consider the case law to see if this provides any general guide. For convenience, procedural requirements commonly provided for by statute will be considered in turn.

Time limits

As stated above, time limits are usually regarded as directory, especially where the consequences of invalidating action taken beyond a time limit would be great inconvenience, for example *Simpson* v *Attorney-General* (1955), where a writ for a general election was issued late, but held to be valid, rather than invalidate the subsequent election.

There will be situations when time limits are strictly imposed, typically in the field of planning, where the administration needs to know it is free to take certain action, such as the compulsory purchase of property because the date for receiving objections has passed. For examples see *Smith* v *East Elloe Rural District Council* (1956).

Matters put in writing

The requirement that certain matters such as the grant of a licence, or notice of appeal, be put in written form tends to be regarded as mandatory by the courts. This is because the requirement arises in cases where written proof is important, for example, in *Epping Forest District Council* v *Essex Rendering Ltd* (1983) the requirement that permission to conduct a noxious trade must be obtained in writing was held to be mandatory, because absence of permission could result in criminal liability.

Prior consultation

A statutory requirement that prior consultation should occur before action is taken is generally regarded as mandatory. Thus, in *Grunwick Processing Laboratories Ltd* v *ACAS* (1978), action by ACAS was held to be invalid because they had not complied fully with a statutory requirement to consult the workforce involved in a dispute before acting.

Similarly, in *Agricultural (etc) Training Board* v *Aylesbury Mushrooms Ltd* (1972) a training scheme that involved the payment of a levy by those involved was held to be invalid, as against the Mushroom Growers Association, because they had not been consulted prior to the setting up of the scheme as statute required.

Financial considerations

Where a measure is introduced that results in some financial burden being placed on persons, the courts tend to regard any procedural steps involved as being mandatory. For example, *Sheffield City Council* v *Graingers Wines Ltd* (1978) where a rating resolution was invalidated because it failed to state the date upon which it would become effective.

Giving of notice

Notice that a particular measure is coming into effect is a requirement that can be either mandatory or directory. Where the measure introduced creates criminal liability for non-observance, notice requirements are likely to be mandatory, for example *R* v *Swansea City Council, ex parte Quietlynn* (1983). On the other hand administrative action will not be invalidated where there has been a technical defect, yet substantial compliance with the requirement of giving notice has been achieved.

In *Coney* v *Choice* (1975) a local education authority posted notices concerning comprehensivisation outside all but a handful of its schools. The court held this to constitute adequate compliance.

Informing of rights of appeal

This procedural requirement is generally regarded as mandatory and failure to comply will invalidate subsequent actions. In *London and Clydeside Estates Ltd* v *Aberdeen Historic Council* (1979) the House of Lords held a certificate issued by the local authority in relation to a compulsory purchase matter to be invalid because it failed to inform the plaintiff of his right of appeal to the Secretary of State. Even if a notice does refer to a right of appeal it may nevertheless be held invalid if it fails to explain how the right is to be exercised: see *Agricultural (etc) Training Board* v *Kent* (1970).

Delegated legislation

A brief word should be included on the difficulties in assessing the significance of procedural improprieties during the making of delegated legislation. A tentative conclusion would be that the courts are reluctant to invalidate such measures on the grounds of errors in procedure, thereby implying that such steps are directory, not mandatory requirements. For example *R* v *Secretary of State for the Environment, ex parte Leicester City Council* (1985), where the court refused to invalidate a draft order which had only been laid before the House of Commons and not before 'Parliament' as the enabling Act required.

SUGGESTED ANSWER TO QUESTION TWO

General Comment

Essentially a natural justice question, the first part requiring students to make the connection between the adoption of over-rigid policies and denial of a fair hearing. The second and third parts require good knowledge of *McInnes* v *Onslow-Fane*, and the development of the doctrine of legitimate expectation as a device for ensuring fair hearings.

Key Points

a • Policy
 • No prior consultation
 • Over-rigid application
 • Denial of a fair hearing
b • Does natural justice require an oral hearing?
 • When are reasons required at common law?
c • Knowledge of case to be met
 • Any reasons for suppressing evidence?

Suggested Answer

The question involves consideration of the way in which a local authority, Sand DC, has implemented a statutory licensing scheme. It is assumed that local authorities are given a discretion under the Act as to when and to whom licences should be granted.

a *Decision to limit the number of licences*

 As Sand DC have a discretion as to whether or not licences are to be issued, they are entitled to develop a policy governing this matter. A preliminary consideration is whether or not there has been a breach of natural justice in resolving to adopt a policy restricting the number of licences without first consulting those likely to be affected by the decision – in this case the Street Traders Association. The Act does not appear to lay down any consultation requirements, consequently the matter falls to be determined by common law. The traders may be able to show a breach of natural justice if they can show that in the past the local authority has consulted them before taking such action, ie that they have a 'legitimate expectation' to consultation. This was one of the arguments relied upon by the appellant in *Council of Civil Service Unions v Minister for the Civil Service* (1984) where the House of Lords indicated that the practice of previous governments in consulting the unions before altering conditions of service gave the union a legitimate expectation that they would be consulted in future; thus a failure to consult could amount to a breach of natural justice.

If there is no previous history of consultation with the street traders they could instead challenge the legality of the policy itself.

On the basis of *R v Port of London Authority, ex parte Kynoch Ltd* (1919), bodies with discretionary powers are entitled to adopt policies, but two requirements must be satisfied. The decision making body must be willing to remain flexible, and listen to any applicant who has something new to say, that might persuade them to alter their policy, and the policy itself must be reasonable, in the sense that it must not be a policy that no reasonable authority would have adopted.

The policy of Sand DC may be valid if they have considered the needs and resources of their area properly and decided that it cannot cope with more than 100 street traders. Reasonableness depends to a great extent on context.

The adoption of an over-rigid policy may also be attacked on the ground that it results in a breach of natural justice. By not considering any applications once 100 licences have been granted, Sand DC are effectively denying a hearing to those applicants. This approach to policies was adopted by the Divisional Court in *R v Secretary of State for the Environment, ex parte Brent London Borough Council* (1982). The Minister in not considering repres-entations on his reduction of rate support grant as a matter of policy, had denied the local authorities a fair hearing on a matter that affected them directly.

One would therefore advise the Street Traders' Association to challenge the adoption of the policy by Sand DC by way of judicial review, always assuming that they are an incorporated body with capacity to make such an application.

b   *Advice to Alf*
In advising Alf it should be noted that the refusal of a licence will seriously affect his ability to earn a living, and that failure to obtain a licence could result in him incurring criminal liability should he nevertheless continue to operate as a street trader.

Following the approach of the court in *McInnes v Onslow-Fane* (1978), licensing cases such as this can be categorised as:

i   application cases
ii expectation cases
iii forfeiture cases.

Where a licensing body is dealing with an application from a person who has not held a licence in the past, (an application case) there is not usually any right for the applicant to be heard, because nothing is being taken away. By contrast, in cases where an existing licence is being revoked, the licence holder generally has a right to be heard.

Alf does not possess a licence, nor does he appear to have been granted one in the past, but the fact that he has been a street trader for many years would seem to place him in the middle category of 'expectation' cases; he has a legitimate expectation of being heard. Megarry VC in *McInnes* v *Onslow-Fane* felt that the expectation cases were closer to forfeiture cases than mere application cases.

Even if natural justice does apply, it does not necessarily require an oral hearing. Here, however, the court will be concerned with a 'livelihood' case, and it has been suggested that in such cases fairness requires an oral hearing. Consider *Pett* v *Greyhound Racing Association* (1969).

There appears to be no statutory requirement upon the local authority to give reasons for their decision, so again the matter falls to be considered at common law. Much depends on the circumstances of the case. Where special considerations apply, the courts are willing to hold that a failure to provide reasons does not constitute a breach of natural justice. For example, *Williams* v *Home Office (No 2)* (1981), where it was held that a prisoner was withheld to be told of the reasons for his being transferred to a special 'control unit'. In the absence of special factors, it is submitted that the approach advocated by Lord Denning in his dissenting judgement in *Breen* v *AEU* (1971) should be followed, that where there is a right to be heard, there is also a right to reasons. This appears to be confirmed by the expansion of the doctrine of legitimate expectation in recent years and the trend towards more openness of decision-making, which has resulted in a duty to give reasons being imposed in many more specific situations than previously: see per Lord Mustill in *R* v *Secretary of State for the Home Department, ex parte Doody* (1993).

Alf would be advised to challenge the refusal of a licence by way of judicial review accordingly.

c   *Advice to Bert*
As in the case of Alf (above), Bert comes within the 'expectation' group of cases, and again the fact that the licensing body has monopoly control over the means by which he earns his livelihood suggests that natural justice will apply to the consideration of his licence application.

One aspect of a fair procedure is that the applicant is informed of the case he has to meet, or the case against him, so that he can refute the evidence accordingly. This would not necessarily involve revealing the contents of the letters, or the sources of information to Bert, but would involve the licensing body in giving him an outline of the evidence against him: see *Re Pergamon Press Ltd* (1971). Any prejudicial points of substance should be put before Bert for him to comment on: see *Maxwell* v *Department of Trade and Industry* (1974). Such information can be made available to Bert without disclosing its source, if this needs to be kept secret, see *R* v *Gaming Board for Great Britain, ex parte Benaim and Khaida* (1970).

Bert would be advised, therefore, to challenge the refusal of the licence by way of judicial review.

SUGGESTED ANSWER TO QUESTION THREE

General Comment

Part (a) of this question is very open-ended. Students should be careful not to let answers to such questions degenerate into a succession of generalities. Note that part (b), whilst being primarily concerned with natural justice, does require some knowledge of the law relating to Crown Service.

Key Points

a
- Natural justice contrasted with the duty to act fairly
- Licensing cases and legitimate expectations
- Decisions not subject to natural justice/fairness

b
- Prerogative decisions – whether justiciable
- Failure to consult – whether breach of the duty to act fairly

Suggested Answer

a   A traditional view of natural justice would be the proposition that it consisted of two aspects; the right to be heard, and the right to an unbiased decision. It was felt that by adherence to these two principles decisions of administrators and those acting in quasi-judicial capacities would be fair. This fairness would be achieved by giving an applicant/complainant notice of a decision, details of evidence, an oral hearing, allowing cross-examination, legal representation, and requiring the giving of reasons. All this, in addition to having any decision taken by an adjudicator having no 'interest' in the issue.

More recently it has been recognised that the requirements of natural justice can be met, without the full panoply of procedural safeguards referred to above. *Re HK (An Infant)* (1967) is often cited as the origin of the 'duty to act fairly' concept. In fact this can be traced back to the dictum of Lord Loreburn LC in *Board of Education v Rice* (1911), where it was stated that there was a duty resting upon anyone given the task of deciding anything, to do so fairly.

The concept of natural justice has thus become slightly blurred. Natural justice should be observed in the interest of fairness; but quite what is required by way of observance of the rules of natural justice to ensure fairness in any given case will depend very much on the circumstances in which the decision is being taken. In *Ridge v Baldwin* (1964) Lord Reid suggested that what was required procedurally to ensure fairness would be related to what was at stake in the dispute, ie look at the rights affected. Alternatively in *McInnes v Onslow-Fane* (1978), the Vice Chancellor linked the requirements of natural justice in the licensing context, to the status of applicants. Mere applicants would be disposed of fairly with the minimum application of the rules of natural justice, having only the right to have their applications dealt with in a process that was not arbitrary, not capricious, and was free from bias. In the case of applicants who had held licences in the past, and who now sought to renew them, or applicants who were threatened with revocation of licences they currently held, fairness required a more complex application of the rules of natural justice, possibly involving a hearing, and the giving of reasons for any decision arrived at. Thus it could be argued that fairness is linked to natural justice on a sort of sliding scale. Where more is at stake for an individual, such as possible loss of livelihood, it is only fair that he should be granted more of the procedural safeguards offered by natural justice in putting forward his case. In other words he has a 'legitimate expectation' to a fair hearing before being deprived of such a status.

It is important to emphasise at this point that the rules of natural justice are essentially procedural requirements. Hence, an applicant for a licence may be refused, and feel that the decision of the licensing body has been unfair, but he will not be able to challenge the merits of any such decision in court by way of judicial review. A decision can appear to be unfair, but if the procedure by which it was arrived at complied with the requirements, the decision should stand.

Finally, it should be noted that there are certain categories of decision making which, even though there may have been unfairness, are not made subject to the rules of natural justice. Thus legislative functions appear to be exercisable without consideration of the fairness of any proposed measure; see *Bates* v *Lord Hailsham* (1972). Where action is merely preliminary to some hearing or investigation, natural justice is excluded, see *Lewis* v *Heffer* (1978). In some cases, bias, or its appearance on the part of the decision maker, is inevitable because there is no one else empowered to decide a matter; see observations in *Franklin* v *Minister of Town and Country Planning* (1948).

In conclusion, therefore, it is submitted that the aim of natural justice is to ensure fair decision making, but that an unfair decision is not necessarily one arrived at in breach of the rules of natural justice.

b   The first question that arises for consideration here is the extent to which the power under which such instructions were issued is subject to control by the courts. The Prime Minister, as Minister for the Civil Service, has powers derived from the prerogative to amend the conditions of service of civil servants. The traditional rule of the courts has been to adjudicate upon whether a power exists under the prerogative or not, and on finding that it does to leave the exercise of that power to the discretion of the relevant minister. Adherence to this view would, therefore, render the instructions in question virtually unreviewable in the courts. The decision of the House of Lords in *Council of Civil Service Unions* v *Minister for the Civil Service* (1985) has altered this traditional view. In that case Lord Diplock took the view that the decision of the Prime Minister to prohibit certain civil servants from membership of trade unions, although made under delegated prerogative power, could be questioned by the courts. His Lordship saw no reason why the origin of a power alone should be cited as a ground for refusing judicial review, and if it had not been for national security, which was involved in the Prime Minister's decision, the court might well have set aside the decision for the failure to consult.

The first question can thus be approached on this basis. The instructions would be challengeable by way of judicial view, despite their being issued under prerogative power, provided the issue raised before the reviewing court was a justiciable one, and not a pure question of government policy on which the courts would not be equipped to decide.

The second question that arises, therefore, concerns the extent to which the minister's action complies with the requirements of natural justice. The instructions could be challenged on the ground that they were not preceded by consultation with trade unions. To establish a legitimate expectation of being consulted the trade unions concerned would have to be able to point to a previous practice on the part of the government of always consulting before materially altering conditions of service, or perhaps by arguing that the changes proposed here are so sweeping, and affect such important rights, that consultation is required in the interests of fairness, this latter argument being based upon the importance of what is at stake for the union's members.

Bearing in mind the reasoning in *Council of Civil Service Unions* v *Minister for the Civil Service*, it is submitted that the trade unions should be able to have the instructions invalidated, subject only to the overriding factor that the government is dealing with a crisis situation which may lead the courts to the conclusion that the special circumstances exclude the application of natural justice.

SUGGESTED ANSWER TO QUESTION FOUR

General Comment

Two main issues to concentrate on when dealing with this question, that of the ouster clause and the applicability of the '*Anisminic* principle' to decisions of the Press Council, and whether the denial of legal representation amounted to a denial of natural justice.

Key Points

- Public law challenges
- Validity of ouster clauses – *Anisminic, Re Racal*
- Denial of legal representation – procedural impropriety?
- Disproportionate penalties

Suggested Answer

It would appear that the Press Council is a body amenable to judicial review in that it is a creature of statute, the Press Council Act; see *R* v *Electricity Commissioners, ex parte London Electricity Joint Committee Co (1922) Ltd* (1924), and subsequent case law. As the dispute between 'The Moon' and the Press Council arises from the Council's purported exercise of its statutory powers, it is submitted that the litigation raises issues of public law, as envisaged by Lord Diplock in his speech in *O'Reilly* v *Mackman* (1983).

On the assumption, therefore, that the correct procedure for challenging decisions of the Press Council is to proceed by way of an application for judicial review, the second issue that arises for consideration is whether or not its decisions are protected by the 'ouster clause' contained in s4 of the Act.

The terms of s4 closely resemble those considered by the House of Lords in *Anisminic Ltd* v *Foreign Compensation Commission* (1969). The Foreign Compensation Act 1950 stated that no determination of the Commission was to be called into question in any court of law. The House of Lords held, by a majority, that such a clause would only protect valid or intra vires decisions of the Commission, as opposed to those that were invalid or ultra vires. In effect, the House of Lords held that an ultra vires decision was a nullity in law, and thus not capable of protection by an ouster clause. Despite some subsequent confusion as to the effect of the *Anisminic* decision, as evidenced by *Pearlman* v *Keepers and Governors of Harrow School* (1979), the correct approach is now indicated by Lord Diplock's speech in *Re Racal Communications* (1981). His Lordship indicated that an important factor in determining whether the courts would intervene to circumvent an ouster clause, by declaring a decision to be ultra vires and thus outside the scope of the protection offered by any such clause, was whether the decision-making body under scrutiny was to be regarded as administrative or judicial in nature. The closer the decision-making body was to a court of law, the more expertise it could be expected to have in matters of law, and thus the less likely it was to have made a serious error of law. Administrative bodies, on the other hand, would not usually have expertise in questions of law, and thus the courts would be more prepared to intervene and quash their decisions.

How then is one to classify the Press Council? In terms of its pedigree it appears to be a typical administrative agency in that it has been created by statute to implement government policy. There is no evidence that it is staffed, or chaired by persons with legal qualifications, and as such one would tend to place it in the 'administrative' as opposed to 'judicial' category. Other factors which might persuade a court to review the Council's decisions regardless of the ouster clause are that there does not appear to be any statutory right of appeal against its decisions, or provision for any form of administrative review, and the ouster clause itself does not appear to serve any readily ascertainable purpose. The problems created by the distribution of a finite fund of money, as in *Anisminic Ltd* v *Foreign Compensation Commission* (above), do not appear to arise here.

If one assumes, therefore, that the courts would be prepared to circumvent the terms of s4 to examine the validity of the council's decisions, are there any grounds upon which it can be said to have acted ultra vires?

The Council's statutory powers enable it to establish principles of decency and fairness in relation to newspapers. The editor of 'The Moon' might seek to contend that photographs of naked men and women are not indecent per se, and that the Council does not therefore have jurisdiction to consider complaints relating to such pictures. If the Council has made a mistake as to the extent of its jurisdiction, then any subsequent determination will be ultra vires, and thus outside the scope of the ouster clause.

Perhaps the strongest ground of challenge to the Council's decision is the contention that it has acted in breach of natural justice by denying the newspaper legal representation at the hearing of the complaint against it. It should be noted that Parliament has entrusted the Council with the task of determining its own procedure, thus it is prima facie permitted to adopt a rule prohibiting legal representation. The rationale behind the prohibition in question is one likely to be accepted by the courts. Newspapers will always be able to afford legal representation, whilst complainants will be able to do so only rarely. It is on this basis that representation by lawyers is prohibited by tribunals dealing with complaints brought by patients against doctors under the National Health Service.

Are there circumstances where adherence to a procedural code prohibiting legal representation might amount to unfairness and/or unreasonableness ? It cannot be assumed that natural justice always requires that legal representation should be permitted. As Lyell J stated in *Pett v Greyhound Racing Association (No 2)* (1970):

> 'I find it difficult to say that legal representation before a tribunal is an elementary feature of the fair dispensation of justice. It seems to me that it arises only in a society which has reached some degree of sophistication in its affairs.'

Where, however, a procedural rule is applied inflexibly, the courts might be prepared to intervene. In *Enderby Town Football Club Ltd v Football Association Ltd* (1971), Lord Denning indicated that where a body adopted a procedure prohibiting legal representation, such rules would be upheld by the courts, provided there was evidence that the decision making body was prepared to make exceptions and grant representation in cases where fairness required it. A factor of crucial significance to the success of the challenge brought by the editor of 'The Moon' is that of the significance of the decision and the extent of the punishment. A denial of legal representation has to be considered in the light of what is at stake for those affected by the decision. A fine of £100,000 is clearly a substantial punishment, and on the basis of *R v Secretary of State for the Home Department, ex parte Tarrant* (1985), it could be contended that no reasonable tribunal, properly taking into account the significance of the case, could have concluded that the exclusion of legal representation was a proper exercise of its powers. See further *R v Board of Visitors of the Maze Prison, ex parte Hone* (1988).

In conclusion, the editor of 'The Moon' might also seek to challenge the punishment decided upon by the Council on the ground that it is out of all proportion with the nature of the newspaper's wrongdoing; see *R v Barnsley Metropolitan Borough Council, ex parte Hook* (1976).

SUGGESTED ANSWER TO QUESTION FIVE

General Comment

This is a straightforward question which requires an outline of the development and application of the concept of a legitimate expectation and the use of case law to illustrate the points made.

Key Points

- Historical development
- Effect of decision in *Ridge v Baldwin*
- Development of concept of legitimate expectation
- Renewal of licences

- Public undertakings and assurances
- Development of 'substantive' or 'reasonable' expectation
- Established procedures

Suggested Answer

It is an important principle of judicial review of administrative action that certain decision making powers must be exercised in accordance with the rules of natural justice. These rules, which are of a procedural as opposed to substantive nature, are designed to ensure that a fair procedure has been followed by the decision maker. They were originally developed in the context of bodies which exercised clearly judicial functions and for the 50 years which preceded the decision in *Ridge* v *Baldwin* (1964) the courts took the view that the requirements of natural justice should be confined to judicial as opposed to administrative functions. In *Ridge* v *Baldwin,* however, the House of Lords rejected this approach and held that what was of critical importance was not the nature of the function but rather what was at stake for the individual affected by the decision in question.

Since *Ridge* v *Baldwin* the range of decisions which are reviewable on public interest grounds has been considerably enlarged. The decision did not, however, provide any precise formula for ascertaining the circumstances in which natural justice is applicable and one particular problem which has confronted the courts has been the position of mere applicants and others who do not have any status or rights as such which are at stake, but may nevertheless have good reason to expect that they will at least receive some form of hearing before a decision which is unfavourable to them is reached.

The concept of legitimate expectation, which has developed in response to this problem, appears to have had its birth in the Court of Appeal's decision in *Schmidt* v *Secretary of State for Home Affairs* (1969). In that case Lord Denning expressed the view that an alien had a legitimate expectation of being allowed to make representations if the Home Office proposed to revoke permission which it had previously given for him to remain in the United Kingdom for a specific period. In contrast, however, no such legitimate expectation arose in relation to a request for further permission to remain for an additional further period.

Subsequent case law indicated that a legitimate expectation (usually of being heard) will arise in three specific contexts. First there is the situation where an individual seeks to renew a licence which he has held for some time. In *McInnes* v *Onslow-Fane* (1978) Megarry V-C expressed the view that in these circumstances the individual concerned would normally have a legitimate expectation of being granted a licence. He did not, however, give any indication as to how long it would be necessary to hold a licence before such an expectation would arise.

Secondly, there have been a number of cases where a legitimate expectation has been held to arise because the decision making body has expressed a public view as to how it intends to act in the future or to the policies that it intends to adopt. A clear example of this is provided by the case of *Attorney-General of Hong Kong* v *Ng Yuen Shiu* (1983) which concerned a decision to deport an illegal immigrant. The Hong Kong government had issued a public statement to the effect that, if illegal immigrants came forward voluntarily, they would be interviewed and each case would be dealt with on its individual merits. The Privy Council held that as the public statement made by the government did not conflict with its statutory duty, it gave rise to a legitimate expectation on the part of those acting in response to it that they would be given an opportunity to explain the merits of their cases.

In *R v Secretary of State for the Home Department, ex parte Ruddock* (1987), Mr Justice Taylor took the view that the doctrine of legitimate expectation was not confined to cases where there was a legitimate expectation of a hearing before some right was affected but also extended to situations where fairness required a public body to act in accordance with public undertakings and assurances. He therefore concluded that repeated assurances by a minister that specified criteria for authorising phone taps would be complied with gave rise to a legitimate expectation that the criteria would in fact be complied with.

This has led to the development of 'substantive' or 'reasonable' expectation, establishment of which might prevent the public body from going back on its promise. It is a controversial development as it seems to conflict with the general principles preventing the fettering of discretion and it was not followed by Laws J in *R v Secretary of State for Transport, ex parte Richmond-upon-Thames London Borough Council* (1994).

It may be that some judges will prefer to rely on the concept of the rule of law as justification for reviewing the merits of such decisions: 'the rule of law enforces minimum standards of fairness, both *substantive* and procedural' (emphasis added): per Lord Stein in *Pierson v Secretary of State for the Home Department* (1997).

The third situation is where a body has developed an established procedure by which it acts. An example of this is provided by the case of *Council of Civil Service Unions v Minister for the Civil Service* (1984). This concerned a directive by the Prime Minister which prohibited membership of trade unions at the government's communication headquarters. The House of Lords held that the long established practice of consulting unions in relation to such matters gave rise to a legitimate expectation on the part of the unions concerned that they would be consulted before a decision was made to prohibit union membership. In this particular case, however, the legitimate expectation was overridden by national security considerations.

SUGGESTED ANSWER TO QUESTION SIX

General Comment

A straightforward question requiring an in depth view of one particular facet of fair procedure. It is logical to divide the answer into sections, dealing first with what common law and statute actually requires, and then moving on to deal with the broader issue of the desirability of reasoned decisions. Some account has to be given of those situations where there are good grounds for not giving reasons.

Key Points

•   Examples of statutory duty to give reasons

- Interpretation of this duty by the courts
- Effectiveness of the requirement
- Duty at common law as an aspect of natural justice
- Whether the giving of reasons promotes good administration and fairness
- Situations where the duty is ousted by other considerations

Suggested Answer

A legal duty to give reasons for decisions can arise only from statute or common law. There is no general statutory duty requiring public bodies to give reasons for their decisions, neither is there a common law rule of general application creating any such duty. There are, however, significant instances of both statute and the common law creating such duties, and these will be considered in turn.

Is there a duty to give reasons?

As a result of the Franks Report in the late 1950s it was felt that tribunals ought to be placed under a duty to provide reasons for their decisions. This resulted in the enactment of a statutory duty to give reasons. This statutory duty applies only to those tribunals listed in the Tribunals and Inquiries Act 1992, and only arises if the tribunal is requested to give reasons before or upon notification of its decision. The nature of the duty under identical provisions in earlier Tribunals and Inquiries legislation has been considered by the courts in *Re Poyser and Mill's Arbitration* (1964). Megaw J, considering the case of an arbitrator who had not given reasons for holding that there had been breaches of an agricultural tenancy, stated that where Parliament required the giving of reasons these had to be adequate, intelligible, covering the substantial points raised.

A statutory duty to give reasons also rests upon a minister who is minded to disagree on a point of fact with the recommendations of an inspector, following the holding of a public inquiry: see Town and Country Planning (Inquiry Procedure) Rules 1992. The courts will quash a minister's decision following a public inquiry if the decisions given for disagreeing with the inspector are unclear: see *Givandan & Co* v *Minister of Housing and Local Government* (1966).

The significance of the duty to give reasons lies partly in the remedies that may become available. The reasons, once given, may reveal an error of law. If the error of law is on the face of the record, there may be an application to quash the decision on this basis. Alternatively the reasons might reveal that irrelevant factors have been taken into account, or that relevant factors have not been given sufficient weight. Either matter could give rise to an application for review of the decision in question.

The mere fact that an administrator is under a statutory duty to give reasons for his decisions does not necessarily mean that the individual affected by the decision will always be able to obtain enough information to launch a legal challenge to the decision. Much depends upon the context within which the decision is taken.

The courts have acted, upon occasion, to provide a common law duty to give reasons, where fairness has required this to be done. The problem is, however, that the requirements of natural justice vary enormously depending upon the context in which a decision is made. In *McInnes v Onslow-Fane* (1978), Megarry V-C considered the case of an applicant for a boxing manager's licence who had been refused by the British Board of Boxing Control. His Lordship proposed that in forfeiture cases, where the applicant had something to lose, natural justice required the giving of reasons if a licence or privilege was revoked. At the other extreme were those cases merely involving the bare applicant, who could be refused a licence without any reason being given, provided that the refusal did not of itself cast any slur upon his character. However, the growth of the doctrine of legitimate expectation since *McInnes v Onslow-Fane* means that even a person who is not faced with forfeiture of a specific legal right may still be entitled to a fair hearing, including reasons for the decision, if he or she is seriously affected by it: *R v Devon County Council, ex parte Baker* (1995).

Ought there to be a duty to give reasons?
It has been a common thread running through administrative law since the Report on Ministers' Powers (1932) Cmnd 4060, through the Franks Report (1957) Cmnd 218 to the present day, that a duty to give reasons is a 'good thing'. It is generally assumed that such a duty will encourage a better standard of decision making within the administration if administrators know that their decisions will have to be justified, or at least explained. The high water mark of this principle is the House of Lords' decision in *Padfield v Minister for Agriculture* (1968). Despite the minister's subjectively worded power to order an investigative inquiry if he saw fit, it was held that he could not refuse to hold an inquiry unless he had good reasons for doing so, and that the courts would be the arbiters of whether or not he had good reasons. In theory at least the effect of this should be to make the minister wary of exercising his powers for any improper purpose.

On a more general basis it might be argued that the giving of reasons ought to be required simply to make the administrative process fairer, or at least to ensure that those affected by it understand why decisions are taken. Whether reasons should be provided is not, however, a matter that can be considered in the abstract. There may be situations where some greater advantage is gained by withholding information.

Where decisions have to be made speedily, it may be counter-productive to saddle the administration with a duty to explain every decision. Where the giving of reasons would involve compromising the source of confidential information, the courts will lean in favour of maintaining confidentiality: see *R v Gaming Board for Great Britain, ex parte Benaim and Khadia* (1970). Similarly where national security issues are involved: see *R v Secretary of State for the Home Department, ex parte Hosenball* (1977)

A pure exercise of academic judgment may be unchallengeable because the court lacks the expertise to evaluate the quality of reasoning, so that in this kind of case no duty to provide reasons will be imposed as it would be pointless to do: *R v Education Funding Council, ex parte Institute of Dental Surgery* (1994).

In conclusion, therefore, it is submitted that whilst a duty to give reasons is clearly desirable, it cannot be viewed as a universal requirement of the decision-making process.

SUGGESTED ANSWER TO QUESTION SEVEN

General Comment

This is a difficult question requiring a thorough understanding of both the theory and the practice of administrative law. In theory ultra vires decisions must be void. In practice, they will operate as if they were valid unless quashed by the court. They appear to be voidable, therefore. Where do the terms 'void' and 'voidable' come from? Do they really belong in administrative law? Explain the practical operation of the presumption of validity.

Key Points

- Origin of 'void' and 'voidable' – their misuse in administrative law
- Definition
- Historical significance
- Confusion arising from presumption of validity
- Previous judicial reasoning
- Practical and discretionary nature of judicial review
- Concluding remarks

Suggested Answer

To use the terms 'void' and 'voidable' in the context of administrative law is a most unhappy use of terminology. It is hardly surprising that the case law has been unable to distinguish between the two with any clarity, for using these terms in the setting of administrative law inevitably becomes paradoxical: the terms 'void' and 'voidable' serve to confuse rather than to explain the operation of the law.

'Void' and 'voidable' are terms drawn from the law of contract, where they are used to distinguish between contracts that are entirely without legal foundation and are invalid from the outset, and contracts which are valid and which must be performed, but which are liable to be set aside by the courts on the application of one of the parties to the contract. The terms have sometimes been applied to administrative law in an attempt to explain the apparent validity that government decisions have before they are set aside by the court upon an application for judicial review. Thus, it is said that these decisions are 'voidable'; that is to say, they must be treated as valid unless and until set aside.

The use of this terminology does have some historical basis within administrative law. Prior to *Anisminic Ltd* v *Foreign Compensation Commission* (1969) a distinction was drawn between errors of law that deprived a tribunal of jurisdiction, and other errors of law within the tribunal's jurisdiction. A tribunal could make errors of law within its jurisdiction, and its decision would not be liable to be quashed unless such errors appeared on the face of the record. Technically, these decisions were intra vires; they were within the jurisdiction of the body concerned. These decisions had legal validity, but were liable to be quashed when the record was produced to the court. These decisions were properly termed 'voidable'. By way of contrast, ultra vires decisions have no legal foundation and are invalid from their outset. Where administrative action is ultra vires, there are no degrees of nullity. An ultra vires decision is void, it cannot be anything else (*Anisminic*). Historically it was, therefore, possible to draw a genuine legal distinction between void and voidable decisions.

This historical distinction between void and voidable decisions has little significance today. It is now accepted as a result of the decisions in *Anisminic* and a body of authority culminating in *O'Reilly* v *Mackman* (1983) that all errors of law go to jurisdiction and render a decision ultra vires, although there has been some modification of that principle so that only relevant or material errors of law will have this effect: *R* v *Lord President of the Council, ex parte Page* (1993). The logical result of this is that the jurisdiction to quash a decision for error on the face of the record is purely vestigial: *R* v *Greater Manchester Coroner, ex parte Tal* (1985). It follows from this that there is no longer any basis to distinguish between void and voidable decisions. Any decision founded upon an error of law will be ultra vires and therefore void; it will be without legal validity from the outset.

Despite the apparently inexorable nature of this logic, confusion still exists within the case law. One main reason for this confusion is that, whatever the legal position of such decisions, as a matter of fact they are presumed to be valid until they are set aside. Although a decision may be ultra vires and therefore lacking in legal validity, it will only be quashed upon a judicial review of the decision by the court. Unless or until it is quashed, it must be presumed to be valid and therefore must be acted upon. It is this 'presumption of validity' which operates to prevent gross disruption to the government process and which has sometimes led to the term 'voidable' being used in respect of ultra vires decisions.

It is perhaps the presumption of validity that has tempted some judges to conclude that ultra vires decisions might indeed be voidable rather than void. For instance, at one time Lord Denning MR certainly favoured the view that a breach of natural justice might only make a decision voidable: *R* v *Secretary of State for the Environment, ex parte Ostler* (1977). Since the court could only quash for ultra vires, such reasoning was very dubious. Current authority favours the view that 'void' is the correct term to apply to ultra vires decisions.

It is questionable whether it is necessary to use even this term to describe the nature of ultra vires decisions. One of the difficulties with the term is that it is in conflict with the practical outcome of administrative decision-making. There may be a number of practical reasons why an ultra vires decision may never be quashed. An application for judicial review may never be brought. Even if an application is made, it may be outside some statutory time limit, in which case the court may not be able to set aside the decision despite its ultra vires: *ex parte Ostler* above. In practical terms, therefore, because of the presumption of validity such decisions will continue to operate and to be binding despite their ultra vires. In this context the use of the term 'void' can only be described as misleading.

Furthermore, it must not be forgotten that the remedies available by way of judicial review are discretionary. The court may, in the exercise of its discretion, decline to quash an ultra vires decision: see *Percy* v *Hall* (1996).

Thus it is that the use of the terms 'void' and 'voidable' leads to an apparent paradox.

Every ultra vires act seems to be both void, in the sense that it is entirely without legal validity from the outset, and voidable in the sense that it will be valid unless and until the court, in the exercise of its discretion, determines to set it aside. As a matter of law ultra vires decisions are void, but as a matter of fact they appear to be voidable. This paradox arises entirely from the grafting of inapposite terminology from the context of contract law to that of administrative law. Rather than using this terminology, we should recognise that ultra vires decisions are never valid, they merely benefit from a presumption of validity. This presumption is entirely practical, and enables the day-to-day working of the government process to escape from the dogma of the law. There is a clear need for this presumption; it is unfortunate that its existence has led to confusion in the use of inappropriate terminology.

Any attempt the courts have made to distinguish between void and voidable decisions is far from commendable. It has served simply to confuse the practical reality of the government process, which is that decisions must be allowed to proceed unless and until the courts set them aside. Government bodies cannot wait in limbo after every decision to see whether a challenge will emerge, and thus their decisions must be presumed to be valid. If the case law has failed to produce an adequate explanation of the terms 'void' and 'voidable' in the setting of administrative law, that is hardly surprising as such terminology does not belong in that setting. Greater clarity will be achieved by an abandonment of these terms altogether and a concentration on the pragmatic realities of administrative law.

8

Reasonableness and Proportionality

Introduction

This chapter is concerned with the extent to which the process of judicial review permits judges to examine the merits of administrative decisions. According to traditional theory, judicial review should be concerned only with the legality of such decisions, since the issue of whether a decision is 'right' or 'wrong' is a matter for an appeal. Further, an examination of merits would involve the review court in an assessment of the political wisdom of many executive decisions and this would be regarded as unconstitutional since Parliament has entrusted the administrator, not the court, with the delegated discretionary power.

However, despite the risk of undermining such traditional principles as parliamentary sovereignty, the separation of powers and the impartiality of the judiciary, common law has developed a particular ground of review, 'total unreasonableness' (sometimes called 'irrationality'), which would seem to require the reviewing court to assess the substantive merits of administrative decisions. Further, the common law may be in the process of developing a doctrine of proportionality which, as a ground for review, would enable the court to set standards against which to measure the appropriateness of the administrative decision under challenge.

Both 'total unreasonableness' and 'proportionality' have been criticised (by judges and academics) for undermining the traditional basis of English administrative law, which has always required judges to exercise second, rather than primary, judgments as to the legality of administrative action. Hence, although there is much practical case law to illustrate the application of these contentious grounds for review, the emphasis for examination purposes tends to be on the constitutional arguments raging around them.

Recent important cases in this area include: *R* v *Ministry of Defence, ex parte Smith and Others* [1996] 1 All ER 257; *R* v *Secretary of State for the Home Department, ex parte McQuillan* [1995] 4 All ER 400; *Pierson* v *Secretary of State for the Home Department* [1997] 3 All ER 577.

Useful articles include ones by Himsworth [1996] PL 46, Lord Irvine [1996] PL 59, Norris [1996] PL 590 and Walker [1995] PL 556.

In regard to examinations, problem-type questions involving various grounds for review, including total unreasonableness and proportionality, are common. In addition, it is not unusual for there to be an essay-type question demanding an exploration of the degree to which judges are prepared to protect fundamental human rights by use of such doctrines as irrationality and proportionality.

Questions

INTERROGRAMS

1   What is meant by '*Wednesbury* unreasonableness'?
2   What is meant by 'irrationality' and how does it differ from *Wednesbury* unreasonableness?
3   What did Lord Bridge mean when he said that judges should give decisions affecting fundamental human rights 'the most anxious scrutiny'? (*Bugdacay* v *Secretary of State for the Home Department* [1987] 1 All ER 940 at 952).
4   Is proportionality merely an aspect of *Wednesbury* unreasonableness?
5   What are the constitutonal objections to the introduction of proportionality as a separate ground for review in English administrative law?

QUESTION ONE

The new Secretary of State for the Environment sends you, his senior legal adviser, the following note:

> 'By s23 of the Housing Act 1980, I am empowered to take over the sale of council houses "where it appears to [me] that tenants … have or may have difficulty in exercising the right to buy effectively and expeditiously". Does this mean that I can do what I like or will the judges expect me to be "reasonable"?'

> Advise the Minister, explaining to him any relevant principles of judicial review.

London University LLB Examination
(for external students) Administrative Law June 1987 Q9

QUESTION TWO

'The *Wednesbury* case was wrongly decided and now *Wednesbury* unreasonableness means whatever the judges want it to mean. It is time to forget *Wednesbury* and to establish a more rational basis for the principle of irrationality.'
    Critically assess this statement in the light of relevant cases.

London University LLB Examination
(for external students) Administrative Law June 1988 Q5

QUESTION THREE

A new government establishes by statute a 'local community contribution', commonly called a 'roof tax'. Property-owners are charged according to the size of their dwelling, as measured by instruments able to determine the exact square footage of a roof from pictures taken by a helicopter or airplane. One local authority, Avantgardia (A), allows all property-owners to see these pictures if they wish to challenge an assessment. The neighbouring authority, Backstothewallia (B), refuses to let those property-owners who live adjacent to an army barracks see the pictures, claiming that 'national security' is at stake. It is well known that the previous Secretary of State for Defence took the view that such pictures of military establishments should not be shown to property-owners and resigned from the government when, as she put it, 'colleagues put electoral popularity above national security'.

Her successor, however, has stated that 'there is no threat to national security'. It is impossible to separate the pictures from the barracks because the measuring method relies on comparison with a public building (in this case the barracks) the size of which is known.

The statute which created the new tax provides that the Secretary of State for the Environment (S) may withdraw central government subsidy from 'any authority where the Secretary of State is satisfied that the authority has acted unreasonably in determining its local community contribution'. S announces that she will reduce by 50 per cent central government subsidy to B 'because it acted unreasonably in denying property-owners an effective challenge and because it has purported to usurp the functions of central government by invoking a defence of national security'. B responds by saying that the issue of access to the photographs is nothing to do with 'determining' the local community contribution, that even if it were the dramatic reduction in grant was inappropriate and out of proportion, and so the Minister has abused and exceeded her powers.

At the same time B applies for judicial review of the decision by S, a property-owner in A called Challengia (C) applies for judicial review of B's refusal to give access to the photographs. C claims 'no special interest beyond that of any member of the public in ensuring good administration and justice for all'.

Advise B as to its likelihood of success in the two cases.

London University LLB Examination
(for external students) Administrative Law June 1990 Q8

QUESTION FOUR

A (hypothetical) Broadcasting Bans Act 1989 states that: 'Where the Minister is of the opinion that the broadcasting of a particular matter or any matter of a particular class would be likely to promote, or incite to, crime or would tend to undermine the authority of the state, he may by order direct any person or company to refrain from broadcasting the matter, or any matter of the particular class, and any such person shall comply with the order.' The Home Secretary issues an order under this Act as follows: 'I hereby require that all television companies to refrain at all times from sending any broadcast matter which consists of or includes any words spoken, whether in the course of an interview or discussion or otherwise, by a person who appears or is heard on the programme in which the matter is broadcast where (a) the person speaking the words represents or purports to represent a terrorist organisation; or (b) the words solicit or invite support for such an organisation.'

The National Union of Journalists seeks your advice as to whether it would be successful in an application for a judicial review to challenge this order in advance of any particular occasion on which a television company wished to broadcast some such matter.

Advise the Union.

London University LLB Examination
(for external students) Administrative Law June 1989 Q8

Answers

ANSWERS TO INTERROGRAMS

1   In *Associated Provincial Picture Houses Ltd* v *Wednesbury Corporation* [1948] 1 KB 223 Lord Greene MR listed a number of examples of ultra vires decision-making which are usually grouped together under the heading of 'Wednesbury unreasonableness'. They include failure to take account of relevant considerations; taking account of irrelevant ones; making a decision on the basis of no evidence or insufficient evidence; acting in bad faith; acting in breach of natural justice; exceeding jurisdiction; and, finally, making a decision which was 'so absurd that no sensible person could ever dream that it lay within the powers of the authority' (what became known as the 'total unreasonableness' principle).

2   In *Council of Civil Service Unions* v *Minister for the Civil Service* (1985) Lord Diplock suggested that 'irrationality' was a better label than 'total unreasonableness' because it was less likely to be misunderstood by judges when exercising judicial review. Lord Diplock described as irrational 'a decision so outrageous in its defiance of logic or of accepted moral standards that no sensible person who had applied his mind to the question to be decided could have arrived at it'. Although Lord Diplock appeared to intend only a re-classification, the new test of irrationality was regarded by some judges and commentors as setting a higher threshold for review because an applicant would have to show that a decision-maker had 'taken leave for his senses' when making the decision in question: see per Lord Scarman in *Nottinghamshire County Council* v *Secretary of State for the Environment* [1986] AC 240. This approach became known as the 'super-*Wednesbury*' test and was criticised for giving too much protection to high level administrative decision-making at the risk of infringing fundamental human rights.

3   In *Bugdaycay* v *Secretary of State for the Home Department* [1987] AC 514 Lord Bridge use the concept of '*Wednesbury* unreasonableness' as justification for taking a 'hard look' at the quality of a decision which affected fundamental human rights (in that case the rights to life and liberty). This approach seems to suggest that the *Wednesbury* test is sufficiently flexible to permit different intensities of judicial review depending on the character of the decision and the effect of that decision on the interests of affected parties. In *R* v *Ministry of Defence, ex parte Smith and Others* [1996] 1 All ER 257 Sir Thomas Bingham MR (as he then was), whilst rejecting as artificial the raising or lowering of the threshold for review, endorsed the view that, under the *Wednesbury* test, the more substantial the interference with human rights, the more the court will require by way of justification before it is satisfied that the decision is reasonable in the *Wednesbury* sense.

4   It is well settled that a disproportionate penalty or punishment imposed by a disciplinary body may be set aside for being *Wednesbury* unreasonable: *R* v *Barnsley Metropolitan Borough Council, ex parte Hook* [1976] 3 All ER 452. However, apart from cases involving disproportionate penalties, the courts have been reluctant to apply the principle of proportionality to the exercise of administrative judgments because to do so would not leave the administrator with the kind of latitude of

discretion left to him by the traditional *Wednesbury* doctrine. For that reason Lord Diplock in *Council of Civil Service Unions* v *Minister for the Civil Service* [1985] AC 374 treated proportionality as a ground for review which is separate in character and effect from the total unreasonableness ground. It may be that the proportionality principle is infiltrating English administrative law as a result of membership of the European Union and the obligations flowing from that membership: see per Sedley J in *R* v *Secretary of State for the Home Department, ex parte McQuillan* [1995] 4 All ER 400.

5   In *R* v *Secretary of State for the Home Department, ex parte Brind* [1991] 1 All ER 720 Lords Ackner and Lowry stated the traditional constitutional objections to the use of the proportionality doctrine by English judges. In their view it would embroil the judiciary too closely in an examination of the 'correctness' rather than simply the 'legality' of executive decisions, thereby turning the process of judicial review into appeal. This would 'politicise' the judiciary by giving the judges, rather than the politicians, the final say on the appropriateness of particular policies. This would undermine parliamentary sovereignty by effectively incorporating the European Convention on Human Rights 'by the back door' when Parliament had so far refused to incorporate it by an Act of Parliament. (The principle of proportionality is well established in the judgments of the European Court of Human Rights.)

It should be noted that the above constitutional objections will be removed or at least diminished if, as expected, Parliament incorporates the European Convention on Human Rights into English law during 1998, because Parliament will be authorising new and stronger powers for the judges in the task of protecting human rights from oppressive exercises of administrative authority.

SUGGESTED ANSWER TO QUESTION ONE

General Comment

A question inviting consideration of the various implied limits imposed by the courts on the exercise of discretion, which is relatively straightforward in itself, but which does require reference to relevant case law.

Key Points

* History of judges' attitudes to subjectively worded discretionary powers
* The need for evidence to support the decision – *Tameside* case
* The need for good faith and rationality – *Norwich* case and *Council of Civil Service Unions* v *Minister for the Civil Service*

Suggested Answer

Provisions such as s23 of the Housing Act 1980 are notable, not simply because it endows the Secretary of State with discretion to intervene in a local authority's affairs, but because it is a subjectively worded power. The minister can act 'where it appears to him ... [that it is necessary to do so]'. Prima facie it is very difficult to find any legal limitations upon the exercise of such a power, Parliament having entrusted the matter to the Minister. In *Liversidge* v *Anderson* (1942), the Home Secretary was empowered to order the detention of persons where he had reasonable cause to believe that a person was of hostile origin or associations. A majority of the House of Lords held that the courts could not inquire into whether the minister had the necessary grounds for his belief. The decision does suggest that the minister has a free hand in such situations, but it should be borne in mind that the House of Lords was there concerned with emergency legislation during wartime. Since 1942 the principles of judicial review have been developed considerably, to the point where the courts are now far more ready to intervene and invalidate ministerial decisions, notwithstanding the subjective nature of the power in question. Much will depend on the context within which the decision is made but, as Lord Scarman commented in *IRC* v *Rossminster Ltd* (1980), 'The ghost of *Liversidge* v *Anderson* … casts no shadow … I think it need no longer haunt the law. It was laid to rest by Lord Radcliffe in *Nakkuda Ali* v *Jayaratne* (1951) … it is now beyond recall.'

It appears to be well settled that the court can enquire into whether there is evidence upon which a reasonable minister would have formed his view. If such evidence is not present, the court will declare the minister's actions to be unlawful.

See, for example, *Secretary of State for Education and Science* v *Tameside Metropolitan Borough Council* (1977). Under s68 of the Education Act 1944, the Secretary of State was empowered to issue directions to a local education authority where it appeared to him that it was proposing to act unreasonably. Again the question arose as to the extent to which the minister's discretion in the matter was unfettered. The House of Lords held that the courts were entitled to examine the evidence before the minister to determine whether or not he was entitled to come to his conclusion that an education authority was proposing to act unreasonably. As Lord Wilberforce explained:

'If a judgment requires, before it can be made, the existence of facts, then although the evaluation of those facts is for the Secretary of State alone, the court must inquire whether those facts exist …'

Section 23 of the Housing Act 1980 was itself the subject of scrutiny by the Court of Appeal in *Norwich City Council* v *Secretary of State for the Environment* (1982). Kerr LJ suggested that s23 went beyond even s68 of the Education Act 1944 in the extent to which it entrusted the exercise of discretion to the minister, and he described it as being 'without precedent in legislation of this nature'. His Lordship also pointed out that unlike s68, the minister could exercise his power under s23 regardless of whether the local housing authority was acting unreasonably or not. He continued, 'I cannot see any basis for reading any words to this effect into the section without rewriting it, which would not be permissible.' Provided, therefore, that the minister had not acted in bad faith or extraneous considerations, or misdirected himself in law or fact, he was entitled to his view that the exercise of his powers was necessary under s23. Although it is true to say that the exercise of such powers is likely to be the subject of close scrutiny by the courts, it is clear that much depends on the objectively verifiable evidence which supports the minister's decision. The compulsory sale of council housing is obviously a contentious political matter, but as Lord Denning pointed out in the *Norwich* case, 'The issues are to be decided according to law and none else'.

In conclusion therefore the minister would be advised that he cannot exercise his power under s23 in bad faith, nor without evidence indicating that such action is needed. Further, his decision in any particular case must not be so totally unreasonable as to be 'irrational': per Lord Diplock in *Council of Civil Service Unions* v *Minister for the Civil Service* (1985).

SUGGESTED ANSWER TO QUESTION TWO

General Comment

This question requires very careful analysis of what was actually decided in the *Wednesbury* case, in addition to a consideration of subsequent developments in this sphere, ie the emergence of irrationality as a ground for review, and the extent to which it differs from *Wednesbury* unreasonableness.

Key Points

- Facts of and decision in the *Wednesbury* case
- Criticisms of the *Wednesbury* case
- Criticisms of the concept of *Wednesbury* unreasonableness
- The modern concept of 'irrationality' – an improvement on the *Wednesbury* test?

Suggested Answer

What did Wednesbury decide?

In *Associated Provincial Picture Houses Ltd* v *Wednesbury Corporation* (1948) acting under a statutory provision that enabled it to grant cinemas permission to open on Sundays, subject to any conditions it thought fit to impose, Wednesbury Corporation granted Associated Provincial Picture Houses Ltd permission to show films on a Sunday provided no children below the age of 15 were admitted. The company sought to challenge the imposition of the condition on the basis that it was unreasonable, but in the Court of Appeal, Lord Greene MR, with whom the other members of the court agreed, held that the condition was lawful, and in the course of his judgment enunciated principles relating to challenge to the actions of public bodies on the ground of unreasonableness which formed the basis of the law in this area in the post-war era.

Lord Greene indicated that an exercise of discretion by a public body might be unlawful because it had misdirected itself as to law, considered irrelevant matters, or failed to take into account relevant matters, and added:

'If [a public body] does not obey these rules, [it] may truly be said, and often is said, to be acting "unreasonably" ...'

His Lordship also suggested that a decision maker might act unreasonably even though he had taken all relevant factors into account, had disregarded all irrelevant factors, and had directed himself correctly as to the relevant law, if his final decision was nevertheless one that no reasonable decision maker in that situation would have arrived at.

Thus it can be seen that the term unreasonableness is both a generic one, covering various forms of unlawfulness, and a substantive ground of challenge in its own right.

Is Wednesbury *wrongly decided?*

To suggest that the case is wrongly decided is obviously a statement of opinion as opposed to law, as it has never been seriously contended that the decision was arrived at per incuriam. It might be contended that the case was wrongly decided on its facts, in that the condition imposed was unreasonable, but this again can only be resolved by reference to some objective standard of reasonableness, which is precisely what Lord Greene MR was attempting to provide in the course of his judgment.

A stronger argument would perhaps be that the Court of Appeal failed to have sufficient regard to the intention of Parliament in enacting the Sunday Entertainments Act 1932, pursuant to which Wednesbury Corporation had imposed its conditions. As mentioned above, the Act endowed the local authority with a subjectively worded power to impose conditions, '… as it thought fit …', yet the effect of the court's decision was to imply many limitations upon this apparently unlimited power, by holding that it had to be exercised reasonably, and that due regard had to be paid to all relevant considerations. The problem with this contention, however, is that Parliament rarely, if ever, expressly states that a power being delegated to an administrative agency must be exercised 'reasonably'; it is assumed by Parliament that this will be the case. Such matters, it is submitted, are rather like the implied terms of a contract, so obvious that the parties involved did not bother to mention them.

Perhaps the real jurisprudential objection to *Wednesbury* is that it represents a move away from review of administrative action on the basis of whether it is legal or not, towards a consideration of whether a decision is, or is not, a 'good' one, thus confusing legality with merits. Consideration of a decision's legality is an exercise involving a far more objective approach on the part of a judge that consideration of its merits.

Thus, to permit review on the grounds of unreasonableness is to open a 'Pandora's Box' of judicial opinion on matters of fact as opposed to law.

Does unreasonableness now mean whatever judges want it to mean?

Administrative agencies cannot be left to operate as laws unto themselves, to do so would be contrary to the rule of law. Hence even where Parliament empowers a public body to decide a matter '… as it thinks fit …', the courts have to be in a position to intervene and invalidate decisions which go beyond the bounds of what Parliament might have intended. In exercising this function judges are frequently cited as the citizen's most important protection against the ever-growing powers of the State, but the difficulty lies in the fact that law, as reflected in the *Wednesbury* decision, simply provides for members of the judiciary to substitute their own notions of what is permissible in place of the public body's. Reasonableness is not a fixed concept. Two judges can arrive at differing views on a particular matter without either of them forfeiting their right to be described as reasonable. To a limited extent at least judges can mould the concept of reasonableness to their own designs – but is this a bad thing? Why should the judges not be trusted with this task?

The answers to these questions are more a matter of politics than law. Many would argue that, given their background, judges faced with a choice between competing political philosophies will generally favour a right-wing, or 'establishment', argument. Advocates of this view would cite the great number of cases from *Roberts* v *Hopwood* (1925), to *Secretary of State for Education and Science* v *Tameside Metropolitan Borough Council* (1977) as evidence of the judiciary's predilection for siding with conservative interests wherever they are given the latitude to do so.

Increasingly, however, there has been a tendency on the part of the courts not to become embroiled in disputes which hinge upon clashes of ideology. In *Pickwell* v *Camden London Borough Council* (1983) the Court of Appeal indicated that one of the reasons that it would not intervene to invalidate a decision by the local authority in question to pay its refuse workers above national average rates of pay, was the fact that if local ratepayers did not approve of this expenditure (which they would themselves be funding at least in part), then the remedy lay in them expressing their feelings through the ballot box at the next local government elections. Thus, even though members of the judiciary might have considerable scope to intervene on the grounds of unreasonableness, they may decline to do so.

Has *Wednesbury* unreasonableness been replaced by irrationality?

In recent years there has been a tendency to use the expression 'irrationality' to describe what has conventionally been regarded as Wednesbury unreasonableness. This development can perhaps be attributed to the speech of Lord Diplock in *Council of Civil Service Unions* v *Minister for the Civil Service* (1985) wherein he stated:

> 'By "irrationality" I mean what can by now be succinctly referred to as "*Wednesbury* unreasonableness"... It applies to a decision which is so outrageous in its defiance of logic or of accepted moral standards that no sensible person who had applied his mind to the question to be decided could have arrived at it. Whether a decision falls within this category is a question that judges by their training and experience should be well equipped to answer, or else there would be something badly wrong with our judicial system ... "Irrationality" by now can stand on its own feet as an accepted ground on which a decision may be attacked by judicial review.'

It is thus submitted that irrationality is perhaps a narrower concept than *Wednesbury* unreasonableness and on that basis is to be preferred by those who would seek to diminish the role of the judiciary in imposing implied limits upon the powers of administrative agencies.

A more rational basis?

There are various ways in which the powers of the judiciary to review administrative action might be curtailed. Review might be limited to situations where a public body purported to act upon no evidence, the existence of such evidence being an objectively ascertainable matter. Legislation could be drafted more tightly so as to limit with greater precision the scope of administrative powers. Neither approach is ideal however as both involve a price that has to be paid in terms of lost flexibility and possible irresponsibility by administrative agencies.

A more rational basis, it is submitted, is to continue to permit judges to invalidate an exercise of discretion on the grounds of unreasonableness, but with the placing of much greater emphasis on the evidential requirements of any such challenge, to the point where evidence of something approaching absurdity has to be established before the courts will intervene. This has the virtue of continuing to allow judges to quash decisions on the grounds of procedural irregularity (including breach of natural justice), but does limit their discretion to deal with extreme cases of unreasonableness.

SUGGESTED ANSWER TO QUESTION THREE

General Comment

A demanding question. Approach the two issues separately. A detailed analysis of irrationality is required as regards the minister's actions. It may not be possible to come to any firm conclusion as to the likely success of challenge. A good knowledge of cases on proportionality is necessary. For the latter part of the answer locus standi is the main issue rather than the grounds of challenge.

Key Points

- Which procedure.
- Grounds of challenge.
- Irrationality.
- Lack of proportionality.
- Appropriate remedy.
- Locus standi.

Suggested Answer

B seeks judicial review of the minister's decision to reduce by 50 per cent central government subsidy. The exercise of discretion by a minister of the Crown is prima facie a matter challengeable by way of an application for judicial review under O.53, and B clearly possesses the necessary locus standi to launch such a challenge. The difficulty for B lies in establishing that the minister has acted ultra vires. Under the relevant legislation the minister may withdraw the central government subsidy where she is satisfied that an authority has acted unreasonably in determining its local community contribution.

B faces a heavy evidential burden in trying to establish that the minister has abused her power by acting irrationally. The use of the test of irrationality can be attributed to the speech of Lord Diplock in *Council of Civil Service Unions* v *Minister for the Civil Service* (1985) wherein he stated:

> 'By "'irrationality'" I mean what can by now be succinctly referred to as *"Wednesbury* unreasonableness" ... It applies to a decision which is so outrageous in its defiance of logic or of accepted moral standards that no sensible person who had applied his mind to the question to be decided could have arrived at it.'

It has been suggested in some quarters that an applicant for review must essentially establish that the decision maker whose decision is challenged has effectively lost control of his mental faculties! In the present case much will depend upon the minister's reasons for her decision. It is significant that the statutory power to penalise certain local authorities by withdrawing subsidy itself involves the minister making an assessment of what is and what is not reasonable.

The situation is analogous to that which arose in *Secretary of State for Education and Science* v *Tameside Metropolitan Council* (1977). There the minister was empowered to direct the local education authority to implement a particular plan if s/he was satisfied that they were proposing to act unreasonably in respect of the discharge of any statutory duties. The House of Lords ultimately held that the minister had misinterpreted the concept of reasonableness, and had erred in concluding that Tameside was proposing to act unreasonably. A crucial factor in the reasoning leading to this conclusion was their Lordships' view that there was little or no evidence to support the minister's conclusion. B would be advised to point out that the previous Secretary of State for Defence took the view that such pictures of military establishments should not be shown to property owners and resigned from the government on a point of principle, and the impossibility of maintaining security because of the measuring method relied upon. It should also be noted that it would be a criminal offence to photograph military installations without lawful authority. A further relevant factor in *Tameside* was that the courts were dealing with the actions of an elected body, and it was felt that the course of action adopted by the local authority must to some extent reflect the views of the local electorate. As such the courts should be slow to intervene. Against this it has to be accepted that the minister has been endowed with considerable discretion by Parliament, and that the basis for her decision is her perception of the national security issue. Where issues of national security are raised by ministers the courts tend to allow them a wide margin of discretion, on the basis that the minister is in a better position to judge than the courts: *Council of Civil Service Unions* v *Minister for the Civil Service*, above.

An alternative argument that might be raised by B is to contend that the minister's action is out of proportion with what is required. Lack of proportionality as a ground for review has had a chequered history in the English courts. The matter was reviewed in *R* v *Secretary of State for the Home Department, ex parte Brind* (1991), wherein it was raised as one of the grounds of challenge to the Home Secretary's restrictions on the broadcasting of interviews with IRA supporters. Lords Acker and Lowry warned that there was a danger that, in considering proportionality as a separate ground of review, the courts might fall into the error of exercising an appellate jurisdiction over the actions of administrative agencies, rather than their proper supervisory jurisdiction. However, the other three Law Lords seemed content to leave the door open to the possible future introduction of proportionality as an independent ground of review. At present, therefore, it remains uncertain as to whether B would succeed with an application for review based upon lack of proportionality.

If B were to succeed with its challenge to the minister's action, the appropriate remedy would be a declaration that the removal of the subsidy would be unlawful.

C applies for judicial review of B's refusal to permit access to the photographs. The main issue here would be as to whether or not C has locus standi to bring such a challenge. Under RSC O.53 r3(7), the court will not grant leave to apply for judicial review unless C can establish that he has 'sufficient interest in the matter to which the application relates'. This term has been interpreted by the House of Lords in *IRC* v *National Federation of Self Employed and Small Businesses* (1982). In the course of his speech, Lord Wilberforce emphasised that litigants should not view locus standi as a threshold requirement to be determined at the outset of litigation, and once satisfied, not considered again.

Locus standi will, therefore, be considered at two stages. First at the time of the application for leave to apply for judicial review, at which C should be allowed to proceed if he can show that he has an 'arguable case'. Secondly, when the substantive application for judicial review is made. It is only at this second stage, in the normal course of events, that B would be represented, and the 'other side' of the case considered. When this new evidence is before the court, it might be found that the applicant for review does not have locus standi. Furthermore, the question of locus standi is dependent to some extent on whether C succeeds in establishing that B has acted ultra vires. It may be significant that in the *Federation* case, the court, in holding that the NFSSB did not have locus standi, took account of the fact that relations between a taxpayer and the Inland Revenue are confidential. By contrast in the present case, the level of local community contribution payable by an individual would seem to be a matter of public record, and the courts might thus be more amenable to C's claim to standing.

It is submitted that if the court regards the actions of B as irrational, then C is likely to have locus standi.

SUGGESTED ANSWER TO QUESTION FOUR

General Comment

This is a complex question and it is important to sort out the issues involved and to deal with them separately. It is important to bear in mind that the order is directed at television companies and not at the union.

Key Points

- Public law issue
- Application of RSC O.53
- Test of locus standi under O.53
- Problems of standing order due to the fact that the order is not directed at the union and has not as yet directly affected its members
- Grounds of review
- Unreasonableness/irrationality
- Proportionality
- Failure to take into account a relevant consideration

Suggested Answer

As the Home Secretary is a public official and the matter involves issues of public law the matter must be challenged by way of an application for judicial review, under O.53 of the Rules of the Supreme Court (see *O'Reilly* v *Mackman* (1983). Under Order 53 an applicant must satisfy the court that he has 'sufficient interest in the matter to which the application relates'. The leading case on locus standi under O.53 is *IRC* v *National Federation of Self Employed and Small Businesses* (1982). This established that the question of standing needs to be considered generally as a threshold issue at the stage of applying for leave and more specifically at the hearing of the application for review. Furthermore locus standi might depend on the extent to which the applicant could establish illegality and, as regards the remedy sought, might be more restrictive in the case of mandamus, than certiorari or prohibition.

In the case of the National Union of Journalists there is a potential standing problem because the order complained of is directed at television companies rather than journalists. Furthermore, in the absence of any occasion on which a television company might wish to broadcast such matters, none of its members have as yet been affected by it. However, there is a nexus between the union and the order in that there will clearly be occasions in the future when television companies would wish to publish the type of material prescribed and when the effect of the order will be to adversely affect the activities of union members. The union is therefore clearly not a mere busybody and arguably has a legitimate interest in protecting the public interest in the freedom of the press. Furthermore, the order is not merely a guideline; it is binding on television companies, which will be obliged to give effect to it unless they can be satisfied that it is ultra vires. It is therefore submitted that the union has a good claim in respect of standing, particularly as it is not seeking mandamus.

Assuming that the union is granted leave to apply for review the next consideration is whether there has been any breach of the principles of judicial review. Has the minister acted illegally, irrationally or unfairly?

The union may argue that the minister acted irrationally in issuing such a broad and inflexible order in that the effect of the order in terms of restricting the freedom of press is out of all proportion to the evil which is sought to be avoided. It is, however, unlikely that it will be able to satisfy the stringent test of unreasonableness as formulated in *Associated Provincial Picture Houses Ltd* v *Wednesbury Corporation* (1948), which requires that the act must be of such a nature that no reasonable person could possibly entertain such a thing. It is also unlikely that it will be able to satisfy the alternative formulation of irrationality in *Council of Civil Service Unions* v *Minister for the Civil Service* (1985). This requires that an action must be so outrageous in its defiance of logic and of accepted moral standards that no sensible person who had applied his mind to the question could so have arrived at it. Here the minister's decision is clearly too broad but it would be difficult to argue that it defies all logic since he is entitled to prescribe the broadcasting not only of a particular matter but also any matter of a particular class and there is a clear link between terrorism and activities undermining state authority. The union may also argue that lack of proportionality is itself a separate ground for review. It should, however, be noted that although the concept of lack of proportionality has long been recognised in Europe, and was cited as a possible but as yet undefined head of judicial review in *Council of Civil Service Unions* v *Minister for the Civil Service*, there has not as yet been any decision where it has been considered as a separate head of review, although dicta of Sedley J, in *R v Secretary of State for the Home Department, ex parte McQuillan* (1995) are sympathetic to the use of the test.

In *R v Secretary of State for the Home Department, ex parte Brind* (1991) which involved an application for judicial review of the Home Secretary's ban on the broadcasting of interviews with IRA supporters, the House of Lords suggested that it was perhaps too early to see proportionality as a separate ground of review. On the facts the claim that the minister's ban was unreasonable was rejected.

An alternative and potentially stronger line of argument is that the minister failed to take into account a relevant consideration namely that the potential threat posed by terrorist organisations will vary according to their geographical sphere of operation and that there are many groups of a non-international nature which do not pose any threat to law and order in the United Kingdom.

Following *ex parte Brind* (above), the NUJ would be unlikely to succeed with the argument that the minister had failed to pay sufficient regard to art 10 of the European Convention on Human Rights. The House of Lords held that resort need only be had to the Convention where domestic legislation was ambiguous, so as to ensure an interpretation consistent with the United Kingdom's treaty obligations. Even if the Convention were to be regarded as a relevant consideration, its term may be found to be wide enough to permit the action taken by the minister.

(*Note*: It is anticipated that the European Convention on Human Rights will be formally incorporated into English Law during 1998, thus making it easier for judges to apply a proportionality test to administrative decisions. But as the advice above concludes, this development would probably not affect the actual outcome of a case similar to *Brind*.)

9

Relevant and Irrelevant Factors; Fettering Discretion

Introduction

This chapter is concerned with some of the more significant heads of ultra vires, whether classified as aspects of *Wednesbury* unreasonableness or as aspects of illegality. They are the failure to take into account relevant considerations and the taking account of irrelevant ones; and the fettering of administrative discretion by policy, contract or other representation (which also leads on to discussion of the scope of estoppel in public law). They are very common heads of review so there is plenty of case law to master.

It will be seen from an examination of the leading cases that much depends on the process of statutory construction in determining what is or is not relevant to a particular decision-making process. Although this ought to be an uncontroversial task for judges, it has on occasion caused criticism when the body under review is an elected and representative body. There is a natural tension between judicial and political perceptions as to the amount of discretion elected officials should enjoy in determining what is relevant to the proper and efficient performance of public responsibilities; see two recent cases as useful illustrations: *R v Somerset County Council, ex parte Fewings* [1995] 3 All ER 20; and *R v Secretary of State for the Home Department, ex parte Venables and Thompson* [1997] 3 All ER 97 (HL). See further Foster (1997) 31 Law Teach 383 and Padfield [1997] CLJ 477.

Recent case law has demonstrated continuing sensitivity as to the issue of relevant considerations, particularly on the context of decisions involving the allocation and prioritisation of scarce resources. Examples of recent cases on this point are: *R v Cambridge District Health Authority, ex parte B* [1995] 2 All ER 129; *R v Gloucestershire County Council, ex parte Barry* [1997] 2 WLR 459; [1997] 2 All ER 1 (see further Hocking [1997] CLJ 472); *R v Sefton Metropolitan Borough Council, ex parte Help the Aged and Others* [1997] 4 All ER 532.

In regard to fettering discretion and estoppel in public law the main issue of academic interest has been the extent to which the growth in the doctrine of legitimate expectation may prevent the revocation of decisions on the grounds of substantive fairness (see Chapter 7). Whilst it is well settled that neither the doctrine of estoppel nor legitimate expectation can 'clothe' a public body with powers it does not legally possess, there remains doubt as to the extent to which a public authority will be bound by an intra vires policy or representation: contrast dicta in *R v Secretary of State for the Home Department, ex parte Ruddock* [1987] 2 All ER 518 with dicta in *R v Secretary of State for Transport, ex parte Richmond-upon-Thames London Borough Council* [1994] 1 All ER 577.

An interesting recent case examining the extent to which the doctrine of ostensible authority (found in the private law of agency) may be invoked in public law to prevent abuse of power is: *Postermobile plc* v *Brent London Borough Council* (1997) The Times 8 December (QBD).

In regard to examinations it is reasonable to expect at least one problem-type question involving various grounds of review which are likely to include the issues of relevancy and fettering discretion. There is also a tendency for essay-type questions to be set demanding critical analysis of the apparently conflicting principles concerning substantive fairness and fettering discretion/estoppel.

Questions

INTERROGRAMS

1   What is meant by the 'margin of appreciation' principle in the context of determining the relevancy of considerations in a decision-making process?
2   Is an electoral mandate a relevant factor in exercising statutory powers?
3   Is an elected administrator entitled to have regard to moral or ethical considerations when exercising statutory discretions?
4   What is meant by the 'margin of appreciation' principle in the context of fettering statutory discretions by policy or otherwise?
5   Can a public body be estopped from acting unfairly or inconsistently?

(*Note*: the following questions may raise for discussion grounds for review covered in earlier chapters.)

QUESTION ONE

'The legislative choice between making a statutory rule and conferring a statutory discretion is very important for the legal control of administrative activity. Rules create duties which authorities must perform; discretions confer choice. Both rules and discretions have their advantages and disadvantages.' (PF Cane)

Discuss.

London University LLB Examination
(for external students) Administrative Law June 1992 Q6

QUESTION TWO

a   'Local authorities are not, of course, trustees for their ratepayers, but they do, we think, owe an analogous fiduciary duty to their ratepayers in relation to the application of finance contributed by the latter' (Jenkins LJ in *Prescott* v *Birmingham Corporation*).

Explain.

b   Local authorities are empowered compulsorily to acquire certain property, compensation being payable. Bishop District Council resolves to use that power in respect of property owned by Dean. Bishop DC knows that one effect of certain legislation which is going through Parliament will be that the compensation payable in the circumstances affecting Dean will be reduced. It therefore deliberately delays the use of the power in question until the legislation is passed. The result is that it has to pay Dean £5,000 less by way of compensation than would otherwise have been the case.

Advise Dean.

London University LLB Examination
(for external students) Administrative Law June 1986 Q6

QUESTION THREE

'Fairness requires consistency: a decision-maker should always act consistently with what he has done before and consistently with what he has promised.'

Do you agree that consistency is desirable in principle? Does English law require a decision-maker to be consistent?

London University LLB Examination
(for external students) Administrative Law June 1991 Q2

QUESTION FOUR

a   Jack wanted to build an extension to his house, and went for advice to Fred, a planning consultant, who had recently opened an office in the town. Fred went to the offices of the District Council to see whether planning permission was necessary for what Jack proposed. He was shown into a room which had on the door 'Deputy Chief Planning Officer'. The person in that room told him that permission was not necessary. Jack made the extension and has now been served with an order by the Council requiring him to remove it on the ground that it was made without planning permission. He considers that the Council is bound by what its officer told Fred.

Advise him.

b   'It would destroy the whole doctrine of ultra vires if it was possible for a statutory power to be extended by means of an estoppel.'

Explain and illustrate.

London University LLB Examination
(for external students) Administrative Law June 1985 Q7

QUESTION FIVE

Critically assess the public law doctrine of estoppel.

London University LLB Examination
(for external students) Administrative Law June 1988 Q4

QUESTION SIX

'Public bodies should be treated like any other body or individual.'
    Discuss with reference to the place of estoppel in public law.

London University LLB Examination
(for external students) Administrative Law June 1990 Q4

QUESTION SEVEN

The newly independent nation of Katawi has modelled its constitution on that of the United Kingdom, and its Supreme Court has indicated that it will accord persuasive authority to English case law.

    The Minister of Justice is currently much troubled by the apparent unwillingness of the Supreme Court to apply the concept of estoppel to the actions of government bodies. She considers that the Court's case law pays too much attention to promoting certainty in citizen/government relations, and is too little concerned with doing 'justice' in hard cases. She would favour a more flexible approach to this issue. She approaches you for an opinion as to how, if at all, that result might be achieved through a development of the Katawian common law.

    Advise her.

London University LLB Examination
(for external students) Administrative Law June 1995 Q9

QUESTION EIGHT

A recent (fictitious) statute, the Places of Entertainment (Safety) Act, makes it a criminal offence to permit the use of premises as places of public entertainment without a licence. The licence is to be obtained from the district council which is empowered to inspect the premises with a view to ensuring that they are safe. The council may, on the grant of such a licence, impose 'such conditions as it thinks fit' and may require the payment of 'such fee as it thinks reasonable'. (Earlier legislation, dating from 1890, fixed the fee payable at £5.)

    Consider the following cases:

a   Mace DC, on granting Basil a licence, imposed these conditions:

    i   Basil is to prevent the use of illegal drugs on the premises.
    ii   No person under the age of 16, whether or not accompanied by an adult, is to be admitted to an entertainment in the premises.

    Advise Basil.

b   Sage DC gave no consideration to the new power to charge what fee it thought reasonable, and continued to charge £5. Advise Rice, a council tax payer.

c   Clove DC decided that the fee should be £500 in each case, taking the view that this roughly represented the fall in the value of money since the £5 fee was fixed in 1890.
    Advise Mint, an applicant for a licence.

d   Salt DC calculated the total cost of examining the relevant premises in its area to be

£200,000 and resolved to raise the sum by the fee payable for licences, the individual fees to be calculated by reference to the size of the premises in question. In the case of Pepper, a licensee, this worked out at £2,500 (the previous fee being, as stated, £5). Advise Pepper.

London University LLB Examination
(for external students) Administrative Law June 1985 Q1

QUESTION NINE

Melvyn is a poet who has had a grant from his local authority arts committee renewed annually for the last five years. But this year his application was rejected. No reasons were given. The committee says that complaints or appeals would be 'futile' as its decision is final. Melvyn knows that the new chairman of the committee had said to the press that he 'had no time for poetry which does not rhyme'. Melvyn's poetry does not rhyme and he suspects that this is the real reason for his rejection. He is, however, hopeful that he might receive a grant next year and so does not wish to make a fuss. But a pressure group, Writers' Rights In The Eighties (WRITE), is considering an application for judicial review to test the committee's behaviour against the principles of administrative law.

a   Will WRITE be given standing?
b   Has there been any breach of the principles of judicial review?

Adapted from London University LLB Examination
(for external students) Administrative Law June 1987 Q7

QUESTION TEN

The Local Government Act (a hypothetical Act) gives a local authority 'a discretion to make such grants not exceeding £1,000 as it thinks fit to any charity'. The Act also states that 'any such exercise of discretion by the authority shall be final and conclusive and shall not be called into question in any court of law'. A local authority announces that as a matter of policy it will never give grants above £500 and that it will never give grants to any lesbian or homosexual organisations. The Gay Action Group (GAG), which is based in the authority's area, has its application for a grant rejected. Could GAG successfully apply for judicial review?

Adapted from London University LLB Examination
(for external students) Administrative Law June 1987 Q8

QUESTION ELEVEN

Alan, an English rugby player, is invited to tour Iraq as part of a 'World XV'. He is employed as a coach driver by a bus company, Business, which has a contract with the Consciencester local authority to take children to and from school. The local authority writes to the bus company warning that the contract, which has been renewed every year for the last decade, will not be renewed again if Alan takes part in the tour 'because the authority does not wish to be associated with Saddam Hussein'. Alan does participate in the tour. The contract with Business is not renewed. Business does not challenge this decision in the courts because it hopes to re-establish links with the authority in the future. Subsequently, the authority enters into a contract with a rival bus company, Dear, which charges £10,000 a year more than did Business. Ernest, who is a council tax payer in the neighbouring authority of Faraway, is the chairman of a pressure group 'Go-to-Iraq'.

Advise Ernest as to whether he could successfully apply for judicial review of Consciencester's decision to give the contract to Dear rather than to Business.

Adapted from London University LLB Examination
(for external students) Administrative Law June 1988 Q9

QUESTION TWELVE

The (fictitious) Funfairs (Licensing) Act imposes strict safety standards on operators of private funfairs and requires them to obtain a licence from their local authority. Local authorities are given a wide discretion as to whether or not to grant a licence and to impose 'such conditions as they think fit'. The licensing requirement applies both to existing operators and to those wishing to establish a funfair for the first time. Applicants must apply before a due date and satisfy a number of conditions; in particular an applicant for a licence 'must give notice in one national newspaper and in one local newspaper circulating in the area where the funfair is to be established'.

Tombola has run a funfair in the area of the Roundabout District Council for many years. The Gloomy Party, which has recently won political control in Roundabout, stated in its election programme that, 'so long as they observe proper safety standards, no established funfair operator need fear that we will harm the commercial viability of their operation'. Tombola expends considerable sums meeting the safety standards and applies for a licence. He is given one on condition that all children under the age of ten and the families of all unemployed people are permitted free access to the funfair on Saturdays and Sundays.

Dodgem applies for a licence to open a funfair in the area of Swinging District Council. The only local newspaper circulating in the area is closed because of a protracted strike. Dodgem is advised by the receptionist at the council offices to put a notice in the magazine sent out by the local church. He does so and complies with all the other requirements of the statute. He is refused a licence because he has not complied with the requirement to advertise in a local newspaper.

Advise Tombola and Dodgem.

Adapted from London University LLB Examination
(for external students) Administrative Law June 1992 Q8

Answers

ANSWERS TO INTERROGRAMS

1   A 'margin of appreciation' essentially means room to exercise discretion, so that in

exercising the secondary judgment of review the court will recognise that, in order for the primary judgment to be made properly, there must be sufficient discretion to decide how much weight to give to a particular relevant factor when assessing all the factors and striking a balance. The margin of appreciation principle also means that a decision will not be ultra vires even though some irrelevant factors were taken into account, provided that the balancing exercise was carried out in a *Wednesbury* reasonable manner and that the dominant considerations which determined the decision were relevant and reasonable ones: *Westminster Corporation* v *London and North Western Railway Co* [1905] AC 426.

2   In *Bromley London Borough Council* v *Greater London Council* [1983] 1 AC 768 Lord Denning MR had remarked that the manifesto commitments made by the governing political party of the Greater London Council (GLC) were 'irrelevant' to the performance of the GLC's statutory powers and discretions, which could only be lawfully determined by having regard to the aims and objects of the legislation conferring those powers and discretions. However, on appeal, the House of Lords, whilst upholding the decision of the Court of Appeal, appeared to disapprove Lord Denning's observation for being too sweeping. Whilst electoral promises could not 'clothe' the GLC with powers it did not possess, they were obviously of political relevance in determining the manner of the exercise of powers within the legal authority of the GLC or other elected body.

3   It appears from the case law that moral or ethical considerations may be relevant when exercising statutory discretions depending on the construction of the relevant statute and the context in which the decision is being made. In a case involving the imposition of planning conditions for land development there was held to be no room for considerations other than purely planning law ones, so that a local authority's imposition of conditions designed to fulfil its moral obligations towards housing the homeless constituted an improper or ulterior motive and was quashed on the basis of irrelevancy: *R* v *Hillingdon London Borough Council, ex parte Royco Homes Ltd* [1974] 2 All ER 643.

Similarly, statutory powers cannot be used to impose a moral viewpoint so as to prevent the lawful activities of others: *Wheeler* v *Leicester City Council* [1985] 2 All ER 1106. In *R* v *Somerset County Council, ex parte Fewings* [1995] 3 All ER 20 the Court of Appeal was divided as to whether the local authority had lawfully taken account of moral considerations when imposing a ban on deer hunting over land which it managed under statutory authority.

4   Judges are prepared to leave a 'margin of appreciation' (room for discretion) to public bodies wishing to adopt policies in order to structure their decision-making or to make contracts or representations in order to obtain commercial services or other benefits. Thus, no unlawful fettering of discretion will occur provided the authority in question retains an open mind in deciding whether or not to adhere to its policy, eg by being prepared to consider the merits of any individual case, any fresh evidence that might be relevant, and an applicant's personal circumstances which might justify making an exception to that policy: *British Oxygen Co Ltd* v *Minister of Technology* [1971] AC 610.

Similarly, the making of contracts or representations will not amount to unlawful fettering of discretion provided those contracts or representations are intra vires the authority making them *and* do not restrict the ability of that authority to take future action which may be required in the public interest: *Birkdale District Electricity Supply Co Ltd* v *Southport Corporation* [1926] AC 355.

5   There are dicta in some cases which suggest that a public body may be acting ultra vires if it unfairly revokes a decision conferring a discretionary benefit on a citizen or if it otherwise acts inconsistently in a situation in which it knows that citizens are relying on it to follow a constant course of conduct: see *HTV Ltd* v *Price Commission* [1976] ICR 70 and *R* v *Inland Revenue Commissioners, ex parte Preston* [1985] AC 835 (discussed in *Administrative Law* by Wade and Forsyth (1994, 7th ed) at pp418–420). The development of a doctrine of substantive fairness as part of the principle of legitimate expectation has also lent weight to these views: *R* v *Secretary of State for the Home Department, ex parte Khan* [1985] 1 All ER 40 and *R* v *Secretary of State for the Home Department, ex parte Ruddock* [1987] 2 All ER 518.

A modified version of the doctrine of ostensible authority may also be invoked to prevent an agent of a public body from making inconsistent statements on its behalf: *Western Fish Products Ltd* v *Penwith District Council* [1981] 2 All ER 204. However, the doctrine of promissory estoppel cannot be relied on to clothe a public body with powers it does not possess, or to prevent that body from performing its public responsibilities for the general public good: per Lawton LJ in *Laker Airways* v *Department of Trade* [1977] QB 643.

(*Note*: the following Answers take account of grounds for review and procedural rules discussed in earlier chapters.)

SUGGESTED ANSWER TO QUESTION ONE

General Comment

This question concerns the different ways of delegating authority. When are rules appropriate? When and why is discretionary power better? When discretion is given, do the courts have significant powers of control? When will a challenge to the exercise of discretion be successful? An awareness of the different uses of rules and discretion is needed, but a lot of the essay will examine the ability of the courts to review the exercise of discretionary power since control by the courts is the issue raised in this quotation.

Key Points

* Appropriateness of rules and discretion
* Judicial control
* Discretion must be exercised
* Duty to listen
* *Wednesbury*
* Abuse

Suggested Answer

It is true that rules create duties and therefore make for a high degree of judicial control over administrative activity. But rules cannot be used effectively for all forms of administration. It is essential that flexibility be built into the administration, particularly where there is a need to be sensitive to local, technical or fiscal matters. Discretion is granted in recognition of the fact that rules have an inbuilt inadequacy to deal with such situations. Although rules allow for a high degree of judicial control, it would not be true to say that the courts have been slow to find ways of controlling the exercise of discretion; they have evolved a number of techniques enabling them to intervene in suitable cases.

The main advantage of rules is their certainty. They impose clear duties upon the authority concerned, and often confer corresponding rights upon individuals. They are highly suitable in those cases where it is vital that clear procedures be followed or where individual rights are to be protected. An example of this would be the field of social security, where there are clear duties to follow correct procedures for determining the entitlements of applicants, and for ensuring that payments are made. It is because the authority concerned is dealing with entitlements that rules imposing duties are so well suited in these circumstances; it is important that, upon default by the authority, the applicant be able to enforce his rights, for example by seeking an order of mandamus to compel performance.

Strong control is not necessary where rights do not need to be protected, in such cases it will often be both more appropriate and more efficient to confer discretion. This is particularly true where some grant or bonus is being conferred. The starting point for judicial control in such cases is the case *British Oxygen Co Ltd* v *Minister of Technology* (1971). Here the Minister had the power to confer a grant upon industries. The applicant did not receive the grant because it did not fulfil certain criteria that the Minister had decided upon; had there been a genuine exercise of discretion? The House of Lords dismissed the applicant's claim, holding that the Minister was entitled to form a policy, so long as he listened to anybody with something new to say in the matter. As matters of general principle, the Lords stated that discretion must not be exercised in bad faith, or in such a way that there was no genuine exercise of discretion.

It is vital therefore that the authority in question should keep its mind open in exercising its discretion; put another way the authority must not fetter its discretion. Thus, for instance, the authority may not abdicate or delegate its power to decide to another authority: *Lavender* v *Minister of Housing and Local Government* (1970). But the formation of policy will often be essential, since it will be impossible to have a full moritorium on each individual case. It is clear from the British Oxygen case that the authority must keep its mind open in such circumstances. It is not clear how far the duty to listen is to be taken, although where an authority has a settled policy which it wishes to change, an applicant may have a legitimate expectation of being heard on the matter: *R* v *Secretary of State for the Home Department, ex parte Khan* (1985). This is an interesting idea, since the authority must keep its mind open with regard both to those who may suffer as a result of some particular policy, and with regard to those whom it benefits; and it should be noted that a legitimate expectation may arise where an authority has undertaken to exercise its discretion in a particular way: *R v Liverpool Corporation, ex parte Liverpool Taxi Fleet Operators' Association* (1972). This last cited principle is at first glance at odds with the Lavender case above, but it is consistent with the general notion that the authority must actually exercise discretion, not mechanically apply rules or policy. To do this the authority must always be careful to take into account all relevant factors, and to exclude those that are irrelevant, in accordance with the doctrine of Wednesbury unreasonableness (*Associated Provincial Picture Houses Ltd v Wednesbury Corporation* (1948)). In this sense, discretions may be more burdensome to the authorities who possess them than the application of rules.

Discretion may be broad, but it will never be unlimited. It must always be exercised in accordance with the reasons for which it is granted to an authority, and the court will always be prepared to construe the legislation which confers that power to ensure that this is the case: *Padfield v Minister of Agriculture* (1968). Thus the court will be prepared to intervene in cases where the discretion is exercised for an improper purpose. This was the case in *Congreve v Home Office* (1976) where the Secretary of State attempted to use his powers of control over television licenses in order to prevent the applicant from renewing his licence early so as to avoid paying an increased licence fee. This is in effect one form of abuse of discretion, which may take place in a number of ways. It will include the use of authority to pursue some illegitimate or ulterior purpose, such as to punish another person unjustifiably, where no offence has been committed as occurred in *Wheeler v Leicester City Council* (1985). But it also includes the pursuit of some legitimate aim, with an ancillary illegitimate aim in mind: *R v ILEA, ex parte Westminster City Council* (1986). It should be noted that such cases are at the extreme end of the spectrum, and thus are somewhat rare.

It can be seen then that, while the failure to observe a rule or carry out a duty will always give the courts stronger grounds for control than the exercise of discretion in a particular way, nonetheless the discretion of an authority is not immune from challenge. An applicant to the authority in any particular case has no right to expect a favourable decision, but the grounds upon which the exercise of discretion may be challenged go a long way towards ensuring that his application is taken seriously.

SUGGESTED ANSWER TO QUESTION TWO

General Comment

Basically a question covering aspects of local authority spending/use of discretion, with emphasis on the interests of ratepayers. Note that part (b) represents a reversal of the problem that usually comes before the courts. Although domestic rates have been replaced by council tax, the fiduciary duty is unaffected so many of the old cases on the rates remain good law.

Key Points

a   •   Concept of fiduciary duty
    •   Case law examples

b • Application of fiduciary duty
  • Remedies for breach
  • Appropriate procedure

Suggested Answer

a   The proposition that local authorities are trustees of ratepayers' money was one which was current during the early years of this century. In *Roberts* v *Hopwood* (1925) Lord Atkinson adopted this view of the relationship between local authorities and ratepayers, but it has subsequently fallen into disuse, the fiduciary relationship principle being used in its place.

What then is the effect and ambit of this fiduciary relationship? In reality it means no more than that a local authority, when making spending decisions, should bear in mind the interests of the ratepayers as a relevant consideration. Failure to give adequate consideration to ratepayers' interests could be a means by which any subsequent action could be invalidated.

An example is provided by the House of Lords' decision in *Bromley London Borough Council* v *Greater London Council* (1983), wherein the GLC's decision to reduce the cost of London Transport fares by 25 per cent not only transferred the £69 million cost of doing so from transport users to ratepayers, but also induced a loss of rate support grant from central government, thus requiring ratepayers to make up a further £50 million deficit. One of the grounds upon which the decision was invalidated, therefore, was failing to give due regard to the interests of ratepayers.

In effect, what the courts are asking local authorities to try and do is to achieve a fair balance between the interests of ratepayers, and those who benefit from services provided by the local authority. Clearly, in *Prescott* v *Birmingham Corporation* (1955) Jenkins LJ felt that the local authority in question had failed to get the balance right (by subsidising senior citizens' travel fares at huge cost to ratepayers).

It should be remembered, however, that the courts will not, or should not, usurp the decision making function delegated to local authorities by Parliament, to determine the allocation of finite resources. In short the courts should not tell local authorities how funds must be spent. In *Pickwell* v *Camden London Borough Council* (1983), Ormrod LJ reaffirmed the view that the fiduciary duty owed to ratepayers was no more than a relevant consideration in the exercise of discretion. In that case, a local authority had agreed a wage settlement with striking refuse workers that was above the nationally agreed figure. The court held that the agreement was valid because the decision to pay higher rates of wages had not been motivated by any ulterior purpose; compare with *Roberts* v *Hopwood*, above (excessive wage increase due to irrelevant desire to redistribute wealth in society).

Finally, it could be said that the fiduciary duty claimed to be owed to ratepayers is based on a misunderstanding of local authority finance. Today, some two-thirds of local authority income is derived from central government funds, ie the general taxpayer. By no means all of the remaining one-third comes from council tax payers. Local authorities receive income from rents, fees for use of amenities, and interest on loans. The result is that the courts may be setting too much store by the interests of council tax payers. To allow the fiduciary duty as a ground for judicial review may result in cases of 'the tail wagging the dog'.

b   Bishop DC has a discretion as to whether or not to proceed with the compulsory purchase order affecting Dean's property. The power to proceed with the compulsory purchase order, or abandon it, must be exercised in accordance with the express limits imposed by the town and country planning legislation, and also in accordance with the implied limits developed by the courts on a case by case basis.

In seeking to delay the use of its compulsory purchase powers, Bishop DC may well have in mind the saving that could be made to ratepayers, if the compulsory purchase order is not issued until the new legislation referred to comes into effect. The question is therefore one of a balance between the interests of Dean, and the interests of the ratepayers.

Bishop DC is under a fiduciary duty to have regard to the interests of ratepayers when exercising its powers, but it must not lose sight of the interests of other parties, such as Dean, who may be affected by such decisions.

An improper delay in taking action is not justifiable simply because the intent or effect is to benefit the ratepayers. Dean would be advised, therefore, to try and convince the court that Bishop DC has struck the wrong balance in trying to determine the interests of the ratepayers and his own.

Dean should also be advised that a public authority that fails to proceed with a compulsory purchase order may be held to have abandoned it, and so to have lost the power to enforce it. Much then depends upon whether the compulsory purchase order has actually been made yet.

Dean should be advised to apply for judicial review under RSC O.53, as this is a public law matter, claiming an order of certiorari to quash the compulsory purchase order or, alternatively, a declaration as to the legal position coupled with a claim for his loss of £5,000, if, for example, he can show that the delay was a deliberate misuse of power amounting to the tort of misfeasance in public office: *Three Rivers District Council* v *Bank of England (No 3)* (1996).

SUGGESTED ANSWER TO QUESTION THREE

General Comment

A question bringing together two issues sometimes considered separately. Consideration must be given to the adoption of over-rigid policies which fetter discretion, and also to the extent to which public undertakings will be binding upon public bodies.

Key Points

* Purpose of policies in the context of discretion
* The leading cases, *Kynoch* and *British Oxygen*
* Importance of context.
* Binding undertakings
* Development of doctrine of legitimate expectation

Suggested Answer

Whether or not consistency in the decision-making process is desirable depends very much on the context within which a decision-making power is being exercised. To the extent that English law requires such consistency it is submitted that it recognises the need for flexibility. Administrative bodies vested with statutory powers are, in theory, supposed to consider each use of discretion in its own right, bearing in mind all relevant considerations. The price paid for giving such bodies discretion may be a degree of inconsistency. For many decision-makers the exercise of discretion is not governed by a system of precedent, so that a claimant denied a discretionary award cannot argue that in a previous similar application an award was made.

Although not necessarily required to do so by law, many inferior bodies develop policies as to how they are to exercise their discretion. The aim is to promote the twin goals of consistency and fairness on the basis that like cases will be treated alike. The desire to promote consistency can be further achieved if a policy can be advertised in advance so that applicants will know what criteria are important, and tailor their cases accordingly.

It would be wrong to assume that consistency through policy necessarily results in rigidity. A decision-maker following a particular policy should be willing to recognise those situations where an exception needs to be made and the policy departed from. It is by this means that a policy evolves, through application and experience. Furthermore, it should be noted that a decision-maker does not necessarily act unlawfully by deciding not to apply a particular policy: see *R* v *Avon County Council, ex parte Rexworthy* (1988).

The attitude of the courts can be divined from an examination of the leading cases. In *R* v *Port of London Authority, ex parte Kynoch Ltd* (1919) the court considered a challenge to the PLA's policy of not licensing certain types of development. The court held that the PLA acted lawfully in rejecting the application, because it had fully considered the arguments raised by Kynoch Ltd and rejected them on their merits. The vital point, commented Banks LJ, was that the decision making body must not 'shut its ears' to an applicant who has something new to say. His Lordship continued:

> 'There are on the one hand cases where a tribunal in the honest exercise of its discretion has adopted a policy, and without refusing to hear an applicant, intimates to him what its policy is, and that after hearing him it will in accordance with its policy decide against him, unless there is something exceptional in his case ... if the policy has been adopted for reasons which the tribunal may legitimately entertain, no objection could be taken to such a course. On the other hand there are cases where a tribunal has passed a rule, or come to a determination, not to hear any application of a particular character by whomsoever made. There is a wide distinction to be drawn between these two classes.'

In *British Oxygen Co Ltd* v *Minister of Technology* (1971) the House of Lords introduced more flexibility into Banks LJ's dictum by pointing out that the legality of adopting a rule to govern the exercise of discretion would vary with the context within which decisions were made. A rule could be adopted provided the decision-making body was still willing to listen to someone with something new to say. Lord Reid stated:

'I do not think there is any great difference between a policy and a rule … What the authority must not do is refuse to listen at all. But a Ministry or large authority may have had to deal already with a multitude of similar applications and then they will almost certainly have evolved a policy so precise that it could well be called a rule.'

It should be noted that an important factor here was the large number of applications dealt with by the Ministry"

Where the context renders the adoption of a policy unsuitable, the courts are likely to invalidate any decision taken in reliance upon it. For example, in *Attorney-General* v *Wandsworth London Borough Council, ex rel Tilley* (1981) the social services committee of a local authority passed a resolution that in cases where the housing department of the authority had determined that a family with young children were intentionally homeless, and the family subsequently approached the social services department, assistance with accommodation would not be provided under the provisions of the relevant Act, although considerations would be given to receiving the children into care if the circumstances warranted it. The Court of Appeal held that a strict policy was inappropriate where the welfare of children was at stake.

Templeman LJ stated:

'… a local authority, dealing with individual children, should not make a policy or an order that points towards fettering its discretion in such a way that the facilities offered to the child do not depend on the particular circumstances of that child or of its family but follow some policy which is expressed to apply in general cases.'

By contrast a housing policy may be essential in dealing with a huge number of applications. Such a policy will be lawful provided that in deciding whether to apply it the housing authority always considers: the merits of an individual case; any fresh evidence that might be relevant; and the applicant's personal circumstances: *R* v *Camden London Borough Council, ex parte Mohammed* (1997)

Whether a decision-maker should always act in a manner that he has promised is a more complex matter. A public body cannot extend the scope of its powers by promising to act in a way that conflicts with its statutory duties or the proper exercise of its powers: see *Western Fish Products Ltd* v *Penwith District Council* (1981).

Where no such conflict occurs, however, it is in the interests of good administration that decision-makers should act as they have indicated that they would act. The growth of the 'legitimate expectation' doctrine underlines the link between fairness and consistency. Such an expectation might be based on some statement or undertaking by, or on behalf of, the public authority which had the duty of making the decision if the authority had through its officers, acted in a way which would make it unfair or inconsistent with good administration to deny the person affected an inquiry into his case.

In its procedural aspect the doctrine merely ensures that a person affected by the change of statement or undertaking is given a fair hearing before the change is implemented. But it has been suggested in some cases that the doctrine has a substantive aspect which can prevent the public body from departing from its representation if the representation is *intra vires* and it would be against the public interest to permit such departure, eg if departure would grossly infringe fundamental human rights: *R* v

Secretary of State for the Home Department, ex parte Ruddock (1987). Reliance on a council officer's advice might therefore constitute a defence in criminal proceedings for breach of the planning laws if it would be an abuse of process for the council in question to prosecute, knowing that it had given misleading advice: *Postermobile plc v Brent London Borough Council* (1997).

In conclusion, it is submitted that, subject to the exceptions noted, a decision-maker should, in the interests of fairness, aim to decide cases consistently, and the case law reflects this view.

SUGGESTED ANSWER TO QUESTION FOUR

General Comment

The whole question concerns the problem of estoppel. The first part is more concerned with an agency problem: who can bind a local authority by a statement as to the use of powers that it does possess? The *Western Fish Products* case is of central importance here. The second part of the question involves the slightly different problem of a body promising to act in a way which it in fact lacks the power to do. It is important to distinguish between the different nature of the estoppel problem in the two parts.

Key Points

a • Who makes the decision?
       – Authorised officer
       – Unauthorised officer
       – Other person
   • Effect on council
   • *Western Fish* principles
   • Other remedies
   • Negligent misstatement
   • Local government ombudsman
b • Distinguish from the problem in part (a)
   • Explain choice facing the courts
   • Need to uphold the ultra vires doctrine
   • Provide illustrations
   • Point out possible exceptions

Suggested Answer

a This problem raises the question of the extent to which a local planning authority can be bound by representations made by another person on its behalf.

   Duties and powers under planning legislation are placed directly on local authorities, but by s101 of the Local Government Act 1972 they can delegate functions to officers and committees. Given that the granting of planning permission, and the determining of whether planning permission is necessary are matters that local planning authorities are empowered by the Town and Country Planning Act

1990 to deal with, they are in theory functions that can be delegated to planning officers.

In the first instance, therefore, if the person by whom the advice was given to Fred is an officer of the local authority to whom the function of determining requests as to whether planning permission is necessary has been delegated, the local authority will be bound by his decisions.

A second, alternative, possibility is that the person giving the representation that planning permission was not necessary was an officer of the local authority, but not one to whom the function of determining such questions had been delegated. The law governing such situations is to be found in the Court of Appeal's decision in *Western Fish Products Ltd* v *Penwith District Council* (1981), where Megaw LJ stated that for an estoppel to arise in such a case, there had to be evidence justifying the person dealing with the planning officer for thinking that what the officer said would bind the planning authority, for example a previous course of dealings where the planning authority had always complied with decisions made by its planning officers. In the present case, the fact that the person making the statement as to the need for planning permission was in a room reserved for the 'Deputy Chief Planning Officer' would not seem to be particularly important, in that it does no more than suggest that the person giving the advice was that officer, not that he was necessarily empowered to do so.

A third possibility is that the person giving the advice was not even a planning officer of the authority. If so, clearly the local authority will not be bound. In effect the onus will be on the developer to discover the authority of the person giving advice.

As an alternative Jack might consider suing the local authority for negligent misstatement, but apart from the problems of proving that the giving of advice fell within the 'operational' sphere of activity, and that the council employee had acted ultra vires, he would have to show he was owed a duty of care in such a situation, and that the local authority were vicariously liable; see *Anns* v *Merton London Borough Council* (1978).

Finally, Jack might consider making a complaint of maladministration to the Local Government Commissioner.

b   The problem of a statutory power being extended by means of an estoppel can arise where an administrative agency promises to take a particular course of action, only to find that it lacks the power to do so. The promisee may have been relying on the promise, and have even acted to his detriment. The choice then becomes a difficult one. Should the administrative agency be kept to its promise, to avoid hardship to the promisee; or should the ultra vires doctrine be observed and the promise declared unenforceable because to carry it out would be to flout the rule of law?

The general rule is that such a promise must be unenforceable, otherwise an inferior body could extend its powers without limit simply by making promises it knew to involve undertakings way beyond its powers.

In *Balbir Singh* v *Secretary of State for the Home Department* (1978), a statement from the minister to an immigrant to the effect that he had a right of appeal to a tribunal from his decision could not confer any such right, where statute did not in fact provide for an appeal.

Similarly, in *Minister of Agriculture and Fisheries* v *Mathews* (1950) a claim by a defendant to a possession order that the plaintiff had granted him a lease, and was therefore estopped from evicting him, failed when the court found as a matter of law that the Ministry was not empowered to grant leases.

A promise by a parish council that a neighbouring authority could make use of its sewers was unenforceable because it lacked power to enter into any such arrangement; see *Islington Vestry* v *Hornsey Urban District Council* (1900).

All the above cases illustrate the principle that the extent of a statutory power is not simply extended by a body making promises it has no power to keep. Note, however, that a statutory body may be held to a promise to waive some statutory procedural requirement if no serious question of ultra vires action arises – and presumably no 'innocent' third party interests have thereby been prejudiced: see *Wells* v *Minister of Housing and Local Government* (1967).

The emergence of a doctrine of 'substantive' or 'reasonable' expectation may also give rise to situations akin to estoppel, though again it appears that the courts will insist that the statement or promise giving rise to such an expectation is intra vires the authority making it: *R* v *Secretary of State for the Home Department, ex parte Ruddock* (1987).

SUGGESTED ANSWER TO QUESTION FIVE

General Comment

The emphasis of the solution should be on the problems posed by the complexities of the relevant law and the manner in which judges have attempted to reconcile the need to do justice with the need not to undermine the foundations of the ultra vires rule.

Key Points

- Definition of promissory estoppel
- Difficulty of application in public law – would it hinder the formulation of executive policies?
- Public interest v private interest
- Doctrine of legitimate expectation: procedural and substantive
- The doctrine of ostensible authority – *Lever Finance, Western Fish, Postermobile* cases
- Conclusions

Suggested Answers

The principle of estoppel, as generally understood, arises when one party makes a promise or gives some undertaking, either as to an existing state of affairs or as to future conduct, to another party, and that party acts in reliance on the promise or undertaking. The party making the promise may then be described as being estopped from going back on its promise or undertaking in the sense that the courts have a discretion to hold a party to such promises or undertakings, even though they are not contractual obligations in the strict sense. The doctrine of estoppel is well established within the sphere of private law.

However, traditionally the concept has proven difficult to import into public law because the public interest may require that public bodies should not be inhibited in the formulation of policy, or prevented from exercising discretionary powers or discharging duties. It may cause hardship to the individual citizen who finds that he/she cannot hold the public body to the statement made to him/her, but this private interest may have to give way to the greater public interest in ensuring proper administration of statutory policies.

However, many judges became concerned at the risk of abuse of power by public bodies if they were to enjoy a large measure of immunity from the doctrine of promissory estoppel. Judicial review began to evolve a set of principles to mitigate the harshness of the traditional refusal to operate a doctrine of promissory estoppel against public bodies. Unfortunately, the result was a very complex area of law, not altogether consistent or logical in its reasoning.

The doctrine of legitimate expectation was developed during the 1970s and 1980s as a device for ensuring that a fair hearing would be given to those affected by a change in a previously published statement or promise by a public body: *Attorney-General of Hong Kong* v *Ng Yuen Shiu* (1983). This did not amount to an estoppel since the public body would be entitled to go ahead with the intended change of position provided it had heard representations from those affected by the change. However, the doctrine began to take on a substantive character when some judges held that a change of position might not be permitted unless the public body could convince the court that it was in the public interest to make the change: see *R* v *Secretary of State for the Home Department, ex parte Khan* (1985) and *R* v *Secretary of State for the Home Department, ex parte Ruddock* (1987). This doctrine of 'substantive' expectation was very close to a doctrine of estoppel and appeared to conflict with the principle that a public body has no power to fetter the exercise of future discretionary powers by a promise or representation. For this reason some judges felt unable to accept the substantive character of the doctrine, eg see per Laws J in *R* v *Secretary of State for Transport, ex parte Richmond-upon-Thames London Borough Council* (1994).

During the 1970s Lord Denning MR made a number of statements suggesting that a doctrine of promissory estoppel could operate against public bodies on the ground that it was an abuse of power for a public authority to act inconsistently in breach of representations made to individual citizens, eg see *Laker Airways* v *Department of Trade* (1977). These were controversial views because they were contrary to House of Lords precedents, and for this reason were repudiated by Lawton LJ in the *Laker* case. However, Lord Denning was successful in making an inroad into the immunity enjoyed by public bodies from the doctrine of estoppel through the concept of 'ostensible delegated authority'. He explained this concept in *Lever Finance Ltd* v *Westminster (City) London Borough Council* (1971):

> 'There are many matters which public authorities can now delegate to their officers. If an officer acting within the scope of his ostensible authority makes a representation on which another acts, then a public authority may be bound by it.'

This case concerned advice on the need for planning permission given by a council officer to developers, and Lord Denning's approach raised fears that the normal decision-making processes for granting planning permission in permanent form would be circumvented by a well intentioned official offering guidance informally over the telephone to an enquirer. Consequently, the doctrine of 'ostensible delegated authority' was later confined to cases where the applicant could show 'tangible evidence' of a 'formal' delegation of power to the official who had given him the advice in question: *Western Fish Products Ltd* v *Penwith District Council* (1981).

The result is that estoppel in public law is only likely to arise in very specialised circumstances where the representation can be shown to be intra vires the authority making it *and* where it would be an abuse of power and against the public interest to permit the authority to renege upon it. A recent example is *Postermobile plc* v *Brent Lonson Borough Council* (1997) where convictions for developing land without the necessary planning consents were quashed because the developers had approached the planning officers of the local authority for advice and had been told that planning permission would not be required in respect of a number of temporary hoardings. It was held that to prosecute the developers in such circumstances would be an abuse of power, particularly as the case concerned the need for only temporary planning permission (ie one month or less). It was on this ground that *Western Fish* (which had involved the need for permanent planning permission) was distinguished. Hence, limited though it may be, there is still some scope for a doctrine of promissory estoppel in public law.

SUGGESTED ANSWER TO QUESTION SIX

General Comment

The question requires a general overview of the law relating to public bodies and the problems that occur when it undertakes to act in excess of its powers. It is important first of all to establish whether or not they are treated like other bodies, and then to consider whether or not they should be.

Key Points

- Define 'public body'
- Consider the origins of the estoppel concept
- Explain various ways in which problems can arise in relation to public bodies
- Explain position following *Western Fish Products* case
- Consider the growth of the doctrine of legitimate expectation

Suggested Answer

For the purposes of this answer the term 'public body' is taken as encompassing both government departments and public corporations such as local authorities, although the vast majority of cases concerning the problem of estoppel in public law involve local authorities.

The problem of estoppel, as generally understood, arises when one party makes a promise or gives some undertaking, either as to an existing state of affairs or as to future conduct, to another party, and that party acts in reliance on the promise or undertaking. The party making the promise may then be described as being estopped from going back on its promise or undertaking in the sense that the courts have a discretion to hold a party to such promises or undertakings, even though they are not contractual obligations in the strict sense. The doctrine of estoppel is well established within the sphere of private law. The application of the doctrine to public bodies has, however, encountered a number of difficulties.

Consideration needs to be given to how the problem can arise in relation to public bodies. Three examples can be given.

First, there is the situation that arises where a public body promises to take action that it does not have the power to take. For example, a local authority empowered by statute to make repair grants to householders of sums up to a maximum of £1,000, promises to make such an award to a citizen to the value of £2,000. Clearly the local authority has promised to do something that it does not have the power to do. Suppose the citizen then spends his savings on installing central heating in his house, in the belief that he does not need the money for repairs as the local authority has promised to pay for them. Is the local authority now to be estopped from denying the undertaking to pay £2,000, or is the citizen to be denied that which was promised to him?

The second, and more complex, problem arises where an officer of a public body appears to make a decision which the body concerned has the power to make, for example a grant of planning permission, but in reality the officer concerned has no actual authority to make such a decision. Is the public body to be bound by the unauthorised action of its officer, or is the developer forced to lose out financially because he does not, contrary to what he might have been forgiven for thinking, have valid planning permission?

The third situation arises where a public body gives a public undertaking which it has the power to make, through an officer duly authorised to do so, indicating some future policy or practice to be adopted by the public body. Can the public body later renege on its undertaking even though citizens may have relied on it?

As to the first of these situations, the law would appear to be reasonably clear; there can be no acquisition of a power through estoppel. In the example of the repair grant considered above, if the courts were to hold the local authority to its promise to make an award above the statutory maximum, it would be forcing it to act ultra vires. Given that one of the functions of the courts is to ensure that public bodies act within the scope of their powers, it is ridiculous to suggest that an estoppel should be allowed here. In any event, it is generally agreed that estoppel is to be raised as 'a shield not a sword', and in cases such as that posited, the householder would be in the role of plaintiff not defendant. The authorities supporting this argument are *Minister of Agriculture and Fisheries* v *Hulkin* (1948), which was cited with approval in *Minister of Agriculture and Fisheries* v *Matthews* (1950).

As suggested above, the second situation is somewhat problematic, in that a member of the public might be regarded as being entitled to rely on the representations of a public officer who appears to be acting within the scope of his authority. Indeed this was the view adopted by Lord Denning MR in *Lever Finance Ltd* v *Westminster (City) London Borough Council* (1971). In that case planning permission had been granted to developers to build houses. On the approved plans the new buildings were shown as being 40 feet away from existing dwellings. As the work progressed, the council's planning officer agreed to variations in the agreed plan in the course of telephone conversations with the plaintiffs' architects. When the buildings neared completion, local residents complained, and it was found that the new buildings were now only 23 feet away from the nearest dwellings. The council invited the plaintiffs to apply again for planning permission to cover the new development. Planning permission was refused. The plaintiffs argued successfully that the council was estopped from denying the existence of valid planning permission. Denning accepted that the plaintiffs were justified in believing that the planning officer had the authority to grant valid planning permission, on the basis of the previous course of dealings between the parties. Moreover, his Lordship thought it outrageous that a member of the public should be unable to rely on the statements of a council officer acting within the scope of his ostensible authority.

This decision should now be considered in the light of the subsequent Court of Appeal decision in *Western Fish Products Ltd* v *Penwith District Council* (1981). Megaw LJ held that a public body could not be estopped from performing its statutory duties, or exercising its statutory powers in the public interest, because of the unauthorised representations of one of its officers, except in two situations.

The first exception arose where a public body waived a technical procedural requirement. Provided third parties were not prejudiced thereby, a public body could not later raise the failure to comply with the technical requirement as a ground of invalidity.

Secondly, an estoppel might arise where an individual acted in reliance upon a decision of an officer, which was within the scope of his ostensible authority, where there was evidence over and above the mere holding of the office to suggest that the officer could so bind the public body concerned. Arguably, the decision in *Lever Finance* is reconcilable with this latter exception, in that the previous course of dealing between the architects and the planning officer provided the evidence upon which the estoppel was justified.

Generally, the decision in *Western Fish* is seen as a return to the principles enunciated in *Southend-on-Sea Corporation* v *Hodgson (Wickford) Ltd* (1962). The result is that estoppel in public law is only likely to arise in very specialised circumstances; indeed the dearth of reported cases since *Western Fish* rather supports this view. A rare recent example is *Postermobile plc* v *Brent London Borough Council* (1997) where developers had approached planning officers on the need for temporary planning permission (one month or less) and had been told they did not need it. After the development they were prosecuted by the council for not obtaining temporary planning consent. They were convicted but the convictions were quashed on the ground that the prosecutions were an abuse of process.

The third situation is one where the courts have been more inclined to hold public bodies to their public undertakings. The extent to which these situations fall squarely within the definition of estoppel as understood by lawyers is perhaps questionable. In *Attorney-General of Hong Kong* v *Ng Yuen Shiu* (1983) the Privy Council held that the immigration authorities in Hong Kong were bound to comply with their public statement , which was to the effect that if illegal immigrants made themselves known to the authorities each case would be considered on its merits. Hence when the applicant presented himself to the authorities and was summarily recommended for deportation, the Privy Council held that the immigration authorities had acted ultra vires. Although this can be seen as a situation where the immigration authorities were estopped from going back on their statement, it can also be seen as a decision on natural justice, in that the public statement gave rise to a legitimate expectation on the part of the applicant that his case would be considered on its merits.

The decision may be regarded as an example of 'procedural legitimate expectation' because the applicant was only entitled to a fair hearing before the public statement could be changed. Yet there are decisions which have gone further by holding that representations by public bodies cannot be changed at all unless it is clearly in the public interest to do so, provided that the representations are intra vires the authority making them: *R* v *Secretary of State for the Home Department, ex parte Khan* (1984) and *R* v *Secretary of State for the Home Department, ex parte Ruddock* (1987). These cases involved fundamental human rights, and the application of a doctrine of 'substantive legitimate expectation' (closely resembling estoppel in effect) was said to be justified in such exceptional circumstances.

Although controversy continues over this line of authority, it may be concluded that the doctrine of estoppel can operate to bind a public body to a promise provided the promise itself is intra vires. An ultra vires promise cannot be binding because it would be against the public interest to treat it as such. Subject to that qualification, estoppel has been successfully imported from private law to public law, though probably subsumed today under the developing doctrine of 'substantive legitimate expectation'.

SUGGESTED ANSWER TO QUESTION SEVEN

General Comment

This question requires consideration of the extent to which estoppel has been permitted in English administrative law. Do the English courts favour the equitable principle of doing justice in hard cases, or are they more concerned with preserving the foundations of administrative law theory? Would the application of English law assist the Katawian Minister?

Key Points

- English law objections to estoppel in administrative law
- The application of those objections to discretionary powers
- Ostensible authority
- Legitimate expectations

Suggested Answer

Recourse to the English common law may not be of great assistance to the Katawian Minister of Justice as a means of persuading the Katawian Supreme Court to take a more liberal approach to the question of estoppel. Indeed, the English courts have themselves taken a very restrictive view of the application of estoppel to the decisions of government agencies. The objections made by the English common law are somewhat different to those apparently raised by the Katawian Supreme Court. Since English law is only persuasive in Katawi, it is hoped that the Katawian Supreme Court might be able to develop their own jurisprudence on this subject, and gradually to depart from the rigid view taken at the moment.

In English administrative law the application of estoppel to the actions of government bodies is very rare, although there are limited examples. The English authorities reveal more than one reason for this. Fundamentally, the English approach does not rest on the desirability of certainty in citizen/government relations, but on the ultra vires doctrine, which is one of the pillars of administrative law. The fundamental objection to estoppel in administrative law is that it would enable authorities to extend their powers beyond the limits assigned by Parliament, or that it would prevent authorities from carrying out their statutory duties. This objection has been expressed in the strongest possible terms. It has even been said by a senior judge that to allow estoppel to bind public authorities would lead to the collapse of the ultra vires doctrine and would enable public officers to extend their powers at will: per Lord Greene MR in *Minister of Agriculture and Fisheries* v *Hulkin* (unreported, but cited in *Minister of Agriculture and Fisheries* v *Mathews* (1950)). A secondary objection is that the operation of estoppel in administrative law would be damaging to the public interest.

It is necessary to distinguish between an authority's public law functions and its actions in private law, since the position is different in both cases. Where public authorities act in their public law capacity, the above objections to the operation of estoppel can readily be grasped. Thus in one case, a planning officer represented to a company that they were permitted to use land for certain purposes. The company spent money in reliance upon that representation and began to use the land for the purposes in question. It was later discovered that the land use was not permitted, and the authority brought enforcement action to prevent that land use. The court held that the authority was not estopped by the representation of the planning officer, since he had no authority to grant planning permission. Had the authority been estopped, the effect would be to give the officer power to act ultra vires, to circumvent the requirements of the planning legislation and to prevent the authority from exercising its statutory powers in planning matters: see *Western Fish Products Ltd* v *Penwith District Council* (1981). Reference to the planning legislation reveals the public interest objection to estoppel that appeared in this case. One of the requirements of that legislation is that members of the public are given an opportunity to object to any application for planning permission. If estoppel operated in such a case, the effect would be to grant planning permission without observing that requirement, and that would be harmful to the public at large.

It is hard to justify the injustice caused to a company or to an individual in such circumstances, even by reference to the interests of the public. Even in the context of private law, estoppel is comparatively rare, and there is no reason to suppose that it would ever become particularly common in the administrative law context were it allowed to operate. Furthermore, the picture of administrative bodies using estoppel to extend their powers freely is quite grotesque and is a poor justification for failing to do justice to an individual who has suffered a detriment by relying on representations given by authorities. Even if it is accepted that the ultra vires doctrine should be protected and that estoppel should not operate to allow authorities to extend their powers, the approach the court has taken has extended beyond that principle. Estoppel is also precluded in the context of discretionary powers. It is difficult to justify such an approach in the context of discretion as opposed to duty.

There is a limited exception to the rule that government bodies may not be bound by estoppel. Where an officer has ostensible authority to make a representation, the public body may be estopped from departing from that representation. In *Lever Finance Ltd* v *Westminster (City) London Borough Council* (1971), a representation made by a planning officer was later held to bind the planning authority. In this case, the authority had a practice of allowing the officer in question to make certain decisions. Although no formal delegation of powers had taken place, the informal practice of the authority had conferred ostensible authority on the officer to make decisions, and to bind the authority. The decision of the officer was held to be intra vires in this context. The difficulty that this case presents is that it will rarely be possible for an individual to know whether an officer will have such ostensible authority or not. Indeed such officers will nearly always appear to have authority. Given that estoppel has its origins in equity and is designed to prevent injustice occurring when a person relies to his detriment on a representation made by another, it is difficult to justify any distinction between the situation in *Western Fish* and *Lever Finance*. Comparison of these cases also indicates that the public interest objection to estoppel is in reality not particularly strong.

See also the recent case of *Postermobile plc* v *Brent London Borough Council* (1997) where it was held to be an abuse of power for the council to prosecute developers who had erected temporary hoardings after being told that they did not need temporary planning consent (of one month or less). *Western Fish* was distinguished for being concerned with permanent planning permission, but the case indicates that estoppel may have a greater relevance in the context of criminal law than had previously been thought.

One potentially fruitful creation of the English common law that could be extended is the doctrine of legitimate expectations. These are sometimes considered to be a type of estoppel, which they are not. In some circumstances, an authority's representations or promises, or its settled policy, may give rise to a legitimate expectation. Unlike estoppel, such an expectation will not operate to prevent an authority from reversing a promise or departing from its policy, but it will give rise to a duty to give an affected individual the right to be consulted and to make representations about the authority's intentions. Where an authority does not consult the individual concerned, the individual will be able to bring judicial review proceedings: *Attorney-General of Hong Kong* v *Ng Yuen Shiu* (1983). This doctrine could possibly be extended to give greater rights to affected individuals, and might be a way to achieve the same results as an estoppel. Thus, in cases involving fundamental human rights, where judges are prepared to give public law decisions 'anxious scrutiny' there may be a willingness to declare that a representation cannot be reversed or departed from unless it is clearly in the public interest for such reversal or departure to take place: *R v Secretary of State for the Home Department, ex parte Khan* (1984); *R v Secretary of State for the Home Department, ex parte Ruddock* (1987).

It is clear from the above discussion of English administrative law that estoppel will be rare indeed in this context, and that English judges have shown a great deal of resistance to the application of estoppel in administrative law. This is an unsatisfactory situation, since it is clear that individuals must often suffer injustice as a result of this failure to use estoppel to hold administrative bodies to their representations. It is hoped that the Katawian Supreme Court might be persuaded to take a more robust view. If they wish to do so, the doctrine of legitimate expectation may be a convenient starting point for any extension of the common law.

SUGGESTED ANSWER TO QUESTION EIGHT

General Comment

A reasonably straightforward question dealing with abuse of power. It is important to remember that it is a statutory licensing power, so the *Wednesbury* principle is especially relevant. Remember, also, to advise on remedies in each case, albeit briefly.

Key Points

- Introduction – nature of statutory discretion – licensing considerations – *Wednesbury* case – absence of appeal
- Basil – unreasonableness – uncertainty – improper purpose
- Mint – improper policy
- Rice – fiduciary duty – locus standi
- Pepper – unreasonableness – irrelevant considerations – proportionality

Suggested Answer

The statute in question, it should be noted, is one that has been passed to give effect to central government policy, that places of entertainment should be regulated in the interests of safety. This function has been entrusted to local authorities, presumably on the basis that they are the most suitable bodies to judge what is in the interests of their areas.

The statute is notable in that it gives two subjectively worded powers to local authorities. The first, to impose 'such conditions' as it considers fit, and the second that the authority may require the payment of a fee 'as it thinks reasonable'.

Despite the wide language of the statute, it is well established that discretionary powers, especially those related to licensing, are subject to certain implied limitations. The starting point of any consideration of these must be the decision of the Court of Appeal in *Associated Provincial Picture Houses Ltd* v *Wednesbury Corporation* (1948).

Here the court was considering a statutory discretionary power to impose conditions upon cinema licences when granted. The Court of Appeal upheld the validity of a condition stating that no child should be admitted under the age of 15. Lord Greene said that the decision to impose such a condition may be one about which reasonable people may disagree, but it was not so unreasonable that no reasonable authority would have imposed it, and that is the basic test to be applied to the facts of this question.

More generally, Lord Greene pointed out that a licensing body's exercise of discretion could be challenged on the grounds that it was wrong in law, based on irrelevant considerations, failed to take account of relevant considerations, was based on bad faith, or failed to comply with the aims and objects of the enabling Act.

It should be noted that the Court of Appeal considered the absence of any statutory right of appeal against the decision to be of significance in deciding whether or not to interfere with the licensing body's decision.

Consideration will now be given, in the light of the foregoing, to the individual cases raised by the question.

a *Basil*

i   The condition that Basil is to prevent the use of illegal drugs on his premises could be struck down on a number of grounds. The strongest argument would be that Mace DC have taken into account an irrelevant consideration in imposing the condition. Whilst their concern at the use of drugs may be laudable, it may well be improper to try and control their use by means of licence conditions.

The condition would be regarded as unnecessary as it would be an offence for Basil to permit the use of illegal drugs on his premises. Further, the condition would be challenged on grounds of uncertainty over the meaning of words such as 'prevent', 'use' and 'illegal drugs'; would this include 'glue sniffing' for example? See *Nash* v *Finlay* (1901) as an example of challenge on grounds of uncertainty.

ii The condition prohibiting persons under the age of 16, with or without an adult may be valid in the light of the *Wednesbury* decision. Basil could attempt to challenge the condition on the ground that it goes too far in not allowing children to be admitted even when accompanied by an adult, but that does not necessarily mean that the condition is so unreasonable, no reasonable authority would have imposed it. Perhaps a better line of argument would be that Mace DC have failed to produce any evidence to substantiate the imposition of the condition.

The fact that the Act does not provide for an appeal may be a factor that sways the court to intervene.

Basil should challenge the conditions by applying for judicial review of Mace DC's actions.

b *Rice*

Rice could challenge the failure of Sage DC to increase the fee payable on the ground that they have a discretionary power to charge 'such fees as they think reasonable' and in continuing to charge £5 they are ignoring the aims and objects of the legislation, and the interests of its council tax payers.

The previous fee was fixed by statute, the new fee is at the discretion of each authority. Parliament must have provided this power to raise revenue for a purpose. Sage DC are failing to take this factor into account.

Following *Prescott* v *Birmingham Corporation* (1955), Rice might argue that Sage DC, in continuing to charge only £5 for each application are not paying sufficient regard to the fiduciary duty owed to council tax payers. Rice's case would be strengthened if he could show as in *Attorney-General* v *Fulham Corporation* (1921) that the service provided by the local authority at council taxes currently charged, was hopelessly unremunerative.

As a council tax payer Rice could have 'sufficient interest' to apply for judicial review of the local authority's actions, possibly requesting an order of mandamus, requiring the local authority to exercise their discretion in accordance with the law.

c   *Mint*

Mint could challenge the legality of what amounts to a policy adopted by Clove DC as to the fee to be charged for applications. Discretion is supposed to be properly exercised in regard to each application. The courts have accepted, however, that in some cases a policy may be adopted as to how a discretion has to be exercised, as an aid to consistency, and to speed up the handling of numerous applications – see *British Oxygen Co Ltd* v *Minister of Technology* (1971).

The two vital questions to ask are:

i   is the policy a reasonable one, based on proper con-siderations?
ii   has the body adopting the policy still allowed anyone with something new to say the opportunity of explaining why the policy should not be adopted in their case? See *R* v *Port of London Authority, ex parte Kynoch Ltd* (1919).

Although Clove DC seemed to have based their decision to charge £500 on sensible considerations, any inflexibility on their part may invalidate it.

On being charged £500 Mint could apply for judicial review to challenge the legality of the authority's actions.

d   *Pepper*

Depending on the size of his premises Pepper could argue that the £2,500 fee was 'manifestly unreasonable': see *Backhouse* v *Lambeth London Borough Council* (1972).

Alternatively, Pepper might argue that Salt DC are using their power to impose fees for an ulterior purpose – see *Congreve* v *Home Office* (1976). This would depend upon whether the purpose of the Act was for local authorities to recover the cost of inspection and licensing through the imposition of fees or not.

Thirdly, Pepper might try to introduce an argument based on 'proportionality' ie. that the fee charged is out of all proportion to the size of his premises – see *R* v *Barnsley Metropolitan Borough Council, ex parte Hook* (1976). The problem with this approach would be that Salt DC have themselves used the proportionality approach to determine the fees payable.

Pepper should challenge the £2,500 fee by way of an application for judicial review.

SUGGESTED ANSWER TO QUESTION NINE

General Comment

A complex question, underlining the need to separate the issues involved and deal with them individually. It is important to bear in mind that whilst Melvyn is the 'wronged' party, the question does require advice to be given to WRITE.

Key Points

a • Locus standi
  - definition of sufficient interest
  - status of pressure groups – the *Greenpeace* case
b • Grounds for review
  - legitimate expectation
  - breach of natural justice
  - duty to give reasons
  - real danger of bias
  - fettering by policy

Suggested Answer

a The Arts Committee of the local authority, as a public body, would be amenable to judicial review, and as the case involves issues of public law, WRITE will have to proceed by way of an application for judicial review if it wishes to challenge the legality of the committee's actions; see *O'Reilly* v *Mackman* (1983).

Applicants for review must establish that they have 'sufficient interest' in the matter to which the application relates. The guiding authority on this point is the House of Lords' decision in *IRC* v *National Federation of Self Employed and Small Businesses* (1982) (the 'NFSSB case'). That decision makes it clear that locus standi is a mixed question of fact and law which arises at two stages in the proceedings. An applicant for review must first obtain leave to apply, a requirement that acts as a sort of filter to weed out the clearly untenable case. The existence of standing will first be considered at this point; if the applicant appears to have an 'arguable case' then the case should proceed to the full hearing of the application for review. The question of locus standi is reconsidered at the full hearing in the light of the arguments put forward there. Their Lordships emphasised that locus standi was not to be looked at as a threshold requirement, but instead was to be regarded as closely linked to the merits of the applicant's case. The stronger the evidence of illegality, the more likely that the reviewing court would find that the applicant possessed locus standi.

Were Melvyn himself to be applying for review there would be, it is submitted, little doubt that he possessed locus standi to challenge the committee's decision. It is more difficult to state with any certainty whether a pressure group or interested organisation will be found by the reviewing court to have locus standi. The answer will depend on the 'nexus' between the group and the decision being challenged, and on the remedy being sought. Recent decisions indicate that the locus standi requirements might be more relaxed were WRITE to apply for a declaration that the committee had acted illegally, than if it were to seek an order of mandamus to compel the committee to act in accordance with law; see *R v Felixstowe Justices, ex parte Leigh* (1987).

As regards 'nexus', the courts will look at the extent and closeness of the links between WRITE and the person affected by the decision, Melvyn. The outcome really depends on the outcome of each case. In *R v Chief Adjudication Officer, ex parte Bland* (1985), the court held that the National Union of Mineworkers had sufficient interest to challenge a decision concerning the payment of welfare benefit to one of its members, but the Trades Union Congress did not because its interests were too remote in the matter. In *R v Inspectorate of Pollution, ex parte Greenpeace Ltd (No 2)* (1994) the pressure group Greenpeace was granted standing to challenge the legality of nuclear waste disposal in Cumbria because it had many supporters living in the region affected by the disposal and could mount a better argued challenge than any indifidual supporter.

It is submitted that WRITE have a strong claim in respect of locus standi, especially in the light of the fact that the group exists for a very specific purpose, which is relevant in this case. WRITE's case might be more compelling were Melvyn to be a member, but this should not be seen as a reason for refusing to allow the application to proceed to a full hearing.

b   Assuming WRITE is granted leave to apply for review, the next consideration is whether there has been any breach of the principles of judicial review. Has the committee acted illegally, irrationally, or unfairly?

WRITE may argue that the committee acted in breach of natural justice in refusing Melvyn a grant without first granting him a hearing. It should be noted however that this is not a 'revocation' case, as discussed by Megarry J in *McInnes v Onslow-Fane* (1978). Melvyn applies annually for his grant, and the fact that his application has been successful in every year for the last five years perhaps creates a legitimate expectation on his part, either that his application will be successful this year or, as seems more likely, that he will at least be consulted before a decision to refuse his application is taken. It is submitted that this previous course of dealings between the parties entitles Melvyn to more than an unreasoned rejection: see *Council of Civil Service Unions v Minister for the Civil Service* (1985).

Even if the absence of any hearing does not amount to unfairness, the failure to give reasons may well do so. Assuming that the committee is not a body listed in the Tribunals and Inquiries Act 1992, and is not under a statutory duty to give reasons, the matter falls to be considered at common law.

A right to be heard frequently carries with it a duty to give reasons, hence a 'mere applicant' has no right to be told why he has been unsuccessful: see *McInnes v Onslow-Fane* (above). Regardless of whether Melvyn was entitled to reasons by virtue of natural justice, the courts may be willing to infer that a failure to give reasons for a decision suggests that there are no good reasons for the decision: see *Padfield v Minister of Agriculture* (1968).

WRITE could contend that the committee's decision is vitiated by the chairman's bias against non-rhyming poetry. it would have to be established that there was a real danger of bias on the part of the chairman: see *R v Secretary of State for the Environment, ex parte Kirkstall Valley Campaign Ltd* (1996).

A further ground of challenge might be that the committee has fettered its discretion by the adoption of an over-rigid policy against non-rhyming poetry. Not only could the policy itself be challenged on the basis that it is irrational, but also on the basis that it has been applied without any willingness to consider exceptional applicants who might have something new to say: see *R v Secretary of State for the Environment, ex parte Brent London Borough Council* (1982).

In conclusion, WRITE would be advised to apply for an order of certiorari to quash the committee's decision, or at least a declaration that the chairman is not fit to serve on the committee.

SUGGESTED ANSWER TO QUESTION TEN

General Comment

The question involves consideration of ouster clauses, fettering discretion by adoption of an over-rigid policy, and general principles of review.

Key Points

- Judicial attitudes to finality clauses andouster clauses – the *Anisminic* principle and *Re Racal*
- Locus standi of pressure groups
- Grounds for review – fettering by policy – bias – total unreasonableness – no evidence to support decision

Suggested Answer

The initial difficulty confronting GAG is the fact that the Act states that the decisions of the authority are 'final and conclusive and shall not be called into question in any court of law'. If this 'ouster clause' is given effect by the courts then there is obviously no prospect of an application for judicial review being allowed to proceed. The judiciary have, however, shown great ingenuity in interpreting such provisions so as to greatly reduce their effectiveness in denying litigants access to the courts.

A statutory provision to the effect that a decision is 'final' will be interpreted by the reviewing court as meaning final on the facts; see *R v Medical Appeal Tribunal, ex parte Gilmore* (1957). It does not prevent judicial review, which in any event is concerned with the legality of the decision, not its merits.

A provision to the effect that a decision is not to be questioned in any court of law is rather more complex. The House of Lords considered a similarly worded provision of the Foreign Compensation Act 1950, in *Anisminic Ltd v Foreign Compensation Commission* (1969). A majority of their Lordships concluded that the provision only protected a valid, or intra vires decision, not one based upon an error by the decision-making body as to the extent of its jurisdiction. Where, therefore, a body made an error of law going to jurisdiction, its decision would be ultra vires (ie invalid) and thus not protected by the ouster clause. Clearly GAG will have to contend that the local authority in this case has made an error of law (misinterpretation of its enabling Act) which has led it to wrongly decline to exercise its jurisdiction. The difficulty lies, however, in determining whether such errors go to jurisdiction or not. Lord Denning in *Pearlman* v *Keepers and Governors of Harrow School* (1979) went so far as to suggest that no inferior body had the power to make an error as to its jurisdiction and that as a result, all such errors must go to jurisdiction. Some guidance in the matter is provided by Lord Diplock in *Re Racal Communications* (1981). His Lordship stated that as far as administrative authorities were concerned, any error of law made in the course of reaching a decision on matters of fact or administrative policy would result in the decision being invalid. To this extent, the view supports the earlier statement of Lord Denning, but Lord Diplock stressed that the same rationale could not be employed in the case of inferior courts which, unlike administrative bodies, possessed some expertise in law. The result is that the courts will not permit ouster clauses to prevent them from dealing with significant errors of law made by administrative agencies. On this basis GAG should be advised that it is likely to be able to circumvent the ouster clause in this case, the local authority undoubtedly falling within what Lord Diplock would have termed 'administrative agencies'.

When applying for leave to apply for judicial review GAG will have to show that it has locus standi or sufficient interest in the matter to which the application relates. On the basis that it is the Gay Action Group, and the local authority has declared that it will never make grants to such groups, it is submitted that GAG should be able to make out a sufficient 'nexus' between itself and the legal issues arising: see *R* v *Secretary of State for Social Services, ex parte Child Poverty Action Group and Greater London Council* (1985).

Under the Act the local authority has a discretion to award grants of up to £1000. In deciding how that discretion is to be exercised, the authority is at liberty to adopt policies provided these do not amount to an unlawful fetter on its discretion. On the basis of Bankes LJ's famous dictum in *R* v *Port of London Authority, ex parte Kynoch Ltd* (1919) the authority should, despite its stated policy, be prepared to listen to any applicant who might have something new to say. The courts will intervene where the evidence suggests that an authority has simply 'shut its ears' and refused to consider an applicant because of its policy. Where the exercise of discretion involves the distribution of public money to applicants the courts recognise that a high number of cases may have to be dealt with, in which case a policy is all the more necessary, but nevertheless the authority must still be willing to listen to someone with something to say: see *British Oxygen Co Ltd* v *Minister of Technology* (1971).

There is a link to be made here also with natural justice and the duty to act fairly. GAG may be a 'mere applicant' for an award, to use the terminology of *McInnes* v *Onslow-Fane* (1978), but it is nevertheless entitled to have its application considered properly without bias or caprice. The connection between the over-rigid application of policy and denial of natural justice is made apparent in *R* v *Secretary of State for the*

Environment, ex parte Brent London Borough Council (1982)., where the minister, in not considering representations on his reduction of the rate support grant as a matter of policy, had denied the local authorities a fair hearing on a matter that affected them directly.

Even if it could be said that consideration had been given to GAG's application, the policy of the authority in not awarding grants to such bodies could still be attacked on the basis that it is irrational, and ignores the aims and objects of the legislation. The policy might be viewed as unreasonable in the sense that no reasonable local authority would adopt it; see *Associated Provincial Picture Houses Ltd* v *Wednesbury Corporation* (1948); alternatively it could be viewed as irrational in that there is no evidence to support it; see *Secretary of State for Education and Science* v *Tameside Metropolitan Borough Council* (1977).

The appropriate remedies in this case would be an order of certiorari to quash the refusal of a grant or a declaration to the effect that the policies are unlawful.

SUGGESTED ANSWER TO QUESTION ELEVEN

General Comment

Two main issues to consider here. Firstly the question of locus standi should be considered in some depth. Secondly the relevance of anti-Iraq policies to the exercise of a local authority's discretion should be considered in the light of relevant case law on this point.

Key Points

*   Locus standi of Ernest: status of pressure groups and council tax payers
*   Grounds for review – irrelevant considerations and improper purposes – analogous cases – *Wheeler* and *ex parte Shell UK Ltd*

Suggested Answer

Since Consciencester, as a local authority, is a public body, and the issue arising is one of public law, Ernest would be required to proceed by way of an application for judicial review in order to challenge the legality of the award of the contract in question to Dear by Consciencester: see *O'Reilly* v *Mackman* (1983). This being the case, the question of locus standi then arises.

Under RSC O.53 r3(7), the court will not grant Ernest leave to apply for judicial review unless he can establish that he has, 'sufficient interest in the matter to which the application relates.' The leading authority on the meaning of this provision is the House of Lords' decision in *IRC* v *National Federation of Self Employed and Small Businesses* (1982). Lord Wilberforce pointed out that the change in the locus standi requirement from 'person aggrieved' to 'sufficient interest' had not removed the question entirely to the sphere of judicial discretion, neither should it be assumed, that because the same wording was used to describe the locus standi requirement for each remedy, that it would be applied in the same way for each remedy.

Subsequent decisions indicate that the courts have adopted a liberal approach to locus standi. In *R v IBA, ex parte Whitehouse* (1985), for example, the applicant was held to have locus standi to challenge the decision of the Independent Broadcasting Authority to show the film 'Scum', on the basis that she was the holder of a television licence. In *R v HM Treasury, ex parte Smedley* (1985), the applicant was regarded as having locus standi to challenge the validity of payments to the European Community by the government, on the basis that he was a taxpayer.

The position of pressure groups such as 'Go-to-Iraq' has always been more problematic. It is really a mixed question of fact and law in each case whether there is a sufficient nexus between the applicant pressure group and the public body concerned. In *R v Secretary of State for Social Services, ex parte Child Poverty Action Group and Greater London Council* (1985), the court held that the CPAG did have locus standi to challenge the refusal of the minister to reopen old case files to discover if applicants for welfare benefits had been underpaid in the past. The GLC was held not to have sufficient interest in relation to the same application, however, because it had no express or implied status to represent welfare claimants, neither was it entitled to adopt the mantle of guardian of the public interest. On this basis, it should be noted that the sole purpose of 'Go-to-Iraq' appears to be the promotion of travel to Iraq, and as such its position is closer to that of the CPAG in the above case, rather than the GLC.

Hence Ernest may be granted a standing in his capacity as chairman of 'Go-to-Iraq'. He would probably be refused standing in his capacity as a council tax payer since he lives in a different local authority area.

On the basis of *R v Felixstowe Justices, ex parte Leigh* (1987) it is submitted that Ernest might be well advised to apply for a declaration as to the decision's illegality, as it would appear that the locus standi requirements in respect of this remedy are more easily satisfied than the requirements of the prerogative orders such as mandamus. In that case a journalist, who sought to challenge the refusal of justices to provide their names and addresses to the press, was held not to have sufficient locus standi for an order of mandamus directing the justices to provide such information, because he was not a party to the litigation. He was held, however, to have sufficient interest to apply for a declaration that the justices' policy of maintaining anonymity was unlawful, as this was a point of general constitutional significance.

Turning to the question of the grounds for the challenge, Ernest would be advised to challenge the local authority's decision on the ground that it is based on irrelevant considerations and an improper use of its contracting powers, and that it is in breach of the fiduciary duty owed to council tax payers by Consciencester.

Ernest's foremost ground of challenge will be that Consciencester has based its decision to award the contract to Dear on an irrelevant consideration, its opposition to Saddam Hussein. A similar issue came before the House of Lords in *Wheeler v Leicester City Council* (1985). Leicester City Council resolved to withdraw sporting facilities from a local rugby club, a number of whose players had chosen to tour South Africa (at that time an apartheid country) as members of a touring side having no connection with the local club. The local authority relied upon its duty, under s71 of the Race Relations Act 1976, to promote good race relations within its area, as justifying its decision to withdraw facilities from the club. The House of Lords held that this had been an improper use of discretion by the local authority, as it had effectively punished the club for something that it was not within its own power to control, and something that was not of itself unlawful, ie club members playing as private individuals in South Africa.

Similarly, in the present case, Ernest could contend that Business cannot prevent Alan from playing in Iraq, and indeed it is not unlawful under English law for him to do so, and that therefore Consciencester is abusing its contracting power by using it to 'punish' Business in relation to a matter beyond its control. This submission is subject to the counter argument that non-renewal of a contract cannot amount to a punishment as such, but it may be that Business had a legitimate expectation of the contract being renewed: see *McInnes* v *Onslow-Fane* (1978).

The contract with Dear is significantly more expensive than that previously held with Business. Ernest may be able to contend that the local authority has given too much emphasis to its anti-Iraq policy at the expense of its fiduciary duty to council tax payers in obtaining good value for money in its commercial dealings. The matter was considered in *R* v *London Borough of Lewisham, ex parte Shell UK Ltd* (1988). Lewisham LBC approved a resolution that stated, inter alia, that it would boycott the products of Shell UK Ltd because of that company's trading links with South Africa, provided alternative products were available at reasonable prices. The company applied for judicial review seeking a declaration that the resolution, and the campaign waged by the authority to dissuade other local authorities from using the company's products, were ultra vires, orders of certiorari to quash the resolution, and an injunction to stop the authority from implementing the resolution. Despite its reliance on s71 of the Race Relations Act 1976, the court held that the local authority could not use its contracting power to punish a company in relation to activity which was not prohibited by English law. The authority's decision could not be attacked on the basis of *Wednesbury* unreasonableness, as it was for the authority itself to determine what would promote better race relations within its own borough, but it was apparent that the council had been motivated by a dominant, ulterior motive, namely to dissuade the company from trading in South Africa, and this rendered the resolution ultra vires. Consequently, the campaign to persuade other councils from trading with the company was also ultra vires.

On this basis it is submitted that if there is evidence that the purpose behind the decision is to pressurise Business into prohibiting its employees from travelling to Iraq then the decision may be questionable. An important distinction between the Lewisham case and that under consideration is that Lewisham LBC resolved to boycott products of companies having links with South Africa only where reasonably priced alternatives were available. Consciencester on the other hand seems to be prepared to spend considerably more council taxes in the pursuit of its ideological aims. The courts recognise that administrators are frequently involved in the difficult task of balancing one set of considerations against another. It is submitted that judicial review should not be granted unless there is evidence that the decision-making body has carried out the 'balancing act' unreasonably, but in this case failure to have sufficient regard to the interests of council tax payers may be fatal to the legality of Consciencester's decision.

SUGGESTED ANSWER TO QUESTION TWELVE

General Comment

This problem raises the issue of the use of licensing powers by authorities. How far must an applicant comply with statutory procedures? When will legitimate expectations arise? May a council use its powers for philanthropic purposes? To what extent will an authority be bound by the advice of its employees?

Key Points

Dodgem
- Advice not binding
- Mandatory statutory requirement

Tombola
- Legitimate expectation
- Existing licensee
- Promise
- Misplaced philanthropy

Suggested Answer

My advice to Dodgem is that he has little chance of bringing proceedings against the council. The conditions imposed by the statute are expressed to be mandatory. Subject to the possibility of challenging the authority's interpretation of the word 'newspaper', Dodgem has not complied with the statutory requirements. Although it may seem unfair that, in the circumstances, he has followed the advice of a council employee, only to be refused a licence, as a general principle an authority is not bound by the advice of its employees. Although the Court of Appeal allowed an applicant to rely upon what he has been told by an officer of a council in *Lever Finance Ltd* v *Westminster (City) London Borough Council* (1971) that case was founded upon the ostensible authority of the officer concerned. Dodgem was advised by a receptionist, and would not be able to claim ostensible authority, a fortiori since the grant of a licence to operate a funfair is subject to strict statutory procedures.

The only case Dodgem may have is that the requirement to advertise in a local newspaper has been substantially observed. By analogy with the cases involving procedures to be observed by public authorities, where procedural requirements are mandatory as opposed to directory they will be construed strictly. In this case the newspaper requirement is expressed in mandatory form. Further, it appears in a statute whose object is the preservation of health and safety, and is thus likely to be construed strictly against Dodgem, and a church magazine is not a newspaper.

Tombola's position is somewhat stronger. His first point of challenge will be that he has a legitimate expectation arising from the fact that he is an existing licence holder: *McInnes* v *Onslow-Fane* (1978). It may also be possible for him to claim a legitimate expectation based upon the express promise of the authority and the fact that he has gone to considerable expense to comply with the safety standards (cf *Council of Civil*

Service Unions v *Minister for the Civil Service* (1985)) although it is doubtful how far a pre-election promise as opposed to a promise by an existing authority can give rise to a legitimate expectation. If Tombola does have a legitimate expectation, then he may be able to challenge the decision on the basis of a breach of natural justice, because the authority should have consulted him before making its decision to impose the condition on the grant of his licence.

A stronger claim on Dodgem's part will be that the condition is unlawful because it is imposed for the wrong purpose. The purpose of the licensing statute is clearly to enhance safety at funfairs, but the council is seeking to use it in a philanthropic manner. It is clear from *Prescott* v *Birmingham Corporation* (1955) that 'misplaced philanthropy' will render a decision by a council unlawful, where the purpose of a power is not philanthropic.

My advice would therefore be that Dodgem does not have strong grounds for complaint. On the face of it he has failed to comply with a mandatory statutory obligation, even though such non-compliance is not his fault. Tombola on the other hand does have grounds for action; he may have a legitimate expectation, and the council's action amounts to an abuse of its powers.

10

The Parliamentary Commissioner for Administration

Introduction

This chapter is concerned with the powers of the Parliamentary Commissioner for Administration (the Ombudsman), and with the impact of this institution on English administrative law since its creation in 1967. In order to assess this impact it is useful to consider the operation of other Ombudsmen-type institutions that exist in the public law, such as the Health Service Commissioner (created in 1973) and the Local Government Commissioners (created in 1974). One of the main themes of this chapter will be the effectiveness of these ombudsmen compared to judicial review as devices for controlling the manner in which public powers are exercised.

Much of the study in this chapter is concerned with the adequacy of the statutory framework under which the ombudsmen operate and with examples of their work. Students need to understand the jurisdiction and powers of the ombudsmen and in particular why the Parliamentary Ombudsman can only be approached through a Member of Parliament. The constitutional relationship between the Parliamentary Ombudsman and MPs is therefore of significance when assessing the effectiveness of the institution.

There is very little case law on the ombudsmen, though one case stands out in establishing that the Parliamentary Ombudsman is subject to judicial review like any other public institution if he exceeds his jurisdiction: *R v Parliamentary Commissioner for Administration, ex parte Dyer* [1994] 1 All ER 375.

However, there are many articles in the law journals which contain critical analysis of, and useful research into, the work of the ombudsmen, notably by Drewry and Harlow (1990) 53 MLR 745, Bradley [1995] PL 345, Clothier [1996] PL 384 and Lord Woolf [1996] NLJ 1701.

In regard to examinations it is reasonable to anticipate at least one essay-type on the work of ombudsmen in a typical examination paper. Usually such a question demands a critical analysis of the impact of the ombudsmen in promoting good government and of the contrasting values of ombudsmen and the courts. It is useful to illustrate the work of the Parliamentary Commissioner by reference to notable investigations such as those into the Sachsenhausen Concentration Camp Affair (1969), the Court Line Holiday Company Collapse (1975) and the Barlow Clowes Affair (1989). Note also reform proposals made by Sir Cecil Clothier, the retiring Parliamentary Ombudsman in 1986: [1986] PL 204.

Questions

INTERROGRAMS

1   Outline the jurisdiction of the Parliamentary Commissioner for Administration.
2   Outline the investigatory powers of the Parliamentary Ombudsman.
3   What is the definition of maladministration?
4   Are ombudsmen merely cheap substitutes for the courts?

QUESTION ONE

Compare and contrast the various ombudsmen within the United Kingdom.

London University LLB Examination
(for external students) Administrative Law June 1989 Q5

QUESTION TWO

'The work of the Parliamentary Commissioner is central to the administrative and political process. Administrative law, however comprehensive and efficient, can never be more than a valuable adjunct to that process.'
   Discuss.

London University LLB Examination
(for external students) Administrative Law June 1985 Q8

QUESTION THREE

It has been suggested

a   that the British ombudsmen should be able to undertake investigations on their own initiative; and
b   that their decisions should be enforceable in the courts.

   Consider the arguments for and against these suggestions.

London University LLB Examination
(for external students) Administrative Law June 1986 Q3

QUESTION FOUR

To what extent are ombudsmen and judges duplicating one another in looking for the same administrative mistakes?

London University LLB Examination
(for external students) Administrative Law June 1988 Q2

QUESTION FIVE

'Ombudsmen are of only marginal relevance to the main concerns of administrative law'.
  Discuss.

London University LLB Examination
(for external students) Administrative Law June 1991 Q5

Answers

ANSWERS TO INTERROGRAMS

1   Section 5(1) of the Parliamentary Commissioner Act 1967 gives the Parliamentary
    Ombudsman power to investigate 'action taken by … a government department … in
    the exercise of administration functions … in any case where … a member of the
    public … claims to have sustained injustice in consequence of maladministration in
    connection with the action so taken'. Schedule 3 to the 1967 Act excludes from his
    jurisdiction the following matters: foreign affairs, extradition, crime, passports, the
    prerogative of mercy, the granting of honours, legal proceedings generally, the
    contractual and commercial undertakings of the Crown, personnel matters arising
    within the civil service or armed forces, Crown appointments generally, and any
    matter on which the citizen has a remedy in the courts which it is reasonable to take.
        The Parliamentary and Health Service Commissioners Act 1987 extended the
    jurisdiction of the Parliamentary Ombudsman to cover about 50 non-departmental
    public bodies such as the Welsh Development Agency, the British Library and
    Industrial Training Boards. The Parliamentary Commissioner Act 1994 further
    extended his jurisdiction to cover, inter alia, the general work of social security,
    disability and medical tribunals and the Child Support Agency Appeal Tribunal.
2   The Parliamentary Commissioner has a right of access to all the files of the body
    under investigation. He may examine civil servants and ministers, and can refer a
    refusal to give evidence to the High Court as a punishable contempt of court. He
    alone decides whether to begin an investigation following a referral of a complaint by
    an MP. And he alone decides whether to continue or discontinue the investigation:
    Re Fletcher's Application [1970] 2 All ER 527. The Parliamentary Ombudsman has no
    power to enforce his findings, but he can make a report on the affair, copies of
    which are sent to the MP who referred the complaint and to a select committee of
    the House of Commons, which may refer that report for debate in the whole House if
    it thinks fit.
3   Section 12(3) of the Parliamentary Commissioner Act 1967 provides that 'nothing in
    this Act authorises or requires the Commissioner to question the merits of a decision
    taken without maladministration …'. Although there is no statutory definition of
    maladministration, the generally accepted definition has become that given by
    Richard Crossman during the debates on the passage of the 1967 legislation: 'bias,
    neglect, inattention, delay, incompetence, ineptitude, perversity, turpitude,
    arbitrariness, and so on'. It is not an exhaustive list because the final three words
    clearly invite holders of the office of Parliamentary Commissioner to adopt a liberal

approach by treating analogous kinds of poor decision-making as within the definition.

4   That the ombudsmen are not mere cheap substitutes for the courts is demonstrated by the provision in Schedule 3 to the 1967 Act which prevents the Parliamentary Ombudsman from investigating complaints where there is a reasonable right of access to a reasonable remedy before a court. (The constraint also applies to the Health Service Commissioner and Local Government Commissioners.)

Whereas the role of the courts is adjudicatory, the ombudsman's role is investigatory and much more informal, allowing him to 'go behind the scenes' to examine departmental files and question officials. Whereas judicial review is confined to ultra vires decision-making, maladministration is a much more political concept denoting a poor quality of decision-making which, whilst not unlawful, has nevertheless caused injustice. Further, whilst judicial remedies are fairly rigid in the form of damages, injunctions and orders of certiorari, the recommendations of the ombudsman take the form of skilled mediation between the administration and the citizen which may help to produce a satisfactory compromise solution to conflicting requirements of bureaucracy and accountability.

SUGGESTED ANSWER TO QUESTION ONE

General Comment

A straightforward question which requires an outline and analysis of the functions performed by the various commissioners for administration in the United Kingdom. Since it would be impossible in examination conditions to examine all of them, it is suggested that attention should be concentrated on the oldest public service ombudsmen.

Key Points

- Ombudsmen in general
- Parliamentary Commissioner, his jurisdiction and powers
- The operation of ministerial responsibility
- Northern Ireland Commissioners, their jurisdiction and powers
- Health Service Commissioner, jurisdiction and powers
- Commissioners for Local Administration, their jurisdiction and powers
- The problem of a lack of mechanism equivalent to ministerial responsibility at the local level

Suggested Answer

The concept of an independent officer or ombudsman to investigate complaints against the administration originated in Scandinavia. Ombudsmen can, however, be found in a wide variety of countries and, although their appointment in the United Kingdom is a comparatively recent development, they can now be found at the national, regional and local level, as well as in the private sector.

The Parliamentary Commissioner Act 1967 provides for the appointment of a Parliamentary Commissioner for Administration. His main function is to investigate complaints of maladministration. These complaints must be made by a Member of the House of Commons at the instance of a member of the public, so that the public have no direct access to him. The term maladministration has been interpreted as requiring an error in the way a decision was reached or in the procedure leading to the decision. In other words a complaint must involve something more than a mere challenge to the merits of a decision.

The Parliamentary Commissioner's jurisdiction is subject to a number of diverse exceptions. For example, he cannot investigate personnel matters or contractual or other commercial transactions other than the compulsory acquisition of land or the disposal of land compulsorily acquired. Furthermore, he cannot investigate a matter where there is an alternative remedy before a tribunal or court though he has a discretion to do so if he is satisfied that in the circumstances it is not reasonable to expect the complainant to resort to it.

If the Commissioner is satisfied that a complaint falls with his jurisdiction he may conduct an investigation, in which case he must give the department concerned and any person named in the complaint an opportunity to comment on any allegations made. He is armed with wide powers similar to those of a High Court judge, for securing the presence of witnesses and production of documents and is protected in the conduct of his investigations by the laws relating to contempt of court.

When the Parliamentary Commissioner has completed his investigation he must report his findings to the Member of Parliament who referred the complaint and to the government department concerned. In addition, if he considers that injustice was caused by maladministration and has not been rectified he may lay before each House of Parliament a special report on the case. He cannot, however, enforce any of his recommendations or rescind or alter any decisions made by government departments. He is, however, supported in his work by a select committee and it is likely that a minister who fails to react to a special report concerning his department will come under political pressure to take some remedial action.

The Parliamentary Commissioner Act 1967 did not apply to Northern Ireland. However, in 1969, the office of Northern Ireland Parliamentary Commissioner for Administration was created to operate under a scheme which is virtually identical to that outlined above, except that he is not subject to an MP filter. Furthermore, if he reports that a complainant has suffered an injustice the complainant can apply to the county court for damages and/or an injunction.

A third category consists of the office of Health Service Commissioner who is empowered to investigate complaints regarding failures in services provided, failures to provide services and acts of maladministration which are alleged to have resulted in someone sustaining injustice or hardship.

Like the Parliamentary Commissioner, the Health Commissioner cannot act except on a complaint and, subject to an overriding discretion, cannot investigate a matter where there is an alternative remedy before a tribunal or court. Likewise he cannot investigate personnel matters or contractual or commercial transactions. In addition, he is subject to a number of other exceptions. For example, he cannot investigate actions taken solely in consequence of the exercise of clinical judgment.

The Health Commissioner has the same investigative powers as the Parliamentary Commissioner and must report the results of his investigations to the complainant, the authority concerned and also to the authority to which that authority is accountable. Where he concludes that a complainant has suffered an injustice or hardship which has not been remedied he may make a special report to the Secretary of State, who is required to lay a copy before each House of Parliament. One major difference from the Parliamentary Commissioner is that the Health Commissioner is not subject to any filter mechanism. However, although a complaint may be made directly to the Health Commissioner, he must give the authority concerned an opportunity to deal with the matter before taking any action.

The final category of ombudsman-type offices in the governmental sphere comprises the Commissioners for Local Administration appointed under the Local Government Act 1974. These are empowered to investigate complaints of injustice suffered as a consequence of maladministration by local authorities, subject to a number of exceptions including personnel matters, contractual and commercial transactions and certain educational functions.

The Local Commissioners are subject to a filter mechanism equivalent to the MP-filter in that complaints must be referred initially to a member of the authority in question and then referred on by that member. However, if a member refuses to pass on a request then the Commissioner is empowered to act on a direct request by an applicant.

The Local Commissioners have the same powers of investigation as the Parliamentary Commissioner. If a Commissioner makes a finding of maladministration his report must be laid before the authority in question which is required to inform him as to what remedial action, if any, it proposes to take. A Commissioner who is dissatisfied with an authority's reply (or lack of one) may make a further report but has no power to take remedial action. In contrast to the position with regard to the reports of the other categories outlined above there is no mechanism akin to ministerial responsibility which operates at the local government level. As a result the Local Commissioners have had more difficulty than the other types of ombudsmen in ensuring that persons who are found to have suffered injustice do in fact receive satisfactory remedies.

SUGGESTED ANSWER TO QUESTION TWO

General Comment

Quite a difficult question if one has not grasped the essential distinction between the Parliamentary Commissioner for Administration (PCA) and the function of the courts. Remember that whenever examiners set essay questions based on such 'opaque' quotations it is wise to start by trying to explain what you consider the quotation to mean. Also, this is not a 'tell me everything you know about the PCA' question. Note that the answer covers a narrow range of issues. It is useful to have a number of illustrative examples in mind when setting about such a question.

Key Points

* Explain quotation
* Identify the differing scope of judicial review and the PCA
* Explain maladministration
* Provide examples of the PCA's work
* Contrast the differences in processes, and the significance of this
* Identify the remedies available
* Generally compare the effect on the administration of the PCA and judicial review

Suggested Answer

The statement under discussion should first be explained. The Parliamentary Commissioner for Administration (hereinafter the PCA) works from within the system. His very title indicates that he is not meant to be some separate body, apart from the workings of government. Judicial review on the other hand is clearly separate from the executive arm of government. The courts are the normal source of remedies when administrative processes are found to be wanting, they staunchly defend their role as the protectors of individual rights from the excesses of the State.

The key to understanding the difference between the operation of judicial review and the investigations of the PCA is to grasp the point that judicial review can only be invoked where an allegation of ultra vires is made out. Much has been done over the past 45 years to develop the concept of ultra vires, but it is still limited to a number of well known heads, such as unreasonableness, acting on irrelevant considerations, failing to take into account relevant considerations, acting on no evidence, bad faith, and so on.

There are many administrative malpractices that are profoundly disturbing and frustrating for the ordinary citizen that do not fit under any of the established heads of ultra vires. Documents may be lost, officials may be rude and offhand, decisions may be delayed, advice may be misleading, or the actions of a government department may simply be incompetent. None of these factors by themselves would be likely to result in a decision being amenable to judicial review, because it would still be intra vires.

The PCA on the other hand, has jurisdiction to investigate written complaints from United Kingdom citizens who claim to have sustained injustice in consequence of maladministration in connection with the actions of a wide number of government departments and quasi-autonomous governmental organisations. Maladministration is nowhere defined in the Parliamentary Commissioner Act 1967 (hereinafter the '1967 Act'), but the oft-cited 'Crossman' catalogue gives an indication of what is involved:

> '... bias, neglect, inattention, delay, incompetence, ineptitude, perversity, turpitude, arbitrariness and so on ...'

As has been stated, these are mostly matters that would be beyond the reach of judicial review, thus illustrating the advantage of using the PCA to deal with such a complaint. As the question suggests, these are not necessarily matters giving rise to great legal issues, but they do involve problems arising at the centre of the administrative process.

Examples of some successes achieved by the PCA will illustrate the point further. In his 1983 Report, Sir Cecil Clothier related how, as the result of a complaint being investigated, the Department of Health and Social Security had to agree to alter a computer programme, so that cheques sent out for benefit payments explained more clearly what the payment actually covered. In November 1984, the PCA reported how an investigation had been launched into delays in payment of benefits by the same department. In the particular case under investigation the department had taken 11 months to settle a claim for industrial disablement benefit. The claimant died eight weeks before any award was made. The PCA received a firm assurance that action had been taken to prevent such delays happening again.

More celebrated was the PCA's investigation of Home Office's failure to review the convictions of prisoners sentenced on the strength of evidence submitted by the subsequently discredited forensic scientist, Dr Alan Clift. The PCA described the five year delay of the Home Office as 'inexcusable' and secured an undertaking from the department to review the convictions of 1,500 prisoners in the trials of which Dr Alan Clift had been involved.

The process by which the PCA works also makes for a marked contrast with judicial review. The PCA has the power to call witnesses from government departments, including ministers, and can call for the production of all papers, except Cabinet documents. The essence of the procedure, however, is investigatory not adversarial. Where possible the PCA seeks to promote an amicable settlement between government and public. Litigation by contrast frequently exacerbates existing problems. Those giving evidence to the PCA are likely to be less guarded and defensive, bearing in mind that his resulting reports do not usually name or identify the ministers, civil servants or other persons involved.

Compared with judicial review, therefore, the PCA's processes are far better suited to the task of fact finding, and he can actually go into a government department to do this.

One further area where comparison between the PCA and judicial review reveals evidence to support the contention that he is more effective in regulating the administrative process than judicial review is that of remedies.

Whereas judicial review is principally concerned with legality, and can only quash a decision found to be ultra vires, the PCA can actually achieve a constructive change in administrative methods. A government department as a result of an investigation by the PCA may agree to re-write an official form, or speed up the processing of claims. In some cases an ex-gratia payment is made – a remedy that is simply not available for ultra vires action. Decisions of the courts on applications for judicial review on the other hand may be ignored by administrators, or be nullified by subsequent legislation.

In conclusion, therefore, it can be seen that the PCA can achieve much more by working with government departments to solve a problem, than can the courts by waiting for an individual to apply for judicial review.

SUGGESTED ANSWER TO QUESTION THREE

General Comment

Note that this question does not invite an answer covering all aspects of the work done by the various United Kingdom ombudsmen – it raises quite specific points. Also note that it is not limited in its scope to the Parliamentary Commissioner for Administration.

Key Points

a • Arguments for and against ombudsmen acting on their own initiative
  • The MP filter system

b • Arguments for and against making ombudsmen's findings enforceable
  • The Northern Ireland precedent

Suggested Answer

a *British ombudsmen dealing with complaints on their own initiative.*

Before considering the arguments for and against such a suggestion it is sensible to state briefly the current position. The Parliamentary Commissioner for Administration (PCA) can only receive complaints of maladministration that have been submitted via a member of the House of Commons. The National Health Service Commissioner can receive complaints direct from members of the public, although such complaints cannot be investigated until they have been brought to the notice of the health authority in question and that authority given a reasonable opportunity to investigate and reply to the complaint.

In the case of Local Commissioners, the complaint must first be made in writing to a member of the local authority against whom the complaint is made, and then referred to the local government ombudsman by a member of the authority with the complainant's consent. Hence, only in the case of the Health Service Commissioner is there anything approaching direct access to an ombudsman.

There are a number of arguments in favour of permitting the various ombudsmen to act on their own initiative. First, there may be instances of maladministration that individuals do not feel sufficiently motivated to complain about, but which collectively lower the overall quality of service provided by the administrative process. It is even possible that working class people are less likely to feel confident about challenging the system than middle class people; consequently an ombudsman acting on his own initiative might be more effective in supervising the administration of social services. Secondly, the very fact that the ombudsman could investigate on his own initiative might have a salutary effect on the administrative processes within the constitution. A former Parliamentary Commissioner, Sir Cecil Clothier, would certainly have supported such a view. In his last annual report published in March 1984, Sir Cecil complained that he had less power as an ombudsman than any of his counterparts anywhere in the world. He added that during his five years in office, he had lost faith in the argument that he should only be empowered to deal with complaints submitted via Members of Parliament. It certainly seems odd that the United Kingdom is alone, apart from France, in not allowing the ombudsmen this power.

In the case of Local Commissioners it could be argued that some citizens are inhibited from complaining about the activities of a local authority for fear of retaliatory action such as eviction, redundancy, or refusal of planning permission. Allowing investigations, on the initiative of the Local Commissioners, would help to circumvent this problem. Similarly, with the Health Service Commissioner, the Select

Committee on the Parliamentary Commissioner, in its first report for 1984-85, recommended that he should be allowed to investigate the actions of health authorities without a formal complaint.

Against such arguments, two main points can be raised. First, how would any of the ombudsmen become aware of maladministration in the absence of complaints from the public? Would they be encouraged to go on 'fishing expeditions' in departments and local authorities hoping to discover evidence of malpractices? Secondly, in the case of Members of Parliament and local councillors, permitting ombudsmen to investigate of their own initiative might undermine the traditional role of such individuals in dealing with complaints from constituents/ward residents.

b *Making ombudsmen's findings enforceable*

It is a common feature of all the United Kingdom ombudsmen, with the exception of the Northern Ireland Commissioner for Complaints (NICC) that they can only report their findings at the end of an investigation; they cannot force a body guilty of maladministration to compensate the member of the public who may have suffered loss.

The NICC makes reports in much the same way as his counterparts, but the difference lies in the fact that a complainant who does not receive the compensation recommended in such a report can apply to the county court, which, on giving notice to the body complained of, may make an award to the complainant. The award should compensate for expenses and loss of opportunity of acquiring the benefit he may reasonably be expected to have had but for the maladministration.

The strongest argument in favour of extending the enforceability of ombudsman's findings arises in the case of the local commissioners. Here there have been numerous complaints that local authorities have been quite happy to ignore both reports, and further reports by local commissioners, sometimes containing quite serious allegations of maladministration. There is no direct sanction available against a local authority that chooses to act in this way. Many agree that it would not be too radical a move for the local commissioners to be given the power to apply to the local county court for an order to enforce their recommendations.

In the case of the PCA, however, the situation is rather different. There are remarkably few instances of government ministers refusing to acknowledge the content of the ombudsman's report and act on it accordingly. This is due in no small measure to the constitutional position a minister possesses in relation to his department. He is answerable to Parliament for its functioning under the doctrine of ministerial responsibility, and it would be politically unacceptable for him to be seen to be flouting the findings of the PCA. In any event the aim of an investigation by the PCA is to reach an amicable settlement of the problem between government department and complainant, in which case enforcement should be an unnecessary weapon.

In summary, therefore, it is submitted that the power to enforce findings should be extended only to local commissioners.

SUGGESTED ANSWER TO QUESTION FOUR

General Comment

Outline the difference in jurisdictions between the ombudsmen and the courts, with reference to the ultra vires doctrine, and the terms of the Parliamentary Commissioner Act 1967. Some specific examples of the ombudsman's work, and a consideration of whether such matters would have fallen within the scope of judicial review is required.

Key Points

- Basic difference between the concept of ultra vires and the concept of maladministration
- Scope of maladministration
- Examples of maladministration
- Areas of overlap – *Congreve* v *Home Office*

Suggested Answer

At the risk of gross over-simplification it might be suggested that, in the context of administrative law, the courts are concerned with the ultra vires actions of public bodies, whilst the ombudsmen are concerned with maladministration committed by those organisations within their jurisdiction. If ultra vires action and maladministration were mutually exclusive concepts, then the short answer to the question posed would obviously be that judges and ombudsmen are not looking for the same administrative mistakes at all. If one accepts, however, that there is at least a degree of overlap in the jurisdiction of the courts and the various ombudsmen, then the question can only be resolved by examining the extent of any such overlap.

The Parliamentary Commissioner Act 1967 ('the 1967 Act'), refers, in s5(1)(a) to the Parliamentary Commissioner ('the Ombudsman') having the power to investigate:

> '… action taken by … a government department … in the exercise of administrative functions … in any case where … a member of the public … claims to have sustained injustice in consequence of maladministration in connection with the action so taken.'

What the 1967 Act does not go on to do, is to provide a definition of what is meant by maladministration. This omission may have been a deliberate one on the part of Parliament, in that if a definition had been provided, the concept of maladministration might have become more limited. As things stand, each Commissioner has a certain amount of discretion as to how he interprets the term, and thus as to how he sees the ambit of his own jurisdiction. During the second reading in the House of Commons of the Bill which came to be passed as the 1967 Act, Richard Crossman suggested that the term maladministration might be taken to cover such matters as:

> '… bias, neglect, inattention, delay, incompetence, ineptitude, perversity, turpitude, arbitrariness, and so on …'

This has become known as the 'Crossman Catalogue' and is now generally regarded as the authoritative definition of maladministration, at least to the extent that it is possible to arrive at such a thing.

The first Ombudsman to be appointed, Sir Edmund Compton, appeared to take a somewhat conservative approach to the extent of his jurisdiction. In particular, there was criticism from the House of Commons Select Committee which monitors the work of the ombudsman, that his interpretation of s12(3) of the 1967 Act was unduly restrictive. The subsection provides that:

'... nothing in this Act authorises ... the Commissioner to question the merits of a decision taken without maladministration ...'

Sir Edmund at first adopted the view that this prevented him from investigating unfair decisions where the procedure leading up to the decision had been unimpeachable. He later accepted that this was an incorrect view, and subsequent holders of the office appear to have adopted a much more robust view as to the concept of maladministration.

This is evidenced by an extract from the Ombudsman's Annual Report for 1973 in which he states:

'[Maladministration] might imply some major administrative failure. But in practice I look upon "maladministration" as including any kind of administrative shortcoming ...'

Again, in the Annual Report for 1977, the Ombudsman wrote:

'... the term "maladministration" is certainly imprecise. But it has been interpreted with great flexibility both by my predecessors and by myself. Moreover the so-called 'Crossman Catalogue' ... surely provides a very broad definition.'

The most accurate guide as to what the ombudsmen understand by the term 'maladministration' are the Annual Reports themselves, which detail the investigations carried out, and the remedies obtained.

Thus, delay on the part of the Home Office in reviewing the safety of convictions of prisoners, which had been obtained on the basis of forensic evidence supplied by the subsequently discredited Home Office scientist, Dr Alan Clift, was castigated as an alarming example of maladministration by the then Ombudsman, Sir Cecil Clothier. Other matters which have been held to constitute maladministration by the Ombudsman are, the giving of incorrect advice on tax liability by the Customs and Excise, errors by the Passport Office which enabled a complainant's divorced wife to take their child out of the country, and the incorrect classification of prisoners of war which led to their being denied war pensions. The Annual Reports of the Health Service Commissioner and the Commissioners for Local Government reveal the wide meaning given to the concept of maladministration by the holders of those offices. In relation to the Health Service Commissioner, he has dealt with allegations of maladministration arising from the closure of surgeries, the inadequate provision of pharmaceutical services, wrong information being given to the families of patients resulting in their suffering unnecessary distress, and improper disclosure of medical records.

To what extent, therefore, are the ombudsmen and the courts looking for the same administrative mistakes? The intention of Parliament, as expressed in the 1967 Act, seems to have been that the jurisdiction of the courts and the Ombudsman should, so far as is possible, have been mutually exclusive. To this end s5(2) appears to prohibit the Ombudsman from investigating any matter in respect of which the person aggrieved has a remedy before another tribunal or court, but the section does go on to provide that the Ombudsman may, nevertheless, conduct an investigation into a complaint if he is of the opinion that, in the circumstances, it would not have been reasonable to expect the complainant to resort to the other remedy.

Thus there may be a measure of overlap in the work of the courts by way of judicial review, and the investigations carried out by the Ombudsman. A good example of this arose when the Home Office decided to penalise all those persons who had renewed their television licences, prior to expiry, at £12 (merely to avoid paying 50 per cent more for their new licences when prices were increased to £18) by revoking their licences after eight months. The Ombudsman investigated the matter despite the fact that those affected (over 20,000 people) did have a right to challenge the revocation of their licences before the courts. In the report laid before Parliament he concluded that although the Home Office may not have been guilty of maladministration, in that it had acted upon competent legal advice, its action had, nevertheless, not been administratively sound, lacking as it did both efficiency and foresight. The subsequent litigation in *Congreve* v *Home Office* (1976) resulted in the action of the Home Office being declared ultra vires.

The conventional wisdom is that the Ombudsman can work within the administration, whereas the courts can only deal with illegality, in the form of ultra vires action. If one refers back to the 'Crossman catalogue', it can be seen that there are some matters referred to there that could give rise to applications for judicial review, such as bias, but there are many matters referred to there which could only form the basis of an application for review in the most extreme cases, if at all. Such matters would be ineptitude, delay, rudeness on the part of officials, and the giving of incorrect information. A government department could fall prey to all these sins without actually acting ultra vires. It is submitted, therefore, that subject to a small area of overlap, the courts and the Ombudsman are certainly not looking for ' the same administrative mistakes'.

SUGGESTED SOLUTION TO QUESTION FIVE

General Comment

A question essentially calling for an examination of the Parliamentary Commissioner for Administration (PCA) as an alternative to judicial review as a provider of remedies within administrative law. Some comparison should be drawn between the ultra vires doctrine as a basis for intervention, and the concept of maladministration. Bring out the fact that the PCA works from within the system.

Key Points

- Compare and contrast the ultra vires doctrine and the concept of maladministration
- The achievements of the Parliamentary Commissioner for Administration

- Advantages over judicial review
- Conclusion

Suggested Answer

Providing an answer to the question set requires some consideration of the main concerns of administrative law. If the main concern is taken to be the quashing of decisions on the ground that they are ultra vires then clearly the ombudsman will be seen as irrelevant to that process. If however a broader view is taken, and administrative law is seen as being concerned with the provision of redress and possible improvements in the quality of the administrative process, then there is much greater relevance to the role of the ombudsman. It might be suggested that, in the context of administrative law, the courts are concerned with the ultra vires actions of public bodies, whilst the ombudsmen are concerned with maladministration committed by those organisations within their jurisdiction.

The Parliamentary Commissioner Act 1967 ('the 1967 Act'), refers, in s5(1)(a) to the Parliamentary Commissioner ('the Ombudsman') having the power to investigate:

'... action taken by ... a government department ... in the exercise of administrative functions ..., in any case where ... a member of the public ... claims to have sustained injustice in consequence of maladministration in connection with the action so taken.'

What the 1967 Act does not go on to do, is to provide a definition of what is meant by maladministration. As things stand, the PCA has a certain amount of discretion as to how he interprets the term, and thus as to how he sees the ambit of his own jurisdiction. During the second reading, in the House of Commons, of the Bill which came to be passed as the 1967 Act, Richard Crossman suggested that the term maladministration might be taken to cover such matters as 'bias, neglect, inattention, delay, incompetence, ineptitude, perversity, turpitude, arbitrariness, and so on ...'.

This has become known as the 'Crossman Catalogue' and is now generally regarded as the authoritative definition of maladministration, at least to the extent that it is possible to arrive at such a thing.

To suggest that these matters are of only marginal relevance is to underestimate the practical significance of the PCA's work. They are all issues which affect the ordinary citizen in his or her dealing with governmental bodies, and as such should be of concern to the administrative lawyer.

The significance of the PCA's contribution has depended to some extent on the approach of successive Ombudsmen to their role. The first Ombudsman to be appointed, Sir Edmund Compton, appeared to take a somewhat conservative approach to the extent of his jurisdiction. In particular, there was criticism from the House of Commons Select Committee which monitors the work of the Ombudsman, that his interpretation of s12(3) of the 1967 Act was unduly restrictive. The subsection provides that:

'... nothing in this Act authorises ... the Commissioner to question the merits of a decision taken without maladministration ...'

Sir Edmund at first adopted the view that this prevented him from investigating unfair decisions where the procedure leading up to the decision had been unimpeachable. He later accepted that this was an incorrect view, and subsequent holders of the office appear to have adopted a much more robust view as to the concept of maladministration.

This is evidenced by an extract from the Ombudsman's Annual Report for 1973 in which he states:

> '[Maladministration] might imply some major administrative failure. But in practice I look upon "maladministration" as including any kind of administrative shortcoming ...'

Again, in the Annual Report for 1977, the Ombudsman wrote:

> '... the term "maladministration" is certainly imprecise. But it has been interpreted with great flexibility both by my predecessors and by myself. Moreover the so-called "Crossman catalogue" ... surely provides a very broad definition.'

There have been important and well documented instances of the PCA obtaining relief for the individual complainant where judicial review may have been unavailable or inappropriate. For example: the PCA's investigation into the delay on the part of the Home Office in reviewing the safety of convictions of prisoners which had been obtained on the basis of forensic evidence supplied by the subsequently discredited Home Office scientist Dr Alan Clift; the giving of incorrect advice on tax liability by the Customs and Excise; errors by the Passport Office which enabled a complainant's divorced wife to take their child out of the country; and the incorrect classification of prisoners of war which led to their being denied war pensions.

The allegation that the PCA is of marginal significance may spring from the fact that the 1967 Act purports to exclude him from investigating any matter that could be dealt with by the courts. Section 5(2) appears to prohibit the Ombudsman from investigating any matter in respect of which the person aggrieved has a remedy before another tribunal or court, but the section does go on to provide that the Ombudsman may, nevertheless, conduct an investigation into a complaint if he is of the opinion that, in the circumstances, it would not have been reasonable to expect the complainant to resort to the other remedy.

The reality, it is submitted, is that the Ombudsman can work within the administration, whereas the courts can only deal with illegality, in the form of ultra vires action. If one refers back to the 'Crossman catalogue', it can be seen that there are some matters referred to there that could give rise to applications for judicial review, such as bias, but there are many matters referred to there which could only form the basis of an application for review in the most extreme cases, if at all. Such matters would be ineptitude, delay, rudeness on the part of officials, and the giving of incorrect information. A government department could fall prey to all these sins without actually acting ultra vires.

In conclusion, one might be tempted to suggest that it is judicial review which is of marginal relevance, since the investigations of the PCA are more likely to manifest themselves in some change in departmental procedures, whereas a decision of the courts may not be implemented to the benefit of the general public.

Old Bailey Press

The Old Bailey Press integrated student law library is tailor-made to help you at every stage of your studies from the preliminaries of each subject through to the final examination. The series of Textbooks, Revision WorkBooks, 150 Leading Cases/Casebooks and Cracknell's Statutes are interrelated to provide you with a comprehensive set of study materials.

You can buy Old Bailey Press books from your University Bookshop, your local Bookshop, direct using this form, or you can order a free catalogue of our titles from the address shown overleaf.

The following subjects each have a Textbook, 150 Leading Cases/Casebook, Revision WorkBook and Cracknell's Statutes unless otherwise stated.

Administrative Law
Commercial Law
Company Law
Conflict of Laws
Constitutional Law
Conveyancing (Textbook and Casebook)
Criminal Law
Criminology (Textbook and Sourcebook)
English and European Legal Systems
Equity and Trusts
Evidence
Family Law
Jurisprudence: The Philosophy of Law (Textbook, Sourcebook and
    Revision WorkBook)
Land: The Law of Real Property
Law of International Trade
Law of the European Union
Legal Skills and System
Obligations: Contract Law
Obligations: The Law of Tort
Public International Law
Revenue Law (Textbook,
    Sourcebook and Revision
    WorkBook)
Succession

Mail order prices:	
Textbook	£14.95
150 Leading Cases/Casebook	£9.95
Revision WorkBook	£7.95
Cracknell's Statutes	£9.95
Suggested Solutions 1998–1999	£6.95
Law Update 2001	£9.95

To complete your order, please fill in the form below:

Module	Books required	Quantity	Price	Cost
		Postage		
		TOTAL		

For Europe, add 15% postage and packing (£20 maximum).
For the rest of the world, add 40% for airmail.

ORDERING

By telephone to Mail Order at 020 7381 7407, with your credit card to hand.

By fax to 020 7386 0952 (giving your credit card details).

Website: www.oldbaileypress.co.uk

By post to: Mail Order, Old Bailey Press, 200 Greyhound Road, London W14 9RY.

When ordering by post, please enclose full payment by cheque or banker's draft, or complete the credit card details below. You may also order a free catalogue of our complete range of titles from this address.

We aim to despatch your books within 3 working days of receiving your order.

Name

Address

Postcode   Telephone

Total value of order, including postage: £

I enclose a cheque/banker's draft for the above sum, or

charge my   ☐ Access/Mastercard   ☐ Visa   ☐ American Express
Card number

☐☐☐☐ ☐☐☐☐ ☐☐☐☐ ☐☐☐☐

Expiry date   ☐☐☐☐

Signature: ....Date: ....